Learning to Think
THINKING TO LEARN

Other titles of related interest

MAND *et al.*

Learning & Instruction: European Research in an
International Context   Volume 2:1

MAND *et al.*

Learning & Instruction: European Research in an
International Context   Volume 2:2

CARRETERO *et al.*

Learning & Instruction: Volume 3

Journals of related interest

Learning and Instruction

International Journal of Educational Research

Learning to Think

THINKING TO LEARN

The Proceedings of the 1989 OECD Conference
Organized by
the Centre for Educational Research and Innovation

Edited by

STUART MACLURE

Editor, The Times Educational Supplement 1969–1989, London, UK

and

PETER DAVIES

Director, The Open School Trust, Devon, UK

Published for the Organisation
for Economic Co-operation and Development by

PERGAMON PRESS

OXFORD · NEW YORK · SEOUL · TOKYO

UK	Pergamon Press plc, Headington Hill Hall, Oxford OX3 0BW, England
USA	Pergamon Press, Inc, 395 Saw Mill River Road, Elmsford, New York 10523
KOREA	Pergamon Press Korea, KPO Box 315, Seoul 110-603, Korea
JAPAN	Pergamon Press, 8th Floor, Matsuoka Central Building, 1-7-1 Nishi-Shinjuku, Shinjuku-ku, Tokyo 160, Japan

First edition 1991

Library of Congress Cataloging-in-Publication Data
Learning to think: thinking to learn: the proceedings of the 1989 OECD conference/organized by the Centre for Educational Research and Innovation; edited by Stuart Maclure and Peter Davies.—1st ed.
p. cm.
Includes bibliographical references.
1. Thought and thinking—Study and teaching—Congresses.
I. Maclure, Stuart. II. Davies, Peter, 1950– . III. Centre for Educational Research and Innovation.
LB1590.3.L45   1991 370.15′2—dc20   91-15159

British Library Cataloguing in Publication Data
Learning to think: thinking to learn: the proceedings of the 1989 OECD conference organized by the Centre for Educational Research and Innovation.
1. Thought processes. Development
I. Maclure, Stuart II. Davies, Peter III. Centre for Educational Research and Innovation
153.42
ISBN 0-08-040646-7 Hardcover
ISBN 0-08-040657-2 Flexicover

Printed in Great Britain by BPCC Wheatons Ltd, Exeter

Contents

Preface

This book has its origins in a conference organized by the OECD Centre for Educational Research and Innovation (CERI) in July 1989. This international event marked the opening of Phase 2 of a project on curriculum reform and school effectiveness, and represented the beginning of a series of activities under the general title "The Curriculum Redefined". The conference was generously supported by Pergamon Press.

The purpose of the conference was to discuss, and hopefully advance, the state of knowledge about how young people think and reason. Interest in this area had already been expressed in member country reports and contributed to *Curriculum Reform—An Overview of Trends* (OECD/CERI, 1990). Of the 120 participants who attended, some 60—the target group—were engaged in psychological and educational research. Ten were teachers, the remainder educational administrators or national delegates with other interests in the area. Unusually for the OECD, there were also two groups of schoolchildren (from Finland and France) who assisted in providing participants with live demonstrations of thinking skills programmes.

This book makes no attempt to be a definitive record of the conference proceedings. Several workshops have not been recorded because it was felt that their subject matter was already covered adequately in the text. The five keynote presentations do not follow the original chronological order but that which we, as editors, feel makes the book more readable. For the record, the keynote presentations and running order were as follows: Edward de Bono with response by Malcolm Skilbeck; Howard Gardner with response by François Bresson, John Nisbet with response by Christiane Gilliéron, Maxine Greene, Hiroshi Azuma. All other papers included in the text were presented either in workshops or in short plenary sessions. For ease of reference, responses are printed in italics.

Whilst it seemed natural to the editors to follow an order which collected the papers into areas of interest, the divisions remain somewhat artificial. If the order therefore seems arbitrary, especially to those who attended the conference, we would excuse ourselves on the grounds of trying to make the material more accessible.

The Introduction serves both as a narrative record of the conference and as a way into the area for the uninitiated. For a more detailed treatment of the subject, refer to John Nisbet's "Methods and Approaches" or to the Background Report by the Secretariat which provides a comprehensive survey of the field.

We would like to acknowledge the assistance and support of a number of people: Marie-Laure Vaillant, who arranged for the French schoolchildren to take part in the conference; Veikko Lepisto for the Finnish pupils; Bill Lucas for his camera work; Touko Voutilainen for his inspiration and hospitality in Finland; and John Nisbet for lending the breadth of his understanding of the subject. Lastly, we thank Pamela Langlais, a final year Economics student at the American University in Paris, who helped to organize the conference.

Stuart Maclure

Peter Davies

Reference

OECD/CERI (1990). Curriculum Reform—An Overview of Trends. OECD, Paris.

Introduction: An Overview

STUART MACLURE

Conference Rapporteur
Distinguished Visiting Fellow,
Policy Studies Institute,
London, United Kingdom

Can Thinking Be Taught?

Homo sapiens can think without being formally taught to think. Thinking is like breathing, a normal activity for every normal human being. Ordinary life depends on the ability to think.

Refining and sharpening the powers of thought have always been prime objectives of formal education, a basic aim of teaching and learning in all disciplines. Education is about acquiring the ability to collect, manipulate and apply information for the purpose of understanding and therefore mastering a given subject matter; it must, therefore, be about thinking and thinking to some purpose.

It has also been assumed that learning to use the power of thought effectively through the disciplines of study in the academic and practical curriculum will benefit other aspects of human existence: other forms of problem solving in other contexts. Attachment to this simple assumption has proved to be stubborn and lasting, even though evidence to support it has been difficult to assemble.

There has also been a traditional belief in something called "common sense", a capacity for handling the daily tasks of living. This is unequally distributed among the population and is not necessarily related to intellectual brilliance or the sensibilities which are explored by education in the affective domain. "Common sense", or what an earlier generation defined by the Greek word *nous*, clearly has a great deal to do with the practical matters of daily life, as also with the entrepreneurial and management aspects of economic activity. Formal education has not usually been held to have much to contribute to the cultivation of this invaluable human resource, although in some countries schools have been expected to contribute, largely through extracurricular activities and the hidden curriculum, to the formation of character and self-reliance.

To ask the apparently simple question "Can thinking be taught?" is to ask whether particular kinds of teaching can improve particular kinds of thinking. It is about the quality of thought: are there ways of teaching children and adults to be more effective thinkers and reasoners, and if so what approaches are most likely to do this most successfully in different circumstances?

The term "thinking" embraces a wide range of cerebral activities. At one end of the spectrum there are the heights of philosophical speculation; at the other, the mundane processes required to fulfil the minimal duties of a humdrum existence. In the modern jargon, thinking needs to be "unpacked" before a meaningful discussion can take place. What kind of thinking are we talking about? Each contribution to the discussion needs a context and some definitions, otherwise the debate is likely to be at cross-purposes.

It has to be said that this degree of precision is often lacking. Protagonists all too often talk past one another. Some argue about ways of raising the quality of specific thinking skills and their application in practical situations. Others are concerned with the fostering of powers of higher-order thinking and reflection. Some aim at developing intelligence in people who have for some reason been held back in early childhood. All claim to be talking about thinking.

Policy makers and educational managers, who want to know whether schools can adapt their programmes to teach children to think more efficiently, have to decide just what it is they are talking about. Are they interested in limited (though nevertheless important) practical skills, or are they concerned with intellectual development of a more elevated kind?

Much of the debate between experts is about the psychology of learning. This is clearly an absorbing study which holds increasing interest for scholars and researchers. It is a truism to observe that differences of priority and concern reflect the differences of interest and professional background among those leading the debate. It seems especially true in regard to questions about the "thinking" debate. Scholars and researchers usually find psychological theory more interesting than the search for competence in thinking at a modest level. Yet this more modest quest may be the priority issue for the policy makers and educational managers.

Three Schools of Thought

When people come together to think about thinking in the context of education, three main groupings emerge:

(i) Those who adopt a "skills" approach or "direct" method. Those who favour a skills approach believe it is possible to teach the skills of thinking explicitly, by means of activities and exercises designed to improve thinking techniques or basic thinking ability which are independent of the subject matter that makes up the rest of the school curriculum. Thinking (under one title or another) thus becomes a subject in its own right. In their very different ways, Dr Edward de Bono, who developed the Cognitive Research Trust (CoRT) methods, and Professor Reuven Feuerstein, the originator of Instrumental Enrichment (IE), come within this category—see Part II.

(ii) Those who favour an "infusion" model. This approach seeks to make more effective thinking a self-conscious aim within the existing school curriculum. It is about devising strategies which will transform the teaching of ordinary school disciplines in such a way as to focus on thinking and strengthen students' powers of thought. Such strategies mean radical changes in the presentation of material and the responses demanded from students; the teaching methods deliberately try to improve reasoning, problem solving and analysis. Examples of "infusion" strategies can be drawn from mathematics, the sciences, the humanities and information technology. Among those who have pioneered such strategies across the curriculum are Professor Antoine de la Garanderie in France and the FACE project team in Finland—see Part III.

(iii) Those who are interested in the application of cognitive knowledge to the teaching of thinking but see thinking as a by-product of traditional disciplines and pedagogy, and who remain agnostic about particular methods.

A Skills Approach

Dr Edward de Bono's CoRT method is one of the best-known examples of what he himself calls a "tool" method of teaching thinking. By a tool method, Dr de Bono means a course of teaching which equips learners with tools to increase the effectiveness of their thinking. The programme provides a series of exercises, undertaken by pupils in groups of four or five, involving problems to solve or ideas to explore using techniques devised by Dr de Bono. These techniques serve as "tools" with which to discover and engage pupils' thinking skills.

Dr de Bono's exposition of his methods (pp. 6–13) gives examples of how the lessons and sequence of lessons are structured. His work is used in schools throughout the world, and has been extensively adapted for use in management training for industry. He acidly observes that his ideas have been taken up more readily in the developing world than in more developed countries, where existing educational structures are entrenched and are characterized by what he describes as "educational complacency, inadequate leadership, jealousies, political in-fighting and confusion". In

Venezuela, a major testing ground for his theory and practice, "all students must spend two hours a week on thinking skills".

The de Bono hypothesis starts from harsh criticisms of conventional education in the advanced countries. As he sees it, Western education operates on the principle that if you can teach people to do enough difficult things to the point where they reach the limit of their capacity and fail, the process of learning which has taken them that far will have instilled the ability to perform lesser tasks. Not so, says de Bono. You may need to teach the lesser things directly because you cannot rely on the automatic transfer of knowledge gained in complex learning assignments to the solution of other practical problems of living. And anyway, for much of the time, problem solving does not depend on knowledge. Perception is more important and needs to be trained.

As he presents his message, de Bono highlights the weaknesses of the conventional wisdom (p. 4). Critical thinking, for example—the bedrock of Western culture—is good if you want to engage in adversarial argument, but of limited value for original and effective thought because it dissipates most of the thinker's energy on defending a position, not the positive exploration of a choice of possibilities. Critical thinking, in de Bono's formulation, is not constructive or creative—it depends on some previous process of creative thought. For all its cultural triumphs, critical thinking, like patriotism, is not enough.

Nor yet is analytical thinking. It is not enough to discover the causes of a problem and to itemize them. In de Bono's terms, analysis must be complemented by design which adds a creative element. People must be taught to generate new hypotheses, not just apply old ones.

De Bono's strength is the simple coherence of his message and his determination to give students an effective way of applying all their thinking capacity (with his tools) to the solution of a problem. Knowledge is important, of course, but, as he puts it wryly, "unless you know everything, what you need is thinking" or—as he calls it—*operacy*: the skills of "doing" which apply all the thinking skills, critical, analytical and creative, together with knowledge, to the matter in hand.

As well as offering a set of tools, de Bono provides a technique for disseminating the use of his methods throughout an education system. A cadre of teachers can be trained with CoRT method, and they in turn can train others. The "cascade" method only succeeds if the message to be conveyed is simple and robust: "robust" is a word de Bono uses frequently. He maintains that he has devised an approach which is coherent enough to be disseminated in this way without losing its vital spark.

De Bono starts from a background of research in neurophysiology, and behind his particular skills package there is a wealth of theory and a lifetime of developing insights. There is also a keen sense of enterprise and the forceful personality needed to turn a set of original ideas into a major venture which does business all round the world.

It is important to separate the ideas from the marketing. The educators have to make up their own minds about what is on offer, being neither dazzled by glossy presentation nor yet put off by the apparatus of commercial promotion.

This raises a more general point which affects many innovators in the field of education. The more successful they become, the more likely they are to be sucked into the commercial process, becoming increasingly dependent on commerce to provide the resources for continued development. This can easily affect the way the message comes across.

In de Bono's case, his brilliant presentational skills are those of a salesman as well as an educator. He is much in demand as a lecturer at business conventions and management courses. It is possible, however, for style to come between speakers and their audiences. Polished presentation can have the effect of dividing an audience composed of both experts and lay people. The lay men and women tend to warm to a speaker with a cracker-barrel wit and a gift of humorous and arresting communication. The academics, on the other hand, are schooled to be suspicious of charisma and this may prevent them from hearing what is being said.

What policy makers and education managers need is a balanced assessment of the results which the CoRT method can promise. Most of the evaluation evidence so far has been less than conclusive. Dr de Bono draws attention to recent work by Dr John Edwards at James Cook University in Queensland, Australia, showing "significant effects on a wide variety of standardized tests". A Schools Council study in the United Kingdom published in 1985 was disappointing. It reported generally favourable feedback from the students but little hard evidence of an improved quality of thinking. Dr de Bono disputes the relevance of the tests used and maintains that many evaluation studies are flawed because the researchers lack the tools for the job. While this debate about evaluation techniques has continued, the policy makers and the managers have had to wait for a clear, independent and conclusive examination of the claims of the CoRT method.

Another approach to the direct teaching of thinking skills to have attracted world-wide attention is Instrumental Enrichment (IE), devised by Professor Reuven Feuerstein, the Israeli psychologist. Feuerstein's original work was with children who had suffered great deprivation—new immigrants to the State of Israel—who needed extensive help before they could be integrated into a regular education programme. A description of Instrumental Enrichment as it has developed as a "three-year series of problem-solving tasks and exercises" grouped in 14 areas of specific cognitive development, is given here in a paper provided by Dr Frances R. Link (pp. 31–47). The prescribed exercises are known as "instruments" rather than lessons because "in and of themselves, they are virtually free of specific subject matter". Their purpose is "to serve as the means or vehicle for cognition-orientated interaction between teachers and students", the aim being to develop, refine and crystallize "functions which are prerequisite to effective thinking".

A paper by Professor Rosine Debray (pp. 49–61) reports on an experiment at one of the schools taking part in the first IE programme in France. In Professor Debray's view:

> Feuerstein's contribution lies in his assertion—supported by both theory and practice—that when intelligence has not developed, at the right time, the disability is not therefore irreversible, because the deficiency is not fixed for ever at adolescence, or even in adulthood. Intelligence in the sense of a capacity to learn intelligent behaviour . . . can thus be acquired.

For most people growing up in a modern Western country, the basic prerequisites are acquired "almost automatically, in the first relations with the mother and father and other important contacts for the child, through educational activities, games, learning, and therefore the transmission of language". If a child has been deprived of this early experience, the deficiency has to be made good later.

Instrumental Enrichment, therefore, fits into the broad category of a skills approach but it is different in aim from the CoRT package. Where CoRT aims to give the learner a set of tools with which to apply native intelligence more effectively, IE is more ambitious; it seeks to develop the learner's intelligence as such. To perform this act of what Debray calls "cognitive resuscitation", it is necessary "to think about the act of thinking itself, analyzing the procedures that come into play in a specific cognitive act and the pinpointing of the deficient cognitive functions".

Essential to the programme which Professor Debray described is an extensive course of training for the teachers taking part—four 15-day sessions over two years, with regular supervision by a psychologist—and the use by this trained staff of specially designed teaching material with small groups of children.

Having quoted statistical evidence, some supportive, some inconclusive, Professor Debray is drawn into a more general discussion of the effect of IE on teaching methods among the first- and second-year secondary pupils and how they developed over the period of the experiment. One of the conclusions which Debray draws concerns the effect of the programmes on the teachers, who feel that their whole pedagogic approach has been changed by participating in it. "The IE frame of mind transformed their way of teaching their own subjects since it threw light on what is involved in thinking and intelligence". It is well known that the teacher's expectation of what a child can achieve is important in raising the child's expectation too. One effect of using the IE method, according to Debray, is to increase motivation and help children to emerge from the pattern of underperformance which has been part of their background.

The picture which emerges is complex, and while it is clear that Debray's conclusions are positive and strongly supportive, it is not clear exactly where the positive influences are located: in the IE materials, the teaching methods, the attitudes of mind of the teachers or all of these in combination. The evidence is presented of an association between the experimental activity with the pupils' success, but it is not possible to attribute cause and effect to any particular element in the IE package. Other teachers might well be able to offer similar examples of success without adopting the package.

A Sceptical Response

How does the teaching of thinking as a subject independent of content fit into the larger pattern of the educational curriculum in the developed countries, represented at the OECD?

This is the question raised by a presentation such as de Bono's, which aims to challenge the status quo. Professor Malcolm Skilbeck, Vice-chancellor of Deakin University, in Victoria, Australia, is one who responds with scepticism (pp. 15–17). He notes that the existing subject-based curriculum is sturdy and of long-standing. This in itself means that those who devise new subjects, independent of the conventional subject content, have a difficult task in trying to break in.

That does not mean, however, that educators have not been interested in thinking—Skilbeck points to Socrates, Abelard and Dewey, spanning more than two millennia, as educational thinkers who believed strongly that students could be taught to think—and witness to this can be seen in the current interest in the subject among the research community.

It remains true, nevertheless, that in the West and the East, teaching has been organized on a subject basis. Why is it that people have universally assumed that thinking would be a by-product of subject teaching, rather than a separate activity in its own right? Could it be that experience had confirmed this belief over time?

It is a fact that Dr de Bono's simple, flexible and practical procedures for the application of thinking skills have been attractive to practitioners, but it is also true that they have on the whole failed to appeal to academics. The researchers have matched the positive testimony of the teachers with their own professional scepticism. Innovators deeply engaged in their own schemes not infrequently complain of excessive scepticism on the part of academics standing on the touchline, but the research community is clearly right to demand hard evidence because the exponents of the skills approach are demanding space in an already overcrowded timetable, space now occupied by other educational activities which have also been perceived to have value.

Professor Skilbeck concedes that one reason why thinking as a separate "subject" has not been placed higher on the educators' agenda in the developed countries could be, as de Bono claims, because of complacency and perversity. But, equally, there could be other reasons, such as a belief that thinking is being taught in other ways, and taught well. Many school teachers would maintain that the subject-based curriculum is a vehicle for teaching children to think; so too would many teachers of adults, believing, as Skilbeck puts it, that "thought must address content".

In considering the suggestions for changing existing practice for the better, Skilbeck sees the choice as between trying (with difficulty) to carve out room for a separate subject called thinking, and the alternative approach (also difficult) of teaching thinking "across the curriculum", that is, building thinking more systematically and self-consciously into existing subjects.

Those who believe, like him, that subject teaching needs to be grounded in knowledge and experience are likely to reckon that this applies also to the teaching of thinking skills. They would lean to the view that approaches such as de Bono's are more likely to be valuable as a stimulus to learning through other subject-based activities, than as the specific techniques for the teaching of thinking which they claim to be.

In trying to accommodate systematic attempts to raise the level of thinking and increase "thinking about thinking" within the existing curriculum, Skilbeck makes the point that it may in practice be easier to pursue an "across the curriculum" approach than to wipe the slate clean and start again with a thinking skills package. The robustness of the tools developed by the CoRT method presents a valuable challenge to conventional ways of teaching subjects but, at a more fundamental level, the critical thinking which de Bono undervalues is unlikely to be set aside in favour of the simplicity of his tools, however robust.

This, then, was the substance of the argument of de Bono's presentation and Skilbeck's response. To the outside observer, the rhetoric seemed irreconcilable, but it did not seem impossible that at ground level there might be ways of drawing on the CoRT method without accepting what de Bono called the full "paradigm shift". It is not difficult to see how, for instance, some of de Bono's tools might be useful for a student preparing a history essay. With or without a proprietary packet, teachers cannot do their job unless they give their students tools, of some kind, to use in tackling academic problems: could they do their jobs better if they used tools developed systematically by an expert exponent of a "skills approach"?

What is also clear is that at the root of the discussion is the question of "transfer": the application of knowledge and skills acquired in one form and one context to solve problems presented in another form and context.

This has been a matter of debate over many years and in many curricular forms. In many education systems, the classics—Latin and Greek—used to be presented as disciplines of peculiar significance because of their transfer potential as a training of the mind in the accurate use of language and precision of thought. Psychologists discounted these claims. Many students of Latin and Greek proved adept at learning other things, but there was no evidence to show that their capacity to learn other subjects was a transfer of skills acquired by learning Latin and Greek. More probably it was the consequence of an aptitude which predated their study of the classics.

Educators used to feel confident in talking generally about education as a "training of the mind" in terms which assumed that training was transferable. This having been discredited, it has to be asked if it can now be reinstated in regard to the teaching of thinking. The question is approached in the background paper to the conference (pp. 201–213): "A critical test of the approach adopted in teaching thinking is whether the competence acquired from instruction can be applied in a context different from that in which it was learned."

The test is clearly difficult to apply in conditions which satisfy both the practitioners and the researchers. Forms of teaching that are generally believed to have great value may have considerable difficulty in satisfying the researcher's objective tests. Wholly appropriate research instruments may not be available or suitable under normal classroom conditions. There is an obvious need for more research and better evaluation, but it is important also to bear in mind the limitations of research technique.

Multiple Intelligence and the Thinking Process

Professor Howard Gardner's presentation (and his paper with Mindy L. Kornhaber, pp. 147–170) leads the discussion in a different direction. His view is that thinking, far from being a single activity, is related to a number of different forms of mental ability and to separate functions of the brain. "The mind," he says, "is not a general problem solver or general thinking machine. Nor is the brain. There is a set of specific devices for dealing with particular problems: linguistic, logical-mathematical, musical, spatial, bodily-physical, interpersonal, and relating to internal self-knowledge."

As far as Gardner is concerned, classical psychologists like Binet were mistaken about intelligence and about intelligence tests. "Ideas about IQ became entrenched but they were simply dead wrong." Dogmas about IQ have had an incalculable influence in the United States, where the hunt is on for "super kids" with outsize IQs, the assumption still being that intelligence is unitary, that everyone has a general intelligence level which can be assessed with some reliability.

Anyone trained in an IQ culture is likely to find difficulty in escaping from it. Howard Gardner's formative experience as a developmental psychologist made him more and more doubtful about "general intelligence". So did his work with brain-damaged children. The brain seemed to him to be "modular", with a number of particular competences rather than a unitary one. The literature supports the idea that there are different kinds of human capacity, and that not everyone is equally capable in all directions. Some people are very good at some things and not at others; for example, prodigies in mathematics or music. Gardner also notes that different cultures place different value on different forms of intelligence, and that this influences the way children develop. He defines intelligence as a capacity to solve problems or to make something that is valued in at least one culture, a definition which automatically broadens the discussion and introduces additional evidence from anthropological inquiry.

The implications of Gardner's theories lead him to urge schools to take individual differences more seriously than they have in the past. Crude assessment instruments are obviously inappropriate if intelligence takes many forms, yet assessment commonly continues to measure a single dimension. It becomes important to look at specific tasks in specific "task-domains", and to help students to select their own problems to work on, along with their own self-assessment.

As for the direct teaching of thinking skills, Gardner concludes that "human beings are not designed to carry out mechanically sound ways of thinking. Good survival reasons make us make selective use of thinking . . . thinking skills need a domain within which to be applied."

Different conclusions about multiple intelligence are drawn by Professor François Bresson of the Ecole des Hautes Etudes en Science Sociales in Paris, who acknowledges (pp. 171–176) that there are various forms of intelligence but maintains that intellectual activities "bring into play a number of processes which exist, as far as we know, in all normal people". Though different forms of intelligence may be controlled by different parts of the brain, they co-exist. "The capacity of knowing how to succeed in some intellectual activities does not mean that we cannot perform as well as in others." Professor Bresson asks:

> Does critical thought and reasoning develop as a general function which is common to all specific intelligence, or is there a function for each intellectual form? Whilst it is impossible to give a precise answer, one can say that these ways of thinking develop only in situations where the specific cognitive capacities can function. Cognitive, affective and social factors make this development possible, and transfer to other intellectual capacities depends on analogous possibilities to exercise them in other situations.

Professor Bresson's arguments lead into a discussion of the relationship between knowledge and what he calls "the procedures of intellectual activity". Verbal activity in pedagogy, he says, "is what the computer scientists call 'declarative'. It allows conscious knowledge to be acquired. But procedural knowledge—know-how, the process that underlies practical actions and their application—is largely implicit and unconscious." In his analysis, "there is no form of direct learning which can develop critical intelligence. One can only try to induce the spontaneous acquisition of these ways of thinking."

The theoretical gulf which separated Bresson and Gardner did not prevent them reaching a common view that there is a need to broaden the curriculum if teachers are to do justice to the wide range of talents which pupils bring with them to school.

Interpretations of the Infusion Model

The infusion approach has attracted considerable interest among developmental psychologists in North America and elsewhere. As the examples referred to below indicate, it offers both less and more than the skills approach: less because it does not provide a set of ready-made tools, more because it can be fitted more easily into existing curriculum structures.

Philosophy

Professor Matthew Lipman, of Montclair State College, Upper Montclair, New Jersey, argues for the teaching of thinking through the introduction of primary and secondary school children to philosophy (pp. 103–113). He has developed teaching materials which aim to make this possible.

Behind this ambitious project is a belief that the curriculum needs to be redefined, with revised aims. Traditionally the aim "has been the passing on of knowledge. The educated person has been conceived of as the knowledgeable person. And one becomes knowledgeable through the process of learning." This, according to Lipman, is no longer enough. The knowledgeable person must also be "reasonable" and "judicious". "The educational process must be one that cultivates reasoning and judgement ... Education is initiation into the process of inquiry." And not just scientific inquiry. There are nonscientific forms of inquiry as well, notably philosophy, which he defines as "inquiry into the generic characteristics of good thinking".

Schools—classrooms as communities of inquiry—figure boldly in Lipman's conception of the curriculum redefined. He believes that traditional philosophy can be "redesigned so as to be welcomed by children" and fitted into the programme of the primary and secondary school, using specially written fictional material to provide the stimulus to the discussion of philosophical principles and procedures "just beneath the surface of the prose".

Lipman's "Philosophy for Children Programme" uses these indirect teaching methods, together with the children's own discussions and contributions, to emphasize five kinds of thinking skills—reasoning, inquiry, concept formation, translation, critical disposition—with direct cross-relationship with other disciplines and areas of study. Among the outcomes should be critical thinking: "thinking that is self-corrective, sensitive to context, and relies upon criteria for the formation of judgements".

Information technology

Faced with a choice between the "skills package" approach and the infusion model, Dr Michel Caillot, who runs a research project on "Science education and the new technologies" at the University of Paris VII, leans towards the infusion model rather than one which aims at teaching thinking independently of any content of study (pp. 95–101). His emphases, however, point firmly in the direction of cross-disciplinary methods and research into the use of computer technology in existing curriculum areas.

Information technology now makes it possible to confront students with a wealth of data and particular ways of using it to solve problems. Examples can be drawn from many disciplines. Caillot quotes a French project conducted by the Institut National de la Recherche Pédagogique (INRP) which uses satellite photography. The pictures are digital images visualized by the computer which can be used in geography or environmental studies: from a mass of material, the student has to develop and test hypotheses.

Other examples relate to word-processing and the development of writing skills; to geometry and the development of powers of deduction; and to various kinds of model-building and simulation. All draw on the possibilities of the computer as a tool for teaching subject-content as well as training the powers of thought. It is clear that the application of information technology for these purposes will become much more sophisticated as time passes and as interactive methods and expert systems become more widely available.

Those who have witnessed false dawns of other technological innovations in the field of education will not underestimate the difficulty of taking advantage of what information technology has to offer in schools where timetables and traditional practices belong to an age before computers. Schools and curricula will have to be flexible enough to seize opportunities which offer enormous benefits, but necessarily involve radical change in working practices.

Mathematics and science

A number of development projects have sought to use teaching in science and mathematics as a vehicle for teaching thinking skills. As the Background Report notes (p. 206), for a long time mathematicians have taught their students by setting them problems to solve with guidance as to how they should set about finding solutions. In the light of this guidance, the students have to apply their knowledge to the solution of other examples of similar problems. There remain the familiar difficulties of transfer. If new examples are closely similar to the context in which a procedure has been learned, there is relatively little transfer; but "in the study of mathematics one hopes for larger leaps and broader generalizations". It is noticeable, however, that many students fail to make these larger leaps and never proceed beyond a modest level of mathematical expertise. The question is whether thinking encouraged and developed through the teaching of mathematics can be transferred as a general skill rather than as particular forms of mathematical knowledge.

Similar questions have been explored in science education ... "the subject of intensive inquiry in many countries". Dr Philip Adey's paper (pp. 79–93) describes attempts to raise the quality of "formal, operational thinking" among 12-year-olds in eight secondary schools over a period of two years. The aim behind the research was to test hypotheses relating to the acceleration of cognitive development through the teaching of science.

The project started from broadly Piagetian psychological assumptions. Children in the experimental group pursued 30 activities, each designed to replace one regular 70-minute science lesson. With this scheme went inservice training for the teachers concerned. In Dr Adey's words:

> The results can be crudely summarized as follows: at the end of the two-year intervention period, there are some real gains in the levels of cognitive development of experimental pupils, but no measurable improvements in their science achievement. One year later, the gains in cognitive development have disappeared, but all the experimental groups show a significantly higher proportion of pupils achieving high results in science compared with controls.

This will be followed up as the pupils move on through the secondary school course and reach the external examination at 16. As a small-scale study, the work which Adey described is unlikely to have widespread influence, but for him there were interesting conclusions to draw from the pupils' initial groans every time the intervention lesson materials were produced, followed, quite quickly, by their enthusiastic absorption in the tasks they were asked to perform. According to Adey,

They groaned because they knew that the next hour was going to require them to think harder than perhaps in the rest of the week . . . but the practice of active engagement in a problem proved . . . to be attractive and motivating . . . What we need in the whole school curriculum, for all abilities, is to release and capitalize on this desire (to exercise their minds), rather than to bottle, channel and eventually kill it.

Arts and humanities

Reference has already been made to the pride of place once accorded to Latin and the claims made for its study as a form of mental training for school pupils. Though the classical languages have lost ground in the face of other competitors for curricular time, a great deal of effort continues to be devoted to language teaching and learning in various forms. The relationship between language acquisition and thinking skills has been extensively studied by developmental psychologists in Europe and the United States. Particularly in Europe, the importance of language learning—grammar, syntax, spelling and understanding—has been seen as holding the key to many of the processes of cognitive development. Language is not only a basic skill for communication and intercourse, but also for the articulation of ideas, feelings, problems and solutions.

Literature also has traditionally played an important part in general education because it provides a way of extending experience vicariously: releasing the imagination, refining the sensibilities, and confronting moral issues. In these ways a study of literature stimulates thinking and provides a needed complement to the modes of thought demanded by the exact sciences.

Some of these ideas are explored in Professor Maxine Greene's paper (pp. 65–77). Professor Greene broadens the discussion by locating the thinking process firmly within a context of moral feeling and its ambiguities. In so doing she brings the argument back to the larger aims of education in human development.

"The passion of thoughtfulness" links the affective domain with the process of thinking—experience and feeling with rationality. For her, the arts and humanities make demands upon the whole person, stimulating imagination as well as thought, passion as well as reason, carrying with them the desire to "make sense, of the lived world . . . the world (we) can see and hear and read".

This kind of thinking, in Greene's presentation, is more likely to lead to unease and anxiety than problem solving. Her package is the antithesis of a tool-kit for problem solving. The richness of the texture of her paper defies brief summary and deserves to be read at length (pp. 65–77). But for educators and educational administrators, it is an intensely refreshing invitation to think about education as an enrichment of the life of the mind—with all the risks implicit in the release of the imagination and the emotions—which she summed up in her last sentence: "I would want to work towards a contextualized, perspectival curriculum beginning in tumult and warmed by passion. I would want to repair a thoughtless age by reaching out towards possibility".

Culture and Content

Professor Hiroshi Azuma emphasizes the importance of context and cultural background in the approach to the teaching of thinking (pp. 191–198). He stresses the need for group activity in the pursuit of thinking skills, as for example in de Bono's CoRT methods, in Feuerstein's Instrumental Enrichment, or in Lipman's "communities of inquiry". Azuma's Japanese cultural background leads him to emphasize the idea of thinking as a shared activity—"much of our thinking proceeds with external and internalized conversation", as Vygotsky had noted—which explained his preference for "quite a high level of noise from discussion" in a class: "I like a class . . . that gets moderately noisy when I want them to think as well as listen to my lecture".

Patterns of thinking among pupils in Japan and the United States reflect differences of cultural values, because thinking takes place within a given context. The content of study is only a part of the context; there are also value priorities which affect thinking because they cause pupils to have different ideas of what facts and attitudes are important, and therefore alter their perceptions. Cross-national studies have shown that, depending on their cultural preconceptions, pupils differ in the pleasure (or frustration) they find in tackling different problems.

The context determines what aspects of a problem interest and excite students, and engage their sympathies and intellectual energies. Cross-cultural studies have shown American students more concerned with originality of thought and opinion, while Japanese rate "insight into other people's feelings more highly".

Professor Azuma's paper suggests that thinking is not just a set of skills which can be analysed and examined separately from the social context and the values in the mind of the thinker. Coming down on the side of an "infusion" rather than a "content-free" approach, he stresses the need:

(i) for the teacher to keep each child in mind as an integral part of the context in which learning takes place;
(ii) for a supportive and co-operative classroom culture;
(iii) for the teacher to be "a thinker who is open to asking and to being asked questions";
(iv) and for incentive schemes to encourage the attainment of self-control in the form of patience and co-operation.

Even so, Azuma ends on a warning note. Because education is so important in social selection, there is every reason to expect that concentrating on this would overshadow the older role of education as individual study. He is anxious to see the thinking powers of the less able recognized, not relegated, quoting as an example the naive but honest question which can be just as important as the more sophisticated contribution from a brighter student.

Reflections and Sidelights

Not all the input to the Conference came in formal papers and plenary session. There were also workshops and discussion groups which gave participants the chance to react to the experts, and to put them to the test of less formal debate.

Among the Europeans, especially, there was a significant representation of those who remained unpersuaded by the advocates of either the "skills approach" or the "infusion" principle. The "traditionalist" view continued to have its defenders who disputed the need for, or the efficacy of, changes in curriculum and method to emphasize thinking. For them there was too much readiness to discuss thinking in the abstract, too much neglect of the essentially contextual nature of thinking. Such scepticism formed a perceptible undercurrent to the discussion, in contrast to the interventionist enthusiasms of some of the plenary contributions.

There seem to be two sets of questions to be answered if deliberate attempts to teach thinking are to gain wider support. The first concerns the nature of the evidence which ought to influence policy. What do we require to persuade us to make changes in the school curriculum that would give more attention to thinking skills? (Such a question, in an international context, does not, of course, address prior questions relating to who the "us" is who can take such decisions.) The practitioners are acutely aware that they have to approach the question of thinking skills in practical terms, in the wider contexts of all aspects of teaching and learning in schools. The psychologists—both the research specialists and those concerned with developing teaching packages—are more concerned with building models. But these theoretical constructions only exist to help explain what is going on in reality, or to predict what will happen. Practitioners and theorists often find themselves arguing about metaphors rather than facts; when they begin to use such metaphors as if they offer realistic accounts of how the brain works, confusion can soon become worse confounded.

The second set of questions relates to practical outcomes: how to bring about changes if it is argued that these are needed. The present curriculum is overcrowded. Behind the discussion there is a certain unreality because in the circumstances in which most people find themselves, the kind of curriculum change required (for example, to introduce an hour or two a week of the direct teaching of thinking skills) is not a real option even if it were thought to be desirable.

This raises broader questions about the school curriculum, relevant to the CERI programme on "The Curriculum Redefined" of which the Conference was a part. There is a long tradition of debate about the curriculum and what it should comprise. This is fed from many different sources: pedagogic, social, political, economic. The debate about thinking skills has to be fitted into this larger debate. Thinking about thinking is not a brand new idea. Is there now evidence to prove the relative efficiency of a particular new approach?

Many of these matters were raised directly or indirectly in the workshop sessions as well as the discussion groups. The nature of the research evidence needed to validate (or discredit) particular approaches to the teaching of thinking was considered in a workshop led by Dr John Edwards from James Cook University, Queensland, to whom Dr de Bono had referred in relation to the evaluation of the CoRT method. He had little difficulty in showing how complicated such evaluation studies were likely to be.

Among the kinds of evidence which Edwards' workshop believed would be needed to reach conclusions there was:

(i) meta-analysis of many studies with constant results across different conditions;
(ii) observed changes in teachers' behaviour and attitudes;
(iii) analysis of the language of children;
(iv) evidence that children were excited about learning and were being stimulated by what they were doing.

It was obvious that there was no single acceptable or "right" method of research in this area. It would be quite easy to erect impossible hurdles for the researchers to clear which would damn valuable innovation in advance by making excessive demands for scientifically verifiable results. One observer concluded that "truth, or at least an approximation to it, can only emerge from the triangulation of many methods including 'hard' (actually probabalistic) data, responses from pupils, teachers and parents, case studies, and ethnographic, in depth, investigation".

Towards Some Conclusions

For the rapporteur attempting to bring the discussion to some interim conclusions, on the basis of three days of often disjointed debate, among the most helpful papers are the Background Report (pp. 201–229) prepared by the Secretariat (with the assistance of Professor John Nisbet, formerly Professor of Education at Aberdeen University, Scotland) and Professor Nisbet's conference contribution on "Methods and Approaches" (pp. 177–185).

There remain the basic theoretical differences between various schools of psychologists. To some extent this division is represented geographically in the conference with the (mainly European) Piagetians who start from strong theoretical convictions about stages in development, and those developmental psychologists (mainly American) who, weaker in theory but stronger in empirical investigation, have begun to take a growing interest in attempts to teach thinking which in some degree challenge Piagetian orthodoxies.

On the basis of the discussion it was clear how the argument divides, and how, in part at least, it is about aims as much as practicalities. Some remain totally committed to the idea of a skills package: a set of tools or aide-mémoire, which focuses attention on thinking procedures and prevents their neglect by busy teachers in a crowded curriculum. Others remain equally convinced infusionists, believing that there is no room in the crowded curriculum for a thinking skills course independent of curricular content and that even if there were, it would be undesirable to divorce thought from content. If there is progress to be made, they argue it should be by developing strategies within the existing subject-based curriculum which promote critical thinking and effective problem solving.

It would be wrong to suggest that the conference divided neatly into these two groups. As has already been pointed out, some remain unconvinced by either the skills or the infusion approach, unwilling to accept that there is any intellectual imperative to make a choice between these two theoretical models.

Though the discussion returns time and time again to the simplistic choice between a skills approach and the infusion model, this argument remains open. The skills approach offers particular advantages of a limited and clearly identifiable kind. If scientific evaluation evidence is limited, there is the experience of many present users to testify to its value at a certain level, and those packages that are available commercially have their own ways of drawing these advantages to the educational world's attention.

On the other hand, there is clearly much more to the study of thinking and how to help students to operate more effectively than can be accommodated in a proprietary package. Many teachers and psychologists are interested first and foremost in attempts to develop better methods of teaching the existing subject-based curriculum, which also promote more effective thinking. They see this as the main task, and believe they can do it in such a way as to enable thinking skills developed in one context to be transferred to another. But the transfer of training remains problematical, as it has done for so long, in these and similar discussions.

There is, it has to be said, always something less than wholly persuasive when a cross-curricular approach is recommended as the answer to a taxing curricular problem. It always seems like a counsel of perfection, so easy to prescribe, so hard to carry through.

What is clear is that the evaluation of such teaching methods has a long way to go before anyone can say with assurance that this or that method works. By building specific teaching aimed at improving thinking into the treatment of a subject like, say, mathematics, teachers can, it is said, enhance the quality of pupils' learning of the subject matter and justify their actions in this way, even if positive evidence of improved thinking skill cannot be established. One of the problems inherent in any evaluation is that the overriding object of the exercise is (or ought to be) good education, not a narrow concern with particular thinking skills, and the latter aim rapidly becomes subsumed within the former.

The practical form taken by many attempts to inject a strategy for the teaching of thinking into the regular curriculum is to develop a problem-based approach to subject teaching. Mathematics is an obvious candidate, along with science. So too is history and social science, and it has been applied to professional studies such as medicine and law. These methods may have much to commend them; whether or not they lead to better thinking, they may be good ways of teaching the subjects.

It is clearly not possible to go far along this road without encountering basic epistemological questions about the nature of knowledge, and whether each domain of knowledge has its own particular style of thinking. As Maxine Greene's paper shows, the arts and humanities have their own intellectual disciplines and thinking styles, enriched by the imagination and the insights of creative thought. Formalized as philosophy, thinking becomes a study on its own, as Matthew Lipman argues in his attempt to use it as the basis of children's learning. And in such a context, too, a moral element enters in: education is not just about the techniques of thinking, but also about the quality of the thoughts and the link between thought and "right" action.

There is already a mounting file of evidence about the possible use of information technology as a subject which could provide a vehicle for the teaching of thinking. Computer programming draws on a method of analysing the thinking process. It is not yet at all clear how far this leads to any transfer of reasoning powers to other activities, but as Dr Caillot's paper shows, the potential of information technology as a tool for teaching thinking has only begun to be investigated, and as work on artificial intelligence moves forward and expert systems become more expert, it seems inconceivable that there will not be a spin-off for education. It would clearly be a matter of great significance if computer games could be used to develop thinking skills; if, that is, any identifiable transfer of learning were to take place.

Again, the argument returns to the diversity of aims which any discussion of the teaching of thinking reveals. Nothing suggests that there is a single effective approach to the teaching of thinking; there is no sovereign method, no single strategy for all situations.

Perkins and Salomon suggest a division between two distinct mechanisms for transfer which seems to fit the distinction between the skills package approach and the infusion approach. A package of learning tools can equip students with a battery of techniques that lead to what Perkins and Salomon call "automatic triggering of well-rehearsed schemata". This is what they call "low road" transfer. "High road" transfer exemplified by the infusion model, on the other hand, involves "active decontextualization and restructuring". This demands more than thinking drills and a tool-kit of mnemonics. There must be "a deliberate mindful abstraction of a principle and its application to a different context".

An analysis along these lines helps make sense of much of the intricate and animated discussion which took place inside and outside the conference room in Paris.

According to the Scottish song, both the low road and the high road arrive at a similar destination, if not by the same route nor at the same speed. That is not the inference to be drawn in this instance. The low road aims at limited but extremely useful competences. Thought of in terms of "education for capability", the low road leads into the realms of personal and social education and the wide range of life skills which the traditional subject-based curricula fail to provide for many less academically gifted pupils.

The exponents of thinking skills packages would argue that education for capability and competence is something that is needed across the board and should not be reserved for those who do not shine in the subjects making up the traditional curriculum.

The high road is more ambitious, more problematical, and aspires to higher-order intellectual skills of reflective thinking. It does not threaten the existing curriculum; it offers to fulfil it: to enhance its educational value. It implies the possibility of systematizing and regularizing the powers of thought that have always been regarded as the priceless by-product of subject-based study, the practical ability to apply the mind to general and particular questions which is an important element in "educated common sense".

Whether Perkins and Salomon would go along with this use of their metaphor is another matter, but it is of the nature of attractive metaphors that they are liable to be applied in ways different from those envisaged by their inventors. Behind both the high road and the low road are the everyday realities of organized learning in schools and colleges and the compromises on which this depends.

I

Learning to Think:
The Direct Method

1

The Direct Teaching of Thinking in Education and the CoRT Method

EDWARD DE BONO

Director of the Cognitive Research Trust,
Cambridge, United Kingdom

Myths and Realities

The direct teaching of thinking as a specific curriculum subject is not a future dream but is already happening in several countries: from Venezuela, where the legal requirement is that all students must spend two hours a week on thinking skills, to the largest community college in North America, to the senior science schools (MARA) in Malaysia. Although there is considerable activity in the United States, Canada, Australia and New Zealand, in general the developed countries are being left behind. This is due to educational complacency, inadequate leadership, jealousies, political in-fighting and confusion. In the developed countries, education has always been more inward-looking and less concerned with the needs of society, although this attitude is beginning to change.

There are two simple matters that need to be considered:

(i) why we need to teach thinking deliberately and explicitly in education;
(ii) how we do it.

Every education system in the world will claim that it already teaches thinking skills. This is because the teaching of thinking skills is so fundamental an aim of education that no educator could possibly admit that it is not already happening. It is also true that some very limited thinking skills are being taught. But underlying the false assumptions that education must, by definition, already be teaching thinking skills are a number of fallacies:

Fallacy 1: Intelligence is the same as thinking skills

This is quite wrong. Many highly intelligent people are poor thinkers. For example, a highly intelligent person may use his or her thinking just to defend a point of view. The more adequate that defence, the less inclined is that person actually to explore the subject. That is bad thinking. Highly intelligent students are good at puzzle solving and reactive thinking. When all the pieces are present they can sort them out. But they are less able in the kind of thinking that requires them to seek out and assess the pieces, like the engine in a car. Intelligence is potential. The skill with which the car is driven corresponds to the thinking skill with which intelligence is used. That is why many programmes for the "gifted" are now starting to use the CoRT Thinking approach.

Fallacy 2: Teaching knowledge is sufficient

Perfect godlike knowledge does indeed make thinking unnecessary, but, since we are always going to fall far short of such perfection, thinking skills are essential to make the best use of existing knowledge and to gain further knowledge. Education is obsessed with knowledge because it is there, because it is easy to teach and because it is easy to test. All knowledge is valuable, and the more you have the more valuable are the next bits you acquire. That is why it is so difficult for educators to make the essential trade-off of knowledge for thinking skills. There is always enough knowledge around to fill several curricula.

Fallacy 3: Surely thinking skills are taught within every subject?

It is perfectly true that some thinking skills are being taught implicitly while any subject is being taught. But these skills are very limited—they are confined to information sorting and analysis, as well as some debating skills—and fall short of the range of thinking skills required both as life skills and for development (decisions, priorities, alternatives, other people's views, etc.).

Fallacy 4: Any thinking that is taking place will develop better thinking skills

This is a most dangerous fallacy. A two-finger typing journalist at the age of 60 has not been short of typing practice, but such practice has only made that person a better two-finger typist. Merely practising a skill only reinforces existing habits. Simply to practise thinking is not enough.

Educators in all countries must stop looking at education as a game unto itself, setting its own targets and feeling complacent about achieving them. Perhaps more than any other educator in the world, I spend a lot of time with business and also non-commercial organizations (IBM, Du Pont, various governments, conservation organizations, etc.). I have worked in 45 different countries with all manner of ideologies and cultures (Protestant, Catholic, Marxist, Islamic, Buddhist, etc.). In all of them there is a great need to teach thinking for the following reasons:

(i) The provision of life skills is necessary so that individuals can operate in an increasingly complex world: making choices, solving problems, taking initiatives.

(ii) In highly competitive industrial societies (and also in developing societies), there is a great need to increase the skills of "operacy". Operacy is the skill of doing. It is a bad mistake to assume that knowing is enough.

(iii) In addition to operacy at a general work level, education must provide the entrepreneurs, organizers and leaders that society requires. Such people need a great fluency in thinking skills: in the skills of wisdom and not just cleverness.

(iv) In any democracy where individuals have to make choices and assessments, a lack of thinking skills means politics by slogan.

(v) If we do not teach thinking skills, then the only intellectual activity open to the intellectually energetic is to be "against everything" because this requires the least thinking skills. That leads to a society that can only progress through disruption and opposition.

At this point my conclusion is that there is a pressing need to teach thinking directly and explicitly in schools, and that this is not happening in many countries at this moment. I would summarize the reasons why education has not taken this necessary step as follows:

(i) Education is both inward-looking and complacent.

(ii) Education is too busy and its curriculum is too crowded with what it is already teaching.

(iii) Education does not really understand what is meant by thinking.

(iv) Education is very confused as to how thinking can actually be taught.

At this point it is clear that we need to move on to consider the practical teaching of thinking as a subject in education. Quite simply, how can we do it?

How To Teach Thinking

I want to review some of the traditional approaches to the teaching of thinking:

Osmosis: The hope is that a brilliant teacher will impart directly to the student his or her habits of thinking. This does work, but it requires a brilliant teacher and a great deal of contact between that teacher and the students over a long period of time. So the method cannot be generalized and is simply not practical.

Intelligent teaching: This usually consists of the asking of questions, the setting of tasks and the making of connections. As with osmosis, this depends on very good teachers. In addition, the type of thinking taught is still concerned with analysis and information sorting, and these skills are inadequate. Thus, the method cannot easily be generalized and even at best is inadequate. The danger is that all education systems claim that their teachers behave in this manner and that this is enough to teach thinking skills.

Rules of logic: At one time in a few schools it was traditional to teach the rules of logic. In general, these were abstract and had little relationship to real life. Even at best, the teaching of logic leaves out the major part of human thinking which is "perception". The bulk of thinking takes place in the perception area, and this is also where most mistakes take place. Correct logic with incorrect perceptions is not only inadequate but dangerous, since the logic breeds arrogance.

Critical thinking: This does indeed have its place amongst thinking skills and is part of the CoRT approach. But there is a very grave danger in assuming that critical thinking is enough. This danger is being played out right now in the United States, where there is a great emphasis on critical thinking. If critical thinking teaches us to avoid all mistakes in thinking, shall we then become excellent thinkers? I would argue that the answer is no. If you want to avoid mistakes in driving a car, the best thing to do would be to leave out the productive, generative and creative aspects of thinking. Without these aspects thinking is sterile. Unfortunately, educators think only of "reactive thinking": how to react to what is put before you. In real life this is only a small part of thinking. Educators must be aware of the insidious danger of concentrating solely upon critical thinking. It has a part to play, but only a part.

Stimulation: The hope is that as a student plays chess or goes through a simulation exercise, the thinking skills demanded by the exercise will stay with the student as skills that can be used anywhere. The difficulty seems to be one of transfer. We can indeed claim that a game like chess must involve strategy, planning, decisions, choices and priorities. Do we find excellent chess players showing these characteristics in their normal lives? It seems that these skills become firmly attached to the subject matter and do not get used elsewhere.

Discussion: This is an attractive approach which has beguiled many educators. Clearly, thinking is taking place. Clearly, the students are motivated and taking part. Again, the problem is one of transfer. The skills exhibited in one discussion do not reappear in subsequent discussions. This is because attention is focused on the subject matter of the discussion and not on metacognitive processes. Unless such processes are made explicit, there is no retention of a skill.

Tool method: This is the method I prefer, and it is also the basis of the CoRT approach. A thinking tool is designed and made explicit. This tool is then used by the students in a variety of situations. The large number of practice situations and their variety is very important, for the only thing that remains constant is the "tool". In this way, skills build up in the use of the tool, which can then be transferred directly to other situations. So the process is direct: tool→practice→transfer. This should be contrasted with the discussion method: discuss→abstract process→verbalize process→apply elsewhere.

The comparison of the different approaches to the teaching of thinking is complex because of the need to be very clear as to what we want. Some of the methods require exceptional teachers or lengthy teacher training. Results will then be demonstrated in a carefully controlled experimental situation. Such results will not easily be generalized elsewhere. Some methods directly teach the skills needed for tackling IQ tests and then proceed to use IQ tests as a measure of improvement in thinking, a dangerously misleading practice.

My own criteria for selecting a method of teaching thinking would be as follows:

(i) The method must be simple, practical and capable of being used by a large number of teachers.

(ii) The method must be robust so that when passed from trainer to trainer and teacher to student it will remain intact. In Venezuela there were five levels of training before 105,000 teachers were trained.

(iii) The "parallel design" method uses a design in which any part on its own is usable and useful even if the other parts are forgotten or misunderstood. This is in contrast to "hierarchical design", in which the whole structure must be remembered or the parts are useless.

(iv) The method must refer specifically to "real life" situations. It is not enough to hope that this transfer will occur.

(v) The method must go beyond "reactive thinking" analysis and information sorting to reach the operacy skills required in real life. This involves an emphasis on perceptual thinking (how we see the world around us).

(vi) The method must be applicable to students of different ages and abilities, with teachers of varying aptitude, with different cultures, ideologies and background. It is only years of experience that will show if a programme is practical.

(vii) The students must enjoy the thinking lessons.

Use of the Tool Method

Let me provide you with a case study using "tools" from the CoRT Thinking programme which I developed: While teaching a demonstration class of mixed 12-year-olds in Sydney, Australia, I asked the class what they thought of the idea of giving every student $5 a week to go to school. All 30 of the students said it was an excellent idea (they could buy sweets, comics, chewing gum, etc.).

I then took four minutes to explain the "PMI" tool, which entailed looking first at the Plus points, then the Minus points and finally the Interesting points. I asked the students to form into groups of five and to go systematically through the PMI. I provided the timing of two minutes for each scan direction.

At the end of the group discussion time, I asked for the output. The Plus points were the same as before. But now there were many Minus points (older students would beat us up for the money; parents would not give presents; less money for teachers; where would the money come from? etc.), as well as Interesting points (would the money be used to ensure discipline? etc.).

At the end of this exercise, I asked the original question again. Now 29 of the 30 had completely changed their minds and decided that $5 a week was a bad idea. This was the result of a broader "scan".

The PMI was just a tool to ensure a broader and more systematic scan. This is no different from a north/south/east/west framework which an explorer might use for scanning a new landscape.

The point I want to emphasize most strongly is that my intervention was only the four minutes needed to explain the PMI tool. I did not argue with the students. I did not ask the students to consider where the money might come from. I did not remind the students of the behaviour of other students. I simply presented the tool which the students used by themselves. That is what I mean by the "tool method". Consider the old saying: "If you give a hungry person fish, that person eats for a day; if you give a fishing rod, that person may eat forever".

Where Do the Tools Come From?

The tools do *not* come from an analysis of the thinking process. There are people who sit down to analyse the thinking process and then seek to teach each part on its own as a sort of "tool". This does not work because the analysis is for the sake of analysis, and tools have to be practical. For example, in the CoRT method there is a tool called "CAF" (Consider All Factors). Then there are two other tools called "C&S" (Consequences and Sequel) and "OPV" (Other People's Views). It is obvious that these two latter considerations are really part of the consideration of all factors. In practice, however, when considering all factors students do not pay sufficient attention to consequences or other people's views, so these get specific scanning tools of their own. This practical approach to the design of the tools is important.

The CoRT lessons could be taught as attitude lessons (looking at the positive and negative points of any situation instead of doing a PMI), but the results simply wash away. The artificial letters of the PMI anchor the operations and make of them an "executive concept" which can be used at any time. The mind is full of descriptive concepts but has very few "executive concepts".

In practice, the design of the CoRT tools comes from two sources: over 20 years of the teaching of thinking skills in both education and the "real world" (including business areas), and a consideration of the basis of perception.

The Nature of Perception

Traditionally, we have only been concerned with one type of information system. This is the passive or discrete system. There are symbols (words or mathematical symbols) which are stored naturally on some passive surface. An outside operator (human mind or computer) then manipulates these symbols according to the rules of logic.

This type of information system has been very good for "processing" (mathematics, computers, verbal and mathematical logic, etc.).

In perception, however, we have an entirely different type of system. We have a system in which incoming information organizes itself into patterns. This is not unlike the way rainfall on a landscape organizes itself into streams, rivers and watersheds. Over the last 20 years we have begun to understand such "self-organizing" systems. In 1969, I wrote a book, *The Mechanism of Mind*, in which I described how neuro-physiological behaviour in the brain gave rise to the patterns of perception. These ideas are now the basis of the advanced neurocomputers.

Without going into technical detail, perception is the result of pattern formation in a self-organizing system. This is what makes life possible.

Without such a system, even getting dressed in the morning would take 48 hours of sorting and analysis to get through the more than 39 million ways of putting on 11 items of clothing!

These perceptual patterns are the basis of the normal point-to-point thinking in which the mind follows the main tracks from one point to the next one. Because of the asymmetry of patterns there is no access to the side tracks. So we need to design specific scanning patterns like the PMI in order to be able to get a broader view of the situation.

It is consideration of the asymmetry of patterns which can give rise to the very simple but highly effective "random word" creative technique. This entails using a random word to trigger off new ideas on any subject, which seems both absurd and totally illogical since, by definition, a random word would work for any subject. Yet it works very well because in an asymmetric system if you start in from the periphery towards the centre, you will uncover patterns you could never have reached when starting out from the centre.

These are the fundamental considerations that lie behind the design of the CoRT Thinking tools. It is not just a matter of someone dreaming up a "tool" which seems to have some relationship to thinking. Because thinking is an everyday process, the thinking skills movement has suffered a great deal from the simple assumption that putting a name to a part of thinking and then teaching it is sufficient. As a result, people have put together a mishmash of ineffective programmes.

A Typical CoRT Thinking Lesson

A CoRT lesson might start as follows:

The teacher would set a simple task: for example, asking younger students to draw a new design for the human head. One student might suggest an eye at the back of the head. The teacher would take this particular design and ask the class for the "good", "bad" and, finally, "interesting" points in having an eye at the back of the head. From this example and exercise the teacher would pull together the PMI tool and explain that this involved a formal way of looking at Plus points, Minus points and Interesting points.

The first exercise would then be introduced. The students would work in groups of four, five or six (depending on class size). They would work on a thinking practice item for two to three minutes. The teacher would then ask for output from each group.

For example, the thinking item might be: "Should all cars be painted yellow?" Some groups would be assigned to work only on the Plus points, other groups on the Minus points and some on the Interesting points.

The teacher would collect the verbal feedback at the end of the allotted time. It is important to keep precisely to the time limit in order to encourage the discipline of thinking. There are various ways of collecting the feedback (one point at a time from each group, or one group giving a full output and the others only adding what has not been mentioned, etc.). The teachers' handbooks that accompany the lessons give full instructions on these matters. The feedback is very important for motivational reasons, but it should be brisk because it can take up too much valuable time that is better used for actual thinking.

The teacher would immediately set the next task from the CoRT student cards. For example, the suggestion that all people should wear a badge showing "their mood of the moment". This time each group would be asked to go through the entire PMI process, taking one stage at a time. The teacher would indicate a switch from Plus scanning to Minus scanning and then on to Interesting scanning after two minutes.

The amount of input required from the teacher will vary with the age of the students. For example, with younger students, it is necessary to explain "Interesting". This is best done with a phrase such as "It would be interesting to see if . . .".

In a lesson, three, four or even five thinking tasks would be covered. It is important that there are several such tasks and that their nature varies so that attention stays on the PMI tool which is the constant. The teacher needs to keep repeating the "PMI" lettering in order to establish this as a deliberate mental operation and not just an attitude.

At the end of the lesson the teacher may have a short discussion on the PMI process: What is its use? Where would you want to use it? The teacher then summarizes the nature and use of the PMI tool.

Structure of the CoRT Programme

For each lesson, reusable student cards are provided. For each of the six CoRT sections there is a teacher handbook which goes into step-by-step detail on each lesson. Many teachers have taken up the use of CoRT without specific training because the instructions are simple and comprehensive.

There are six CoRT sections of 10 lessons each:

CoRT I: Breadth of perception
CoRT II: Organization of thinking
CoRT III: Interaction, argument, critical thinking
CoRT IV: Creative thinking with specific tools
CoRT V: Information and feeling
CoRT VI: Action (framework for step-by-step thinking).

The CoRT programme is designed to cover the creative, the constructive and the critical aspects of thinking.

It is important that CoRT I always be done first. After that, it is possible to use the other sections in any order desired. For example, one school might use CoRT I, CoRT IV and CoRT V. Another school might use CoRT I and CoRT III. Yet another might choose CoRT I, CoRT IV and CoRT VI. Some schools choose to work through the entire programme, taking each section in turn.

The thinking tasks show a mixture of fun, remote items (not immediately part of the student's life) and problems. This mix is very important. In order to develop the "tool" as such, it is important that the tool be practised on "fun" items that do not have too much emotional or experience content. Once the tool has been "acquired", then the tool can be used on serious, backyard problems to show that these thinking tools are applicable to real everyday life.

Results

It has always been the policy to encourage CoRT users to do their own research with local conditions. To set up some centralized research in idealized circumstances often has very little relevance to real educational use. Research has been done in Venezuela, Bulgaria, Australia, Canada and the United Kingdom, and is being initiated in many other countries, including the United States.

No adequate test of thinking "performance" has been developed. In general, education is completely lacking in tests of composite performance (how do you test if someone can play the piano well?). Therefore, results have fallen into three categories: soft data, thinking performance and standardized tests.

There is a lot of feedback from teachers, principals, parents and students. The CoRT-trained students are more constructive. They are more willing to listen to others and to explore alternatives. These students consider themselves as "thinkers" and are therefore willing to apply their thinking. Thinking is not of the argument and challenge type but is constructive in nature.

Thinking Performance

In spite of the lack of developed thinking performance tests, there have been various attempts to analyse the results of written thinking output (essays, notes, expository paragraphs). These range from a simple listing of ideas to more detailed analysis. The Venezuelan project showed statistically significant increases in ideation, as did the Singapore Government project and various research efforts in Canada and elsewhere. In the United Kingdom, a Schools Council project (Hunter–Grundin, 1985) showed a statistically significant increase in the number of relevant ideas, following the use of CoRT training. Rather curiously, since the difference in total ideas was not statistically significant, the report was perceived as negative. This is manifestly absurd since irrelevant ideas have no value, and the statistically significant increase in relevant ideas clearly supports the value of thinking training. This point indicates the dangers of performance measurement, even to sophisticated researchers. In these matters it must be noted that with students the variance is so huge that statistical significance is very difficult to achieve.

Standardized Tests

The Bulgarian research showed statistically significant improvement in IQ tests (Raven's matrices). In Australia, John Edwards at the James Cook University in Queensland has carried out very comprehensive research and shown significant effects on a wide variety of standard tests. For example, using the standard tests of the Australian Council for Educational Research, he showed that after CoRT training, 52 per cent of the students in a school were placed in the top two mathematics categories, compared to a norm of 31 per cent and the six-year performance of the school at 24 per cent.

The Way Forward

All educational authorities need to take a serious look at the direct teaching of thinking as a skill in schools.

Point 1: In the modern world, every person needs to develop thinking skills to use as life skills. These are needed to make sense of an increasingly complex world, to allow the democratic process to work clearly, and for industrial development and competition to proceed.

Point 2: No matter how much educators may disagree, thinking skills are simply not taught adequately in traditional education. There is a need not just for knowledge analysis and the skills of argument, but for constructive and creative thinking skills. There is as much need for operacy as for literacy and numeracy. Whatever the present state of thinking skills is assumed to be, it can be greatly improved through direct and deliberate attention to such skills.

Point 3: Thinking must be taught directly and deliberately as a subject and not simply infused into other subjects, because the latter method is far too weak for metacognitive training. There is a need for a single (or double) period per week devoted to thinking skills throughout a student's education.

Point 4: There are established methods of teaching thinking directly as a skill. Some (like this programme) have been in use for many years across a wide range of cultures, ideologies, ages, abilities and teacher abilities. It is best to use an established programme that has proved its practicality.

Point 5: A core body of teachers can be trained in the direct teaching of thinking. After building up their own experience, they can then become trainers for others. This model has been very successful in the rapid spread of training in the direct teaching of thinking. For this to work, the method must be simple and robust.

References

Bono, E. de (1969). *The Mechanism of Mind*, Pelican, London.
Hunter–Grundin, E. (1985). *Teaching Thinking*, SCDC, Schools Council, London.

Commentary by Malcolm Skilbeck

Vice-Chancellor of Deakin University,
Geelong, Victoria, Australia

I will deal first with the practical situation and the policy environment in OECD member countries as they relate to Dr de Bono's proposals for teaching thinking. Then I shall draw out some of the issues and problems as I see them, in the approach he has recommended to us. Finally, I will suggest two or three lines of thought and action for further consideration.

Turning first to the policy environment and the political situation in OECD member countries, I can but underline de Bono's contention that the teaching of thinking as such is quite low on the agenda. A "state of the art" report which I and others have recently completed for the OECD found little evidence in the countries where curriculum policies and major programmes are reviewed that thinking is identified as a major target in the organization of the curriculum of basic education. By "basic education" I mean the primary or elementary school, together with the first three to five years of the secondary school: what in most countries constitute the compulsory years of schooling. In the later, postcompulsory years leading to such public examinations as the baccalaureate, abitur, "A" levels and so on, there may be courses in philosophy, scientific method, science and society and so forth, when the focus is not so much subject content as modes of reflection, analysis and critical inquiry or problem solving, but these are on the whole for a minority of students, and in any case fall outside what I take to be the main lines of de Bono's argument. His thesis is that some clearly articulated thought processes of a problem-solving kind should be separated or abstracted from the normal context of content-based teaching in schools and made into a central theme in the curriculum.

For more than a century, most member countries have had experience of highly organized curricula arranged in systems of sequential public schooling. In several countries the period has been longer. Yet thinking in de Bono's sense has not achieved a central place in the curriculum. It is necessary, therefore, to ask why this should be so. As a pioneer and an advocate, de Bono offers some important, not to say hostile, reasons. He refers to "educational complacency", "inadequate leadership", "political in-fighting" and "confusion". He blames the educators for being inward-looking, and too little concerned with societal needs. Like a missionary faced with a wall of indifference, however, he finds light where he can and affirms that though the situation is bad, it is changing. I doubt, however, if it is changing in the direction he recommends, since it seems to me that the changes are less towards the concept of teaching thinking and more towards a consolidation of the subject-centred curriculum on the one hand (for example, through a resurgence of interest in subject-defined core curricula in the United States, the United Kingdom, France, the Netherlands, Australia and New Zealand) and, on the other, towards multi-skilling and work-related education and training. Neither of these major trends addresses in any central or significant way the teaching of thinking through what de Bono describes as the tool method. But it would be foolish indeed to conclude that the trends and the overall framework for the curriculum and pedagogy are not centrally concerned with thinking in a wider sense of the term than de Bono addresses in his paper.

The debate, therefore, can scarcely proceed unless we pay closer attention to the concept of thinking and to the various ways in which thinking is indeed taught in our educational systems. While I am prepared to concede many of the criticisms de Bono makes of schooling—and have made many of them myself—I am not able to agree that thinking is not taught or, as he implies, that it is usually badly managed where it is taught at all. It would come as a great surprise to educational policy makers, administrators and teachers to learn that the teaching of thinking does not occur. Perhaps we all need to be surprised, but if so the case had better be well founded on argument and evidence.

De Bono manages to present his case without actually defining thinking at all. He does give us a few examples, mostly of a negative kind. He takes such processes as critical inquiry—itself, by the way, an extremely amorphous concept that philoso-phers as diverse as Socrates, Descartes, Bacon and Dewey have tried to pin down to procedural rules and methods—or the skills of analysis and information sorting, and simply dismisses them as inadequate. He is able to do this by adopting what is, in fact, a long-established rhetorical procedure: namely the use of the worst case and the selection of features which in themselves neither give a full or fair account of the procedure in question (e.g. discussion, analysis, evaluation, simulation etc.), nor exhaust the range of meanings of "thinking".

As I said, de Bono himself does not define thinking. He moves as quickly as he can on to his own favoured methodology. He reminds one of the rhetoricians of ancient Athens and Rome, and the experts on the teaching of reading who frequented the courts of the lesser European princes in the seventeenth and eighteenth centuries. He has a method to promote rather than a subject matter to examine.

Perhaps I can illustrate this argument by asking two questions. First, why is no consideration given to such aspects of thought as the poetic association of ideas and images, the construction of metaphors, iconography, the systematic organization of knowledge, criteria for the selection and evaluation of evidence, and the application of codes and formulae? Each of these aspects of thought is drawn from the field of educational practices in as much as they are used, and widely used, in teaching subjects such as literature and the arts, chemistry and geography, history and social studies, physics and mathematics. My second question on this point is: what are the criteria de Bono himself promotes for the validity and efficiency of his tool methods?

As far as I can judge, there are essentially two criteria that he offers. Firstly, there is the claim that it works. But the question then is: what work does it do? We need a great deal more than de Bono offers in his paper if we are to address that question in any depth. Secondly, de Bono justifies his method by reference to the psychology of perception. I claim no expertise in this field, but when I read in de Bono's paper that "neurophysiological behaviour in the brain gives rise to a pattern of perception" and that "perception is the result of pattern formation in a self-organizing system", I feel the need for rather more explanation, not to say rigorous analysis than we have been given. De Bono offers no empirical evidence for the efficiency of his model, other than his own successful experiences, which of course may tell us more about his personality and intellect than about the CoRT method. Moreover, his remarks about patterns of perception, the asymmetry of patterns, the use of random words and so forth do not to my mind constitute a clear or coherent explanation of why CoRT should be treated as the royal road to the teaching of thinking. At best it could be regarded as one way in which some thought processes might be given more attention in formal education than they now are. De Bono says CoRT is "not just a matter of someone dreaming up a 'tool' which seems to have some relationship with thinking". He has in this remark put into words precisely the view I formed in reading his paper.

Is my conclusion then a negative one? In the words of a much earlier teacher of thinking, Peter Abelard, yes and no. I do not believe that de Bono has sustained his larger and bolder claims. He has taken the relatively easy course of attacking the conventional practice of education for not teaching thinking without either defining thinking—except in the limited and incomplete operational terms of his own CoRT method—or documenting the educational policies or practices with which he is dissatisfied. Thus, every educational policy statement I have seen includes the teaching of thinking and thought, and subject teachers collectively and individually can rightly claim to be teaching the organization of thought. But even if de Bono had successfully made a case for the universalization of CoRT in schools, his paper gives us no idea as to how such a change might occur. His criticism of education for being inward-looking applies with even greater force to his own analysis.

I said that my conclusion would be both positive and negative. The real interest and significance of CoRT, as I see it, is that it has prompted a useful stimulus for thinking about the school curriculum and approaches to teaching and learning. It is one example which has demonstrated its own practicability and robustness in many different educational and business settings around the world. While it is neither an exhaustive nor comprehensive model of thinking and thought, and while its intellectual rationale lacks the conviction necessary to influence large parts of the academic community, CoRT, its protagonist Edward de Bono and various other exponents have properly challenged the educational establishment to focus more sharply and precisely on the teaching of thinking as a principal aim of education. As to whether de Bono himself is not running the risk of mechanizing and technologiz-ing thinking by isolating and hypostatizing certain processes is a matter of debate.

Our subject-orientated curriculum, as he points out, is not always a "vehicle for the teaching of thinking and provides an insufficient context for the teaching of thought and its application in everyday life". But its proponents—and that means practically the whole educational establishment world-wide—have more on their side than de Bono is prepared to concede. This conference as it proceeds will, I am sure, repeatedly re-examine issues raised by a consideration of de Bono's paper.

Note

In preparing this paper I had the benefit of comments from two of my colleagues at Deakin University, Professor Richard Bates and Professor Barry Coussins.

2

Research Work on the CoRT Method

JOHN EDWARDS

*Department of Pedagogics and Scientific Studies in Education,
James Cook University of North Queensland,
Townsville, Australia*

For many generations, the academic disciplines and teacher-centred pedagogy have been relied upon to transmit to students the thinking skills they need. Increasingly, it is becoming clear that this faith has been misplaced. Studies such as that of Gunstone and White (1980) show that even the best products of our secondary schools have impoverished thinking skills. There is also evidence (e.g. Edwards and Marland, 1984) that what is going on inside the heads of children in classrooms is far removed from what educators may desire.

Over the last 20 years there has been a resurgence in interest in the direct teaching of thinking skills. This is related to a range of views about learning and brain functioning (de Bono, 1969; Feuerstein, 1980). A fundamental position emerging from this is that the learning of thinking skills as a by-product of studying academic disciplines is relatively inefficient and ineffective.

This paper reports on the third in a series of studies undertaken to reveal the effects of a thinking skills programme on students. The programme used was de Bono's (1981) CoRT-1 programme, a set of 10 lessons intended to teach children a set of thinking tools they can use to broaden their thinking. The total instructional time involved is about eight hours.

The first study (Edwards and Baldauf, 1983) involved incorporating the CoRT-1 programme into a Grade 10 science class (approximate age 15 years). Students, teachers and parents reported positively on the effects of the programme. Students showed large increases in the number of ideas, quality and structure of answer on a familiar essay topic, and in the novelty and number of ideas generated on an unfamiliar essay topic. The improvements were independent of the students' IQ level. The results also suggested that learning of the CoRT-1 skills had produced improved performance on the end-of-year science examination.

In the second study (Edwards and Baldauf, 1987), 67 Grade Seven students (approximate age 12 years) completed the CoRT-1 programme over a four-week period. They were tested with a broad range of measures before starting CoRT-1 and again 11 weeks after completing the programme. The students showed statistically significant gains in: scholastic aptitude, as measured by the Otis–Lennon (1982) School Ability Test (OLSAT), Intermediate Form R; self-concept as a learner, as measured by Waetjen's (1967) Self-Concept as a Learner (SCAL) Scale; and flexibility and originality of thinking, as measured by the Torrance (1984) Test of Creative Thinking.

The study reported in this paper aimed to blend the strengths of instruments used previously with newly designed instruments, to incorporate a sizeable control group, and to include personality as a dimension for study.

The CoRT-1 Materials

The CoRT-1 programme (de Bono, 1981) is a set of 10 lessons each presented on a separate sheet. A brief overview of each sheet is given in Table 2.1. There are five other CoRT packages, each also containing 10 lessons. CoRT-1 aims to broaden student perception by demonstrating a number of different directions that thinking can follow. Students are encouraged to use specific thinking tools to develop the habit of broadening their thinking.

Working through each CoRT-1 sheet takes about 45 minutes. So, in total the CoRT-1 programme covers about eight hours of instruction. Students work from individual copies of the sheets. First the particular thinking skill is described and explained by the teacher using an example. Then the students apply the skill to two or three practice items, working in groups of three or four. A brief whole-class feedback and discussion session is held after each practice item. After this there is a whole-class discussion of the use of the thinking skill and the principles that apply to it. Usually students also do a short homework project to apply the skill.

The Study

Two hundred and two Grade Seven students, in the last year of their elementary schooling, participated in the study. The students were from seven classes, three in a co-educational Roman Catholic school and four in a state primary school. These were the two largest schools of their type in a large rural city in North Queensland, Australia. Two classes in each

TABLE 2.1   *CoRT-1 Thinking Lessons: Brief Overview adapted from CoRT-1 Teacher's Notes*

Sheet 1:	PMI (Plus, Minus, Interest). Involves looking for the plus (P), minus (M), and interesting points (I) in any idea. The aim is to enlarge one's view of a situation and to provide a means of bypassing the natural emotional reaction to an idea.
Sheet 2:	CAF (Consider All Factors). Involves the exploration of a situation before coming up with an idea. The aim is to attempt to be as complete as possible in considering all the factors in any situation.
Sheet 3:	Rules. Provides an opportunity to practise PMI and CAF. PMI is used on an existing or proposed rule, CAF when making a rule.
Sheet 4:	C&S (Consequence and Sequel). Deals with what may happen after a decision is made. Immediate, short-term (1 to 5 years), medium-term (5 to 25 years) and long-term (over 25 years) consequences are systematically explored.
Sheet 5:	AGO (Aims, Goals and Objectives). Introduces and emphasizes the idea of purpose. Both aspects—"because" and "in order to"—are investigated.
Sheet 6:	Planning. Provides an opportunity to practise C&S and AGO, and to a lesser extent PMI and CAF.
Sheet 7:	FIP (First Important Priorities). A focusing device, directing attention to what is important. This is only done after using the earlier skills to generate as many ideas as possible.
Sheet 8:	APC (Alternatives, Possibilities and Choices). Encourages the student to generate possibilities beyond the obvious and satisfactory ones. It is used as an antidote to emotional reaction or rigid thinking.
Sheet 9:	Decisions. Provides an opportunity to practise FIP and APC and, in a general way, the earlier skills.
Sheet 10:	OPV (Other Point of View). Directs attention to other people's point of view. It is used to balance the focus in the earlier sheets on one's own point of view. The possible differences between viewpoints are emphasized.

school formed the treatment group, a total of 115 students. The other three classes formed a control group of 87 students. The classes were mixed-sex and mixed-ability groups according to school administration. All seven teachers volunteered to be treatment teachers, and the allocation to treatment or control was made to provide an even spread of teacher personality types in each group, as determined by the Myers–Briggs Type Indicator.

The treatment classes each were taught the 10 lessons of the CoRT-1 programme by their normal classroom teacher. This involved a total of approximately seven to eight hours' instruction. The control classes continued with their normal curriculum. Training of the four treatment teachers consisted of exposure to the CoRT-1 programme and a brief demonstration and discussion, a total of about three hours. After this brief introduction the teachers worked solely from the CoRT-1 Teacher's Notes. The teachers individually designed ways of creating time to squeeze the CoRT-1 instruction into their already crowded programmes. The 10 lessons were taught at the rate of two lessons per week over a five-week time-span. There was a two-week school holiday in the middle of that time, and due to the continuing illness of one of the treatment teachers, the teaching time for the CoRT-1 programme in the state school was put back one and a half weeks.

Both treatment and control groups underwent a series of tests in a pre-, post-, and delayed posttest design. The time between pre- and posttests was 10 weeks in the Roman Catholic school and 11 weeks in the state school, and in both cases the delayed posttest was four weeks later.

Instrumentation

Nickerson, Perkins and Smith (1985) and Polson and Jeffries (1985), in reviewing the effects of thinking skills programmes, clearly outline many of the weaknesses in testing programmes and research studies. As de Bono (1976, p. 200) so aptly puts it, "testing thinking is extraordinarily difficult and beset with pitfalls".

In this study an attempt was made to draw from the strengths of instruments previously used successfully and to combine these with the development of new instruments, as well as the testing of another well-established instrument not previously used in this area of research.

The previous study in this series (Edwards and Baldauf, 1987) showed that both the Otis–Lennon School Ability Test, Intermediate Form R (Otis and Lennon, 1982) and the Torrance Test of Creative Thinking, Verbal Test Booklets A and B (Torrance and Ball, 1984) were reliable measures, and so these were used again in the present study. The Self-Concept as a Learner Scale (SCAL) (Waetjen, 1967) was shown to be an unsuitable instrument for this population (Baldauf, Edwards and Matthews, 1985). Similarly, the use of essay tests appeared to be of questionable value (Matthews, 1985), since the students' perceptions of the type of essay required by the teacher seemed to dominate their products.

The normal test-based subject achievement ratings by teachers used in midyear and end-of-year school reports were incorporated in the study, as were questionnaires asking parents to comment on changes, if any, in their child's thinking.

Four new instruments were introduced in this study: the Myers–Briggs Type Indicator, a widely used instrument for personality assessment (Hoffman and Betkouski, 1981); the Self-Concept as a Thinker (SCAT) Scale, designed by the researchers for this study; the Student Thinking Assessment (STA) Scale, a teacher's version of SCAT; and the Thinking Approaches Questionnaire (TAQ), another scale developed for this study to allow student self-assessment in areas specific to the CoRT-1 programme.

The Myers–Briggs Type Indicator (MBTI)

Previous research (Edwards and Baldauf, 1987) and common sense suggest that a programme such as CoRT is likely to work differently for different teachers, different students, and different teacher–student combinations. The Myers–Briggs Type Indicator has been widely used as an investigative tool in education (Hoffman and Betkouski, 1981; Briggs Myers, 1962) and, although there was some concern as to the ability to self-reflect of children in the 12- to 13-year-old range, it appeared to be the most promising instrument available. Form G, a 126-item shortened version of the MBTI (Briggs and Briggs Myers, 1976), was used in this study.

The Self-Concept as a Thinker Scale (SCAT)

Since no other suitable instrument could be found, it was decided to design a new scale to measure self-concept as a thinker. Following extensive reading of the literature on the teaching of thinking, 80 potential items for inclusion in the scale were developed. These covered the major components of self-concept as a thinker. This 80-item scale was administered to 143 Grade Seven students in a school other than those used in this study. The 30 items which had the strongest correlations to the full-scale score were used to form the 30-item version of SCAT in this study.

Student Thinking Assessment Scale (STA)

This scale is a teacher's version of SCAT which allows the teacher to assess each student on the same items as covered by student self-assessment on SCAT.

Thinking Approaches Questionnaire (TAQ)

Two 52-item parallel forms of this questionnaire were designed to allow students to self-assess their approaches to the seven thinking skills targeted in the CoRT-1 programme. Seven items were developed for each thinking skill with three extra items added. The questionnaires were used with the 143 Grade Seven students who had participated in the development of SCAT. As a result of this trial, two parallel 28-item versions of TAQ were produced for use in this study, with four items in each version covering each thinking skill in CoRT-1.

Research Design Summary

Pretest	Posttest	Delayed Posttest
Otis–Lennon Tests		X
Myers–Briggs Type Indicator		X
Student Thinking Assessment		X
School Achievement Ratings:		
Language Arts		X
Social Science		X
Science		X
Mathematics		X
Torrance Tests (Verbal Form A)	X (Verbal Form B)	
Self-Concept as a Thinker	X	X
Thinking Approaches Questionnaire	X	
Parent Questionnaires		X

Results and Discussion

TABLE 2.2   *Performance of Treatment Group Compared with Control Group*

Measure	Relative Change	Significance Level
Scholastic aptitude	Improvement	< 0.02
SCAT	No change	N.S.
STA	Improvement	N.S.
TAQ	Improvement	< 0.05
Torrance Tests:		
Fluency	Improvement	N.S.
Flexibility	Improvement	< 0.05
Originality	Improvement	< 0.02
Achievement:		
Language Arts	Improvement	< 0.02
Social Science	Improvement	< 0.03
Science	No change	N.S.
Mathematics	No change	N.S.
Overall	Improvement	< 0.05
MBTI:		
E-I	More extraverted	< 0.04
N-S	More intuitive	N.S.
F-T	No change	N.S.
P-J	More judging	N.S.

Sample size: 97–112 for the treatment group; 79–85 for the control group.

Scholastic Aptitude (SA)

The SA gains of the treatment group in this study almost exactly matched those obtained in the previous study (Edwards and Baldauf, 1987), giving strong confidence that statistically significant improvements in scores on the Otis–Lennon School Ability Test occur during CoRT-1 treatment.

A possible complicating factor in this study was that one of the treatment classes had a significantly higher SA than the other six classes, resulting in a statistically significant difference in SA between the treatment and control groups. However, the data from this study and from the previous studies (Edwards and Baldauf, 1983, 1987) reveal that all gains are independent of SA. For example, the lowest SA group in the present study was also a treatment group, and their SA gains matched those of the highest SA group.

Self-Concept as a Thinker

The CoRT-1 programme appeared to have no effect, over the 15 weeks of the study, on self-concept as a thinker, as measured by SCAT. Scores for both the treatment and control groups were stable across the pre- and posttests. Both groups showed slight parallel improvements in SCAT scores between post- and delayed posttesting.

As a result of this study, an improved 40-item version of SCAT has been prepared for use in future research. Validation of items in SCAT was achieved by sending the original 80 items, plus the best 20 items from the Self-Concept as a Learner Scale, to all of the contributing authors to the Association for Supervision and Curriculum Development (ASCD) publication Developing Minds (Costa, 1985). Twenty-three of those authors rated each potential item as suitable or not suitable for inclusion in a self-concept as a thinker scale. These data did not arrive in time to inform the development of the 30-item SCAT Scale for this study, yet 26 of the 30 items on the scale were rated as valid items by over 70 per cent of the validators. The new 40-item SCAT scale includes only items rated as suitable by over 75 per cent of the validators and whose scores correlated at least at the 0.4 level with total scale scores from the trial.

Student Thinking Assessment (STA)

While there was a slight improvement in STA scores for the treatment group compared to the control group, it was not statistically significant. This indicated that the treatment teachers had not significantly changed their ratings of student thinking skills during the study. The relationship between the teacher ratings and student self-assessments is not a simple one, and no clear correlation emerged in preliminary analysis of the data.

Thinking Approaches Questionnaire (TAQ)

The TAQ asked students to self-assess their thinking approaches in areas covered specifically by CoRT-1. In the pre-test, half of each group were given Form 1 and half were given the parallel Form 2. In the posttest, the forms were reversed. The treatment group showed a statistically significant gain in scores between pre- and posttests when compared to the control group, with the effect levelling off slightly between post- and delayed posttests. This result indicates that one of the direct objectives of the

CoRT-1 programme was achieved, a shift towards a more positive self-rating as a thinker. That this effect was not revealed in the more general SCAT measure raises questions of transfer in the area of self-concept. The improvement in scores on the TAQ was the only improvement maintained at a statistically significant level from posttest to delayed posttest.

Academic Achievement in School Subject Area

The scores used for academic achievement were teacher ratings on a 1 to 5 scale in each academic subject based on the normal teacher-designed school examinations. These paper-and-pencil examinations were the traditional examinations based on subject content. The treatment group showed an overall increase in academic achievement, with a particularly large increase in the area of language arts and a large increase in social sciences. The areas of mathematics and science were not affected. This is interesting in that these results are completely in keeping with de Bono's (1976, p. 141) claims for CoRT. In that respect they do not agree with the incoherent trends in academic achievement revealed in Edwards and Baldauf (1987). These results suggest that there appears to be some transfer from CoRT-1 training to performance in content-based academic examinations.

Creativity

The trends in results on the Torrance Test of Creative Thinking were the same here as in the previous study in this series (Edwards and Baldauf, 1987). There was a large statistically significant increase in originality, there was also a statistically significant increase in flexibility, and there was an increase in fluency which was not significant. In the previous study both the originality and the flexibility gains were statistically significant. The replication of the trend is convincing evidence. It appears that CoRT-1 has greatest effect on originality and least on fluency. In all cases the absolute gains in scores are large and impressive. The issue of the relationship between Torrance scores and real-world creativity (Nickerson, Perkins and Smith, 1985) is an important consideration when looking at these results.

Personality

It was hoped that use of the Myers–Briggs Type Indicator would allow investigation of the differential effects of the CoRT-1 programme with students and teachers of different personality profiles. However, comparisons of the pre- and delayed postscores on the MBTI showed that only 39 of the 202 students recorded the same personality type. This precluded any simple treatment of the personality data. As a result it was decided to look initially at any shifts in group continuous scores on the MBTI. On the extravert–introvert (E–I) dimension the control students had become more introverted whereas the treatment students had become slightly more extraverted, resulting in a statistically significant relative shift toward extraversion for the treatment group. No clear hypothesis emerges as to why the control group students should shift so far towards introversion during the last 15 weeks of their elementary schooling. On the sensing–intuitive (S–N) dimension the treatment group shifted towards being more intuitive. This tendency to go beyond reliance on the senses could be expected as a possible outcome of exposure to CoRT-1. On the thinking–feeling (T–F) dimension both groups shifted in a parallel manner towards being more feeling. The co-operative learning which is so much a part of the CoRT programme could be expected to encourage such a shift towards concern with more personal and interpersonal factors. On the judging–perceiving (J–P) dimension the treatment group shifted towards being more judging while the control group shifted towards being more perceiving. This tendency towards being more organized and structured could be hypothesized for a heuristic-type approach to thinking such as CoRT; however, the programme could also be seen as encouraging spontaneity, a more perceiving characteristic. While the trends revealed here are tentative, they are also fascinating and suggest great potential in the more thorough investigation of the relationship between personality profiles and the teaching and learning of thinking skills.

Parent Questionnaires

The response rate to the parent questionnaires was very disappointing. Only 20 per cent of parents responded, with approximately an even split between those noting a change in their child's thinking and those seeing no change.

Typical comments for those seeing no change:

> "No noticed changes."
> "Hardly any change; she didn't like the programme, couldn't see any benefit from it."

Typical comments for those seeing a change:

> "Sean seems to ask more questions and expects detailed explanations from us."
> "I have noticed a marked improvement in Nicolas's presentation of his written notes and yes, he does seem a little wiser and less eager to jump in without some forethought."

"Glenn seems better able to evaluate information and other materials in research-type projects. I don't know whether this is an outcome of the thinking skills programme, intellectual development, or classroom teaching."

Then, there are always comments that are hard to classify:

"Whether it was the thinking skills programme or not, Susan tends to be thinking and talking all the time; she never shuts up."

Conclusion

Inclusion of a large control group in this study gives it much greater significance than those which preceded it in the series (Edwards and Baldauf, 1983, 1987).

The significant positive shifts in scholastic aptitude and originality are in keeping with earlier results. Similarly, the relative shifts in the measures from the Torrance test confirm previous results in that originality is most improved, followed by flexibility and then fluency.

No effects were noted on self-concept as a thinker using the SCAT scale, and no significant effects were noted on teacher ratings of student thinking skills. However, significant improvements were found for the treatment students in their self-ratings on specific CoRT-1 thinking skills as measured by the TAQ. The shift in TAQ scores was the only improvement maintained at a statistically significant level from posttest to delayed posttest.

A particularly interesting result in this study is the improvement in performance by the treatment students on their normal teacher-designed content-based academic test results. As well as the overall improvement in performance, the very large gains in language arts, gains in social science, and lack of shift in mathematics and science, present valuable insights into the nature of these disciplines and how they are taught and tested. These results provide evidence of potential transfer of CoRT-1 skills to performance in academic disciplines.

Results in the area of personality using the Myers–Briggs Type Indicator need to be examined with caution. It is clear that there were reliability problems with the MBTI in this study. At the same time the shifts toward extraversion, being more structured and organized, and more concerned with interpersonal factors, are indicators worth further investigation.

The Self-Concept as a Thinker Scale, both in the 30-item form used in this study, and the new 40-item form developed from this study, appears to have great potential as an instrument for general measurements in a wide range of studies in the area of teaching thinking. For research on the CoRT-1 programme specifically, the two forms of the Thinking

Approaches Questionnaire are promising scales. A recent report on the use of the 40-item SCAT can be found in Melchiar and Edwards (1989).

When one considers that the total instruction time involved in the CoRT-1 programme is from seven to eight hours, the gain scores are highly impressive. The next step is clearly to investigate the effect of the full 60-lesson CoRT programme to see if the trends in results reported here are maintained and build throughout a longer intervention. Such a study has just been completed with impressive results which will be published shortly.

References

Baldauf, R. B. Jr, Edwards, J. and Matthews, B. (1985) "The reliability and factorial validity of the self-concept as a learner (SCAL) measure for year seven students in Australia", *Educational and Psychological Measurements*, **45** (3), pp. 655–659.

Bono, E. de (1969). *The Mechanism of Mind*, Pelican, London.

Bono, E. de (1976). *Teaching Thinking*, Temple-Smith, London.

Bono, E. de (1981). *CoRT-1 Thinking*, Pergamon Press, Oxford.

Bono, E. de (1983). "The direct teaching of thinking as a skill", *Phi Delta Kappa*, 57, June, pp. 703–708.

Briggs, K. C. and Briggs Myers, I. (1976). *Myers–Briggs Type Indicator, Form G*, Consulting Psychologists Press, Palo Alto, CA.

Briggs Myers, I. (1962). *The Myers–Briggs Type Indicator-Manual*, Consulting Psychologists Press, Palo Alto, CA.

Costa, A. (ed.) (1985). *Developing Minds*. ASCD, Alexandria, VA.

Edwards, J. and Baldauf, R. B. Jr (1983). "Teaching thinking in secondary science", in Maxwell, W. (ed.), *Thinking: The Expanding Frontier*, Franklin Institute Press, Philadelphia, PA, pp. 129–138.

Edwards, J. and Baldauf, R. B. Jr (1987). "The effects of the CoRT-1 thinking skills programme on students", in Perkins, D.; Lochhead, J.; and Bishop, J. (eds.), *Thinking: The Second International Conference*, Erlbaum, Hillsdale, NJ, pp. 453–473.

Edwards, J. and Marland, P. (1984). "What are students really thinking?", *Educational Leadership*, **42** (3), pp. 63–67.

Feuerstein, R. (1980) *Instrumental Enrichment: An Intervention Programme for Cognitive Modifiability*, University Park Press, Baltimore, MD.

Gunstone, R. F. and White, R. T. (1980). "A matter of gravity", *Research in Science Education*, **10**, pp. 35–44.

Hoffman, J. L. and Betkouski, M. (1981). "A summary of Myers–Briggs Type Indicator research applications in education", *Research in Psychological Type*, **3**, pp. 3–41.

Matthews, B. (1985). "The effects of CoRT-1 training on year seven students' self-concepts as learners and as thinkers". Unpublished honours thesis, James Cook University, School of Education, Townsville, Australia.

Melchiar, T. and Edwards, J. (1989). "The effects of the CoRT-1 thinking programme on student self-concept as a thinker". Paper presented to the tenth International Conference on Thinking, San Juan, PR.

Nickerson, R. S., Perkins, D. N. and Smith, E. E. (1985). *The Teaching of Thinking*, Erlbaum, Hillsdale, NJ.

Otis, A. S. and Lennon, R. T. (1982). *Otis–Lennon School Ability Test: Intermediate Form R (Australian Adaptation)*, Australian Council for Educational Research, Victoria.

Polson, P. G. and Jeffries, R. (1985). "Analysis-instruction in general problem solving skills: An analysis of four approaches", in Segal, J. W., Chipman, S. F., and Glaser, R. (eds.), *Thinking and Learning Skills*, Vol. 1, Erlbaum, Hillsdale, NJ.

Torrance, E. P. and Ball, O. E. (1984). *Torrance Tests of Creative Thinking*, Scholastic Testing Service, London.
Waetjen, W. B. (1967). *Self-Concept as a Learner Scale*, W. B. Waetjen, Cleveland State University, OH.

3

Instrumental Enrichment: A Strategy for Cognitive and Academic Improvement

FRANCES R. LINK

Director, Curriculum Research Association, Washington D.C., United States

Background

What lies behind a student's failure to think? All too often we attribute an inability to perform a given operation to a lack of knowledge of the principles involved or, worse, to a low intelligence that precludes the student's understanding of those principles. What is overlooked is that the specific deficiency may reside not in the operational level or specific content of the child's thought processes but in the underlying functions upon which successful thinking depends.

This distinction is crucial to any useful understanding of students' corrective needs, which should take into account not only what they cannot do but why they cannot do it. Consider for a moment a problem requiring the mental classification of objects or events. Its solution necessarily involves subordinate mental functions such as systematic and precise data gathering, the ability to deal with two or more sources of information simultaneously, and the comparison of objects or events to be classified. A student incapable of performing and applying these prerequisite operations can hardly be expected to perform the overall task. Clearly, if teachers fail to identify the specific source of the child's cognitive weakness, corrective actions in this area will suffer.

Improving the overall cognitive performance of the low-achieving adolescent demands a broad-scale strategy of intervention aimed at the process of learning itself rather than any specific skills or subject. Instrumental Enrichment (IE) is such a programme: a direct and focused attack on mental processes that, through their absence, their fragility, or their inefficiency, are to blame for poor intellectual or academic performance.

The core of the IE programme—developed by Reuven Feuerstein, an Israeli clinical psychologist—is a three-year series of problem-solving tasks and exercises that are grouped in 14 areas of specific cognitive development. They are called instruments rather than lessons because in and of themselves they are virtually free of specific subject matter. Their purpose is to serve as the means or vehicle for cognition-oriented inter-actions between teacher and students. Each instrument's true goal is not the learner's acquisition of information, but the development, refinement and crystallization of functions that are prerequisite to effective thinking (see Table 3.1). In terms of behaviour, IE's ultimate aim is to transform retarded performers by altering their characteristically passive and dependent cognitive style so that they become more active, self-motivated, independent thinkers.

There are six major goals of IE:

(i) to correct weaknesses and deficiencies in cognitive functions;
(ii) to help students learn and apply the basic concepts, labels, vocabulary and operations essential to effective thought;
(iii) to produce sound and spontaneous thinking habits leading to greater curiosity, self-confidence and motivation;
(iv) to produce in students increasingly reflective and insightful thought processes;
(v) to motivate students towards task-oriented abstract goals rather than towards objectives of impulsive self-gratification;
(vi) to transform poor learners from passive recipients and reproducers of information into active generators of new information.

TABLE 3.1 *Instrumental Enrichment Cognitive Functions*

Gathering all the information we need (input)

1. Using our senses (listening, seeing, smelling, tasting, touching, feeling) to gather clear and complete information (clear perception).

2. Using a system or plan so that we do not skip or miss something important or repeat ourselves (systematic exploration).

3. Giving the thing we gather through our senses and our experience a name so that we can remember it more clearly and talk about it (labelling).

4. Describing things and events in terms of where and when they occur (temporal and spatial referents).

5. Deciding on the characteristics of a thing or event that always stay the same, even when changes take place (conservation, constancy and object permanence).

6. Organizing the information we gather by considering more than one thing at a time (using two sources of information).

7. Being precise and accurate when it matters (need for precision).

Using the information we have gathered (elaboration)

1. Defining what the problem is, what we are being asked to do, and what we must figure out (analysing disequilibrium).

2. Using only that part of the information we have gathered that is relevant—that is, which applies to the problem—and ignoring the rest (relevance).

3. Having a good picture in our mind of what we are looking for or what we must do (interiorization).

4. Making a plan that will include the steps needed to reach our goal (planning behaviour).

5. Remembering and keeping in mind the various pieces of information we need (broadening our mental field).

6. Looking for the relationship by which separate objects, events and experiences can be tied together (projecting relationships).

7. Comparing objects and experiences to others to see what is similar and what is different (comparative behaviour).

8. Finding the class or set to which the new object or experience belongs (categorization).

9. Thinking about different possibilities and figuring out what would happen if we were to choose one or another (hypothetical thinking).

10. Using logic to prove things and to defend our opinion (logical evidence).

Expressing the solution to a problem (output)

1. Being clear and precise in our language to be sure that there is no question as to what the answer is. Putting ourselves into the shoes of the listener to be sure that our answers will be understood (overcoming egocentric communication).

2. Thinking things through before we answer instead of immediately trying to answer and making a mistake, and then trying again (overcoming trial-and-error).

3. Counting to 10 (at least) so that we do not say or do something we will be sorry for later (restraining impulsive behaviour).

4. Not fretting or panicking if for some reason we cannot answer a question even though we "know" the answer. Leaving the question for a little while and then, when we return to it, using a strategy to help us find the answer (overcoming blocking).

Why do Students Fail?

Numerous causes have been suggested to explain poor cognitive perform-ance, ranging from heredity to environment. At one extreme, Jensen (1969, 1973) held that mental ability is largely determined by genetics and thus is inaccessible to substantial modification. He proposed a dichotomous model of intelligence in which humanity is divided according to genetic endowment: people whose capacities are limited to simple mental acts of an associative and reproductive nature, and people able to use complex transformational, operational and abstract processes. Jensen suggests we accept the limits imposed by heredity, and adjust educational goals downward for those with low intelligence. This is the position of defeat.

At the opposite extreme, we encounter the notion or fantasy that the retarded performer's failure can be traced to unreasonable demands imposed by an insensitive and alien school system. This theory, the "cultural difference" position, implies that merely altering the student's learning environment will produce the desired changes and will eliminate poor performance. This gross oversimplification fails to recognize that deficient cognitive functioning is neither culture-bound nor limited to the classroom, occurring as it does in many different situations. A student may master education's "three Rs", yet still be incapable of adapting to new information, demands and responsibilities, both in school and later in life, for lack of the fourth R: reasoning.

Between these opposite points of view lie a host of intermediate theories, all of which share the belief, either implicit or explicit, that the persistence of poor cognitive performance beyond childhood is a condition beyond remedy. All are fundamentally at variance with the goals and strategies of Feuerstein's IE (Feuerstein, 1980).

Retarded Performance: A Temporary State

In contrast with the views discussed above, IE is firmly rooted in the concept of cognitive modifiability as the working channel for improving the underlying processes of thought. The programme's essential aim is not merely remediation of specific behaviours but basic structural changes that alter the individual's whole course of cognitive development.

One common misconception to be overcome is the belief that regarded performance is an irreversible state. The term *retardation* has unfortunately come to imply that an individual's capacity for development is fixed. Yet evidence is mounting that, except for the most severe cases of organic impairment, the human mind is open to modification at all ages and stages of development. The term *retarded performance*, therefore, is meant to stress that what is regarded is no more than the individual's manifest cognitive ability at the time. It is not a label for any supposedly stable and immutable characteristics of the individual's ultimate potential.

Although it is a pervasive state, regarded performance is neither permanent nor irreversible. Retarded performers do not make connections based on former experiences in learning; they do not spontaneously build relationships; they view the world and learning in an episodic manner; they do not seem to learn from direct exposure to experience. By changing the cognitive structure rather than selected dimensions of behaviour, we can achieve a permanent stable state of capacity for improvement.

Cognitive Modifiability: To Adapt, To Survive

To understand what is meant by cognitive modifiability and why it is such a valuable human attribute, one must appreciate the difference between structural changes in cognitive development and other kinds of developmental processes. In the normal course of events, a child undergoes a series of changes: these may be of a maturational nature, such as the transition from crawling to walking, or they may result from exposure to specific sets of circumstances, such as learning a particular arithmetic operation or a foreign language.

Unlike development spurred by random experiences, structural changes reflect a person's entire manner of dealing with and responding to information and stimulation. Modifying this cognitive structure demands a particular kind of mediation or intervention by the parent or teacher, which renders individuals receptive and sensitive to sources of information and stimulation from which they would otherwise be incapable of benefiting.

Cognitive modification promotes continuous growth by opening the channels for adapting to the demands of life and of the environment. The survival of any organism depends on its ability to respond, not to a stable environment but to situations and circumstances continually in flux. Ultimately, the IE curriculum attempts to provide learners with the means for their survival in school and throughout life.

The Mind as a Container: Open or Closed

Instrumental Enrichment's active modification approach contrasts sharply with the passive acceptance approach, which attempts to adjust external conditions to suit the limited abilities currently manifested by retarded performers. A case in point is special education, where both the modes of training and its goals are based on so-called "realistic limits" indicated by current levels of functioning. Special education deems the child's cognitive structure an immutable entity, and keeps attempts to elicit change within this presumed capacity. This approach sees the mind as a rigid container with predetermined limits as to what it may contain. It does not view the mind as a dynamic, flexible system with the capacity and structure to change through adolescence and beyond, as do learners' latent functions when interacting with new situations.

At the heart of the matter lies the issue of whether the mind is an open or closed system. When intelligence is conceptualized in quantitative terms as a fixed product of ability that is constant through life, passive acceptance of the present condition is the outcome. Attempts to modify an individual's course of development come to be regarded as futile, even unfair, because they demand the "impossible".

The common response is to confirm the observed low level of performance, using tests specifically designed to measure such performance.
Students' low achievement in school is confirmed by poor performance
on tests. After testing, students are classified, labelled and left at their
current stage of functioning. This exercise in self-fulfilling prophecy,
needless to say, holds devastating implications for the ultimate destiny of
students.

The Instruments: What They Do

The instruments provide sufficient material for one-period lessons given
two to five days a week. Although a three-year sequence is recommended,
the programme may be implemented in two years, depending on the class
curriculum and students' needs. IE is not intended to replace traditional
content areas but as a supplement to help students get the most out of all
opportunities to learn and grow. It is a form of general intervention
enabling the teacher and students to make bridges to both specific and
general subject areas. The instruments are tools for learning to learn.
The goal is the development of higher mental processes, not minimum
competencies.

First-Year Curriculum

Organization of Dots

The aim of this initial instrument is to produce in the student the
spontaneous ability to discern relations among data that may not be
clearly organized. Students find the relations—shapes, figures and other
attributes—among a field of dots, much the way one picks out constella-
tions in the night sky. In this way students begin developing strategies for
linking perceived events into a system yielding comprehensible information that can be a basis for understanding and logical response.
Perceptual problems, spatial, planning, and organizational abilities are
mediated by use of this instrument.

Orientation in Space I

This instrument promotes the creation of specific strategies for differenti-
ating frames of reference in space, particularly with regard to the student's
personal frame of reference. Left, right, front and back are the major
concepts developed. This instrument also helps illuminate the important
differences between systems based on relative measures or quantities, as

opposed to those dealing in absolutes, and demonstrates how strategies for dealing with each must adjust accordingly. The development of "point of view" in personal, political, literary and social relationships is the focus of bridging activities.

Comparisons

The spontaneous and efficient comparison of behaviours, ideas and events is an ability crucial to continuous cognitive development. This instrument therefore fosters precise perception, the ability to discriminate by attribute (equal/unequal, similar/dissimilar), and the judgement necessary to identify and evaluate similarities and differences.

Analytic Perception

This instrument addresses the ability to analyse component parts in order to find how they relate to each other as well as how they contribute to the overall character of the whole they compose. Students learn to recognize how systematic analytical processes may be applied in a variety of ways to physical structure, to the different parts of an activity or operation, to the reasons through which an act is explained, and to the creation of logical propositions.

Second-Year Curriculum

Categorization

In this instrument, students learn not simply how to sort objects or events but the underlying principles and strategies for creating conceptual sets and categories, a vital prerequisite for higher mental processing. By finding the common attributes that go into the formation of categories, students develop the abilities to perceive, label and compare, as well as to differentiate between relevant and irrelevant information.

Instructions

Instructions emphasize the use of language as a system for both encoding and decoding operational processes on levels of varying complexity. By requiring students to read and carry out directions precisely, it promotes systematic, ordered thought and response. Exercises also focus on criticizing instructions, rewriting them to supply missing relevant data, and creating instructions for others to follow.

Temporal Relations

This instrument addresses chronological time, biological time and other temporal relations. Students learn to isolate the factors involved in evaluating or predicting outcomes—time, distance, velocity—and to find the interrelation among those factors. Problems force students to seek all relevant information, such as starting points, routes, distances and terrain, before attempting to compare and summarize, thus restraining impulsiveness and stressing the need for planning.

Numerical Progressions

This instrument promotes the ability to perceive and understand principles and formulas manifested in numerical patterns. By searching for the principles involved in ascending and descending numerical progressions, students learn to establish relations among events and to discover the rhythms by which relations repeat themselves.

Family Relationships

Although the title of this instrument suggests the study of relationships among kin, its larger goal is the promotion of a clearer understanding of how individual roles in hierarchical organizations define the network of relationships that are encountered in daily life and work. In short, family relations helps bring into focus the complexity of relationships within the human family and in all hierarchical structures.

Illustrations

This is a collection of situational cartoons that present, in graphic form, problems which students must perceive, recognize and interpret. Its aim is to encourage a spontaneous awareness that a problem exists, an analysis of why it exists, and a projection of cause-and-effect relations. Unlike other instruments, illustrations need not be taught sequentially but can be interspersed among other instruments, as needed, to assess mastery or correct specific operations.

Third-Year Curriculum

Transitive Relations and Syllogisms

These two instruments, usually taught together, foster the higher level abstract and inferential thought for which the student has been prepared by mastery of earlier instruments. Transitive relations deals with drawing inferences from relations that can be described in terms of "greater than", "equal to", or "less than". In effect, the student learns the rules governing transitive thinking and learns to connect separately presented statements by means of a common reference point. Syllogisms deals with formal propositional logic, and aims at promoting inferential thinking based on local evidence. Students learn the laws governing sets and their members, as well as how to construct new sets by such operations as logical multiplication. In addition to learning formal syllogistic thought, students learn to evaluate analytic premises and propositions.

Representational Stencil Design

One of the most advanced instruments in the programme, representational stencil design calls into play a broad range of higher level thought processes addressed in previous instruments. Completing its tasks requires an intricate series of steps: analysing a complex figure, identifying its components, and recreating the whole mentally in colour, shape, size and orientation.

Orientation in Space III

This final instrument deals with spatial relations according to standard conventions: north, east, south and west. It complements the earlier instrument in spatial orientation by extending students' understanding of relative positions from a personal orientation to the stable external system represented by the points of the compass. Personal and external orientations are integrated in a way that permits students to use both simultaneously.

The Means: Mediated Learning Experience

The development of higher mental processes cannot be understood without the powerful adjunct concept of mediated learning experience (MLE). This refers to a particular kind of experience, which, for all its technical-sounding name, is a familiar and integral part of growing up for most of us.

In its early manifestations, MLE is the way parents and, later, teachers instruct children and transmit cultural elements. Guided by intentions, culture and emotional investment, "mediating" agents select and organize the child's world of stimuli towards a particular goal of behaviour and attitude. As a result of such mediation, children acquire the learning sets and operating structures for mentally organizing, processing and acting on information gathered from internal and external sources.

MLE may be viewed as the means by which nascent, elementary cognitive sets and habits are transformed into the bases for effective thinking. Consequently, the earlier and more often that children are subjected to mediated learning experience, the greater will be their capacity to perceive, understand and respond efficiently to information and stimulation in and out of school. The less mediation children experience both in quantity and quality, the less prepared they will be for school and for life.

If this concept is accepted, one can readily see that evidence is accumulating for IE as a substitute for early MLE. By interposing the IE programme, the teacher can facilitate the organization and transmission of information at increasingly complex, abstract and efficient levels of functioning. MLE of this kind hastens the development of the prerequisite cognitive structures that enable a human being to learn and grow. At stake is not merely the acquisition of particular skills or abilities but the opportunity to create a radical change in the adolescent's stubborn course of failure and to institute a pattern of growth and development. In summary, Feuerstein's concept of mediation and intelligence lies more in its active construction than in its measured product.

Teacher Training in Instrumental Enrichment

Whatever the particular focus of an instrument, its larger purpose is always the further development of students' conscious thought processes, of their discovery of practical applications, and transfer of those processes in and out of school. In this effort, teachers play a crucial role as mediating agents.

To perform this role, teachers require special training in IE's basic precepts, materials and teaching strategies. They must learn how to extract the thinking processes and principles from an instrument and how to help students learn to "bridge" or apply them. Teachers, moreover, must focus the educational experience set in motion by the exercises to help students understand in cognitive or problem-solving terms what their performance means. This focusing will help students overcome the frustration and alienation engendered by past failures to learn or by a limited opportunity to think on higher cognitive levels.

The teacher as a human mediator learns to apply the important aspects of MLE, which include:

—intentionality of meaning
—transcendence
—mediation of meaning
—mediation of feeling of competence
—mediated sharing behaviour
—mediated regulation and control of behaviour
—mediated individuation and psychological differentiation
—mediation of goal-seeking, goal-setting and goal-achieving planning behaviour
—mediation of challenge: the search for novelty and complexity.

Teacher training thus involves a minimum of 45 hours of inservice annually, plus on-the-job use of exercises in the classroom, if possible while training is in process. Training programmes are custom-designed to fit the inservice schedules of school systems.

Teacher training concentrates on the following three areas:

(i) understanding and accepting IE's fundamental theories and concepts;

(ii) mastery in classroom use of the instruments, by learning to plan lessons that focus on the six subgoals of IE;

(iii) special techniques for mediating, bridging, developing insight and applying cognitive processes to specific subject matter and to life experiences.

Many school systems have been conducting evaluation studies. The three reported in this chapter demonstrate the variety of methods of evaluation. The changes in self-image, motivation and intellectual growth across a variety of populations, and the improvement in teaching, seem to be consistent results in all these studies.

Cognitive Modification for the Hearing-Impaired Adolescent: The Promise

A pilot study of the effects of the cognitive intervention programme of IE for hearing-impaired adolescents was conducted at the Model Secondary School for the Deaf in Washington, D.C. (see Martin, 1980). Experimental and control groups were contrasted in regard to general cognitive functioning, problem-solving strategies, and reading comprehension. Experimental subjects demonstrated improvements in the following areas: (a) systematic approaches to problems; (b) analysis of problem situations, (c) vocabulary size, (d) analysis of source of error in problem-solving situations, (e) completeness, organization, and planning in problem-solving situations, (f) peer co-operation in problem solving, (g) abstract thinking, (h) precision, and (i) development of multiple strategies to solve a problem. These results establish the efficacy and strong potential of systematic cognitive intervention programmes for improvement of thinking skills in the hearing-impaired adolescent.

At the end of the second pilot year, hearing-impaired students who had systematic experiences in "cognitive education" (a) showed consistent improvement in problem-solving interviews in regard to the practicality, completeness, organization, and systematic planning of their problem solutions; (b) significantly improved their non-verbal logical thinking as shown on the Raven's Matrices; (c) more frequently expected themselves to be precise, were able to describe several strategies to solve a problem, and defended their opinions on the basis of logical evidence, as shown by teacher observation checklists; (d) demonstrated important gains in reading comprehension; and (e) made considerable progress in mathematical computation.

Cognitive education for the hearing-impaired does seem to hold promise for the improvement of spatial reasoning skills (Parasnis and Long, 1979), of the ability to consider two or more sources of information simultaneously (Ottem, 1980), to carry out analogical reasoning, to develop the concept of comparison and opposition (Furth, 1963), and the ability to understand cause-and-effect relations (Johnson, 1981). To the degree that memory is involved with the reading comprehension and mathematics computation subtests of the SAT-HI (Stanford Achievement Test— Hearing-Impaired), there is also promise of improvement in deaf performance in the cognitive laboratory (Karchmer and Belmont, 1976). In addition, the emphasis on metacognition activities during IE lessons must be considered as at least one factor in the improvement of experimental students; this interpretation should corroborate the finding of Peterson *et al.* (1977) that students who can explain why they have understood a cognitive task tend to have higher achievement scores.

From these results, the following recommendations emerge for future efforts in cognitive education of hearing-impaired adolescents:

> (i) Systematic (as opposed to incidental) cognitive intervention is important in the context of the school curriculum.
>
> (ii) Adolescence is apparently not "too late" in the development of a hearing-impaired learner to make important and measurable modifications in cognitive functioning.
>
> (iii) In-depth teacher training in cognitive education is an essential prerequisite to the success of any cognitive intervention programme with students.
>
> (iv) Future studies should investigate the apparently positive perceptions of teachers who are engaged in cognitive education: what are the reasons for their enthusiasm?
>
> (v) Larger student samples and more complex evaluation designs are needed to measure accurately in statistical terms the effects of this intervention for hearing-impaired adolescents. Included in such studies should also be an investigation of possible aptitude–treatment interactions.

The continuing enthusiasm of the original pilot teachers led to the involvement of a total of 39 teachers in cognitive education for 1984–85 at the Model Secondary School for the Deaf, a sign of strong professional commitment to the idea that positive growth was occurring in the problem-solving skills of the students in this population. Such professional commitment and enthusiasm may be the most important indicator of all.

New York City Special Projects Evaluation Report[1]

A study of regular education students who qualified for remedial instruction was conducted in New York City. In the fall of 1980, the IE programme trained eight teachers in the non-public school Chapter I programme.[2] IE classes began in November 1980 with 134 students. In September 1981, 135 students were in the programme; 96 were second-year students. In the fall of 1982, 203 students were participating; 65 were third-year students and 14 were second-year students. The evaluation found that after the second year, students made achievement gains ranging from 2.2 to 8.0 normal curve equivalents.

Although the programme served more students in 1982–83, the same eight teachers who were initially trained continued with the programme. Each teacher taught IE to as many as three groups of eight to ten students two or three times a week in 45-minute or 60-minute sessions.

Based on severity of need, eligible students were placed in Chapter I remedial reading or mathematics pull-out groups. From the groups that met five times a week, 21 classes were designated to receive IE instruction two or three times a week. The 21 classes selected included students who were continuing in the programme and students whose remediation needs were greater.

The major objectives of the non-public school IE programme are listed below:

> (i) The reading achievement of IE students will be greater than that of a group of non-IE students, as measured by the reading comprehension subtest of the California Achievement Test (CAT).
> (ii) The mathematics achievement of IE students will improve as measured by the applications subtest and the total mathematics score on the Stanford Achievement Test (SAT).[3]
> (iii) Students in the IE programme will develop positive attitudes about their participation in IE.
> (iv) The IE programme will be implemented as designed by programme developers.

Evaluation Methodology

The 1982–83 evaluation of the IE programme was guided by three questions, derived from the programme's objectives:

(i) To what extent did students improve their reading and mathematics skills? How do the reading scores of IE students compare with randomly selected non-IE, non-public school students receiving remedial reading or mathematics services?

(ii) To what extent do students have positive attitudes towards the IE programme?

(iii) Was the programme implemented according to the training received? What were teachers' attitudes towards the availability, comprehensibility and continued use of IE materials?

Conclusions and Recommendations

The IE programme has been successful in terms of student achievement, students' perceptions and teachers' perceptions. IE students made substantial gains, which were greater than those of non-IE students. Responses to the student questionnaire were very positive, and teachers were unanimous in their enthusiasm for the programme.

Observations of IE classes gave evidence that teachers adhered to the programme design. The overall dynamics in the classroom in terms of activities, interactions and the students' display of skills were consistent with the programme design. This close match between what teachers should be doing and what was observed was one source of the programme's success in the non-public school Chapter I classes. The teachers were able to execute the programme successfully due to the intensive teacher training they received during the first year and the support they continually received from the programme's administrators.

Another source of the programme's success was the motivation it provided for students to achieve, with teachers asserting that students have a chance to state their opinions, right or wrong. This helps them understand how to live with errors, and as a result they are not afraid of making mistakes. Other behaviours observed by the teachers that contributed to the students' success were less impulsivity, more task-orientation, higher tolerance for frustration, a sense of accomplishment, and increased self-esteem and confidence.

The third source of the IE programme's success is summarized by one IE teacher: "I expect more of the students, more thinking, and I see them as more capable of handling any task." It is well known in the educational community that when a teacher has this kind of positive attitude towards the students, the students will perform better than they would with a teacher who has lower expectations.

"Making Up Our Minds"

In the United Kingdom, a case study approach (Craft and Weller, 1983) was designed for a wide variety of age groups and populations. In 1980 the OECD, the then Schools Council and five Local Education Authorities (LEAs) agreed to mount a two-year study of IE in United Kingdom schools. Each LEA selected two to four institutions to take part in the study.

IE was taught in 17 establishments in Inner London, Somerset, Coventry, Manchester and Sheffield Education Authorities. One college of further education was involved, together with an equal number of special schools and comprehensive high schools.

Local evaluators from universities were asked to visit each class at least once every term and to submit a record of observations to the Schools Council. Evaluators and LEA co-ordinators also wrote short progress reports early in 1982 and kept records of discussions. A cumulative record of experience, therefore, has been available to Schools Council co-ordinators, and it provides the basis of Craft and Weller's interim review.

Institutions organized IE teaching in a wide range of different ways: some offered short intensive courses; others employed extended light programmes. In consequence, pupils' weekly contact time with IE varied widely. Some teachers worked alone, whereas others benefited from ancillary help and team-teaching techniques. Often, particularly in the special schools, teachers taught IE to classes with whom they spent a large part of the week. Pupils receiving IE teaching were mainly between 11 to 15 years of age; most were retarded performers, and some had behaviour problems.

There was a strong general impression that pupils, including retarded performers, were benefiting from IE. The evidence was mixed but was largely positive, in some cases extremely so. Evaluators' observations have frequently shown that pupils enjoy lessons: they are interested, motivated, and gain in self-confidence. Pupils were felt to be learning in most lessons observed. One evaluator remarked on the apparent ability of even seriously handicapped pupils to keep up with the group. In some cases, teachers reported improvements in attendance and behaviour, and noted increases in pupils' spans of concentration. In others, greater concern for accuracy and planning was observed, and pupils were described as less impulsive and as being concerned with checking their work more carefully. In two schools, pupils joined examination courses as a result of improvements attributed to IE.

Teachers inevitably needed time to gain confidence in the new materials and teaching strategies. Some were still working on handling discussions and on relating work covered in IE to other subjects and contexts ("bridging"). However, there is evidence that the materials have had a significant effect on teachers: many were spending much time preparing IE lessons and, in consequence, were thinking harder about their teaching strategies; many also said they had revised upwards their expectations of pupils. In the words of one teacher: "A number of children have shown insights, used language or solved problems that I would previously have thought unlikely."

In summary, it can be said that IE has been generally well received by teachers and pupils in the United Kingdom. The work has not been without its problems, but many of these have organizational roots that would apply to any curriculum innovation. A closing comment from an evaluator may give something of the flavour of the work: "The children were consciously thinking problems through ... the teacher wondered whether working with the materials had alerted her to the nature of problems and changed the way she taught."

As a result of this study, in 1985, throughout the United Kingdom, 25 LEAs trained teachers to implement IE.

Notes

1. The Project Director was Larry Larkin, New York City Special Projects Division.
2. Non-public schools were selected if they were providing Chapter I corrective reading, reading skills, or mathematics at least five times per week in grades 4 to 7, and if teachers had at least two years of experience in Chapter I. Chapter I services were provided by public school teachers under the supervision of the Office of Special Projects, Bureau of Non-public School Reimbursable Services.
3. Because the number of mathematics students in IE in each grade level was small, no comparisons were made with a non-IE group.

References

Craft, A. and Weller, K. (1983). *Making Up Our Minds: An Exploratory Study of Instrumental Enrichment*, Schools Council Publications, London.

Feuerstein, R. (1980). *Instrumental Enrichment*, University Park Press, Baltimore, MD.

Furth, H. (1963). *Thinking Without Language*, Free Press, New York.

Jackson, Y. F. (1983). "Identification of potential giftedness in disadvantaged students." Doctoral dissertation, Columbia University, Teachers College, New York.

Jensen, A. R. (1969). "How much can we boost IQ and scholastic achievement?", *Harvard Educational Review*, **39**, pp. 1–123.

Jensen, A. R. (1973). *Educability and Group Differences*, Methuen, London.

Johnson, J. (1981). "Hearing-impaired learner with special needs". Presentation at a symposium, Lincoln, NE.

Karchmer, M. A. and Belmont, J. M. (1976). "On assessing and improving deaf performance in the cognitive laboratory". Presentation at a meeting of the American Speech and Hearing Association, Houston, TX.

Martin, D. (1980). "Cognitive modification for the hearing-impaired adolescent: The promise", *Deafness and Child Development*, University of California Press, Berkeley, CA.

Ottem, E. (1980). "An analysis of cognitive studies with deaf subjects", *American Annals of the Deaf*, **125** (5), pp. 564–575.

Parasnis, I. and Long, G. L. (1979). "Relationships among spatial skills, communication skills, and field dependence in deaf students", *Directions*, **1** (2), pp. 26–37.

Peterson, P. L., Swing, S. R., Stark, K. D. and Waas, G. A. (1977) "Students' reports of their cognitive processes during classroom instruction." Research report from the University of Wisconsin presented at a Conference of the American Educational Research Association, Montreal.

4

Reviving Thought Processes in Pre-Adolescents

ROSINE DEBRAY

Professor of Clinical and Educational Psychology,
Université de Paris-V René Descartes,
Paris, France

Towards a Dynamic Conception of Intelligence: It Is Possible To Learn How To Think

I intend to deal only with the important problems surrounding the notion of intelligence which still exist in the field of psychology, the extreme positions being:

> (i) that intelligence is hereditary and determined once and for all, an idea which is defended in particular by Eysenck (1975); or, on the contrary,
>
> (ii) that intelligence develops only in relation to the environment, an idea which is backed by sociologists and psychosociologists.

Both these perspectives have had their hour of glory. Today, however, a more reasonable consensus exists around an interactionist conception of intelligence where what is genetically inherited is reinforced, backed up or inhibited by the weight of environmental factors. Our notion of a given individual's intelligence, whether a child, an adolescent or an adult, often appears to be a statement of inescapable fact that seems objective because based on a psychological examination, particularly if it is careful and thorough (Sanglade–Andronikov and Verdier–Gibello, 1983; Debray, 1982).

To be able to teach children branded "disabled" how to think—that is to say, for them to learn how to use the procedures of intellectual reasoning— is in France a novel, if not revolutionary, idea. In fact, it is contrary to trends in psychiatry dating back to Esquirol as early as 1838 and continued by Binet and Simon (1907), all of whom saw mental retardation as incurable. Thus, there is a considerable cultural tradition which encourages specialists in mental retardation to accept that the intellectual capacities of children described as not very intelligent are limited. Yet the opposite can be observed when what I call "cognitive resuscitation" is applied.

Feuerstein's Theory of Mediated Learning Experience and its Application Through Instrumental Enrichment (IE)

Professor Reuven Feuerstein's theory of mediated learning and its application through IE[1] provides a method to teach, or teach again, procedures of intelligent thinking that are by definition deficient in mentally handicapped children. The causes of the deficiency are not important in this context: in trisomic children it is genetic, whereas it is essentially environmental in those described as "culturally deprived". The problem is not to find out why a deficiency is present but rather how we should remedy it. There is no point in asking if there is a remedy, since the answer is of course yes, as is shown convincingly by the results of the various experiments I have been carrying out since 1983 and which are outlined below (for details see Debray, 1989).

The theory of mediated learning stresses above all the importance of the human mediator's role in the act of transmitting knowledge. It insists on one basic fact: children learn—that is, develop their intelligence—when they are captivated by a lively and stimulating interpersonal relationship. Teachers know this only too well, as do loving parents who are concerned about the development of their child's capacity to think. Feuerstein's contribution lies in his assertion—supported by both theory and practice—that when intelligence has not developed at the right time, the disability is not therefore irreversible, because the deficiency is not fixed for ever at adolescence or even adulthood. Intelligence, in the sense of a capacity to learn intelligent behaviour and hence solve problems, can thus be acquired. In our Western industrial cultures, this happens almost automatically in the first relations with the mother and father and other important contacts for the child, through educational activities, games, learning and the transmission of language. When family environments are stimulating and encouraging, babies, and then young children, discover the world and learn to fend for themselves, thanks to their parents who make their surroundings intelligible and let them demonstrate that they can cope.

Feuerstein, through IE, proposes a method for re-educating intelligence by teaching those who have missed out on this human mediation how to learn; this is indispensable for what I call *l'appareil psychique* (the psychological/mental apparatus) and Feuerstein calls intelligence. The essential agent in re-educating intelligence is the human being, the teacher, the only person capable of giving a sense to the knowledge he or she is conveying to the students.

One needs to think about the act of thinking itself, analysing the procedures that come into play in a specific cognitive act, and pinpointing the deficient cognitive functions with the help of what Feuerstein calls a "cognitive map".

Learning to Think in the Junior Years of a Low Socioeconomic Status Secondary School

The SES classes (Specialized Education Section) of this school have benefited from the very first IE programme in France. Given the positive effects observed on both the pupils and the teachers, the extension to first- and second-year secondary school classes seems highly desirable.

Eleven teachers out of a total of 58, recruited on a voluntary basis and teaching various subjects (French, English, maths, physics, music, natural science, history and geography, fine arts and physical education), paired off to make up three IE sessions a week in two different classes. Ten classes in the first year of secondary school were given IE, and at the beginning of the experiment there were 227 pupils (October 1986). But this total was found to have dropped to 91 at the end of the second year. At the end of the first year of secondary school, a number of students were moved to a new school which had just opened.

A test/retest procedure was set up at the end of the experiment to try to assess the progress of the students receiving IE. Their results were compared with those of a control group made up of students from four classes in the first year of secondary education from a neighbouring school who had not been given IE. There were 93 students at the start of the experiment and 53 at the end. The following tests were applied:

(i) PMS 38 (Progressive Matrices Standard), which aims to measure the logical and non-verbal level of intelligence;

(ii) Analytic Intelligence Tests (AIT), which are intended to provide an assessment of the student's verbal, numerical and spatial aptitude;

(iii) drawing a picture.

Description of the Population

On the whole, the first-year students in the school come from what one could describe as modest, if not disadvantaged, sociocultural backgrounds. Their fathers are mainly manual workers or lower-level white collar, and nearly 10 per cent of them are unemployed. Most of their mothers are housewives and 25 per cent of them are employed. Families are large, with three, four, five or more children, far above the national average, which is closer to one or two children. Lastly, the ethnic origin of the pupils is extremely varied. French children form the largest group (44.4 per cent), but a high proportion are foreign: no less than 32 different nationalities are represented, mainly from North Africa, Portugal, Asia and sub-Saharan Africa.

These general characteristics do not mean that all the students in the first year of secondary school are "culturally deprived" in Feuerstein's sense, though some, usually the older ones, may well be. The age range is wide, from 10 to 16, the majority of the 227 students being between 11 and 14 years old.

Statistical Analysis[2]

A comparison of the progress of the experimental group (EG) and the control group (CG) comes up against a major problem: the averages of the two groups are not identical to the pretests (AIT = 70.2 for the EG and 81 for the CG; PMS 38 = 35.5 for the EG and 42.2 for the CG). When this happens, it is difficult to compare progress, since the CG is clearly better than the EG. The reason for this no doubt lies in the fact that the experimental school takes children with greater difficulties than the neighbouring schools used as the CG. This difference in levels at the start forces us to use special statistical techniques.

(i) An analysis of covariance

This statistical technique transforms the starting marks (using linear regression) so as to make the two groups comparable and then assesses the significance of the two factors involved.

The analysis was carried out on 144 students (EG = 91, CG = 53). The results obtained from the AIT (numerical, spatial, verbal and total) and PMS 38 tests were then examined. The marks obtained from the pretest were treated as independent variables, as were those for the two groups, experimental and control. The results from the posttests are dependent variables.

The variations between the two groups reveal the differences in progress between the students given IE and those following normal schooling, without any other external influence. Table 4.1 provides the values of Snedecor's F-test for each individual activity, with their level of significance.

TABLE 4.1 *Values of Snedecor's F-Test*

Activity tested	Value of F	Significance
Numerical AIT	0.134	p = 0.715
Spatial AIT	3.632	p = 0.059
Verbal AIT	0.857	p = 0.356
Total AIT	2.076	p = 0.152
PMS 38 Total	1.750	p = 0.188

Thus, only the Spatial AIT test reaches the 5 per cent level of significance. The overall scores on AIT and PMS 38 were significant, though barely. The verbal and numerical tests had by far the highest significance levels.

(ii) Analysis by paired groups

This second technique does the same thing as the covariance analysis. In this particular instance, the idea is to pair off a student from the EG and one from the CG with the same original marks and so construct two comparable groups by getting rid of the differences in pretesting.

This approach has many drawbacks because of the size of the two groups and the disparity of the marks obtained. Since the control group had only 53 members, almost half the students in the experimental group (N = 91) had to be dropped in order to make the pairing. In addition, pairs could not be found for some EG students because they did not match the CG exactly, so that in the end only 40 pairs remained.

A second problem has been described by Bacher (1983). The pairing of two disparate groups leads to better students being selected from the weaker group and matched with relatively poorer members of the stronger group. This has a "differential regression effect", which pulls up the average of each of the subgroups closer to the average of the group to which it belongs, that is, the comparison of the averages of the two groups paired off will be distorted by an effect which accentuates their differences. In our case, this will make it all the more difficult to demonstrate a difference between the two groups in progress on the posttests.

We nevertheless managed to pair off the two groups, experimental and control. There were in fact two distinct pairings: the first was carried out on the basis of the total marks obtained in PMS 38, where a difference of ± 1 point in the pretest scores was deemed acceptable and so 44 subjects were grouped. The second was based on the overall AIT figures. These scores are much higher and a difference of ± 2 was tolerated in each group, hence 43 pairs could be made.

An analysis of the marks obtained in the numerical, spatial and verbal subtests did not lead to new pairings being made; that is, the pairings based on the overall marks were retained.

Results obtained in PMS 38:

(i) Figure 4.1 shows the change in the averages for the two paired groups, as well as the pre- and posttest margins.
(ii) The starting points were virtually the same (CG = 40.68/ EG = 40.57) with almost identical dispersions (σ CG = 5.77/σ EG = 5.86).

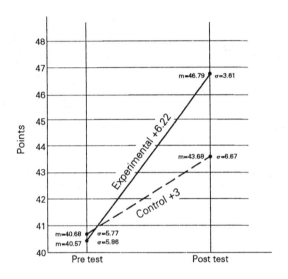

PMS 38 Test: total scores
(t significant to p=0.01)

FIG 4.1   Progress of scores obtained in PMS 38 in the two paired groups (44 subjects).

But the experimental group made considerably greater progress than the control group (CG: m = 43.68 and σ = 6.67/EG: m = 46.79 and σ = 3.61), that is, + 6.22 points against + 3 points (Student's t significant at p = 0.01).
Results obtained at the AIR (total score):

As for PMS 38, Figure 4.2 shows the close identity of the starting levels (CG: m = 77.74 and σ = 16.14/EG: m = 77.72 and σ = 15.97).

Once again the improvement is much greater in the experimental group (CTG: m = 98.21 and σ = 14.71/EG: m = 102.77 and σ = 12.69), that is, + 25.05 points as against + 20.46 points (Student's t significant at p = 0.05).

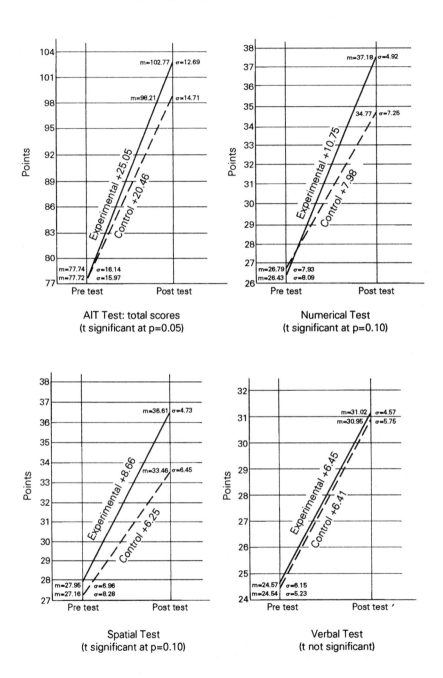

4.2. Progress of scores obtained in AIT in the two paired groups (43 subjects).

Results obtained from the numerical, spatial and verbal tests of the AIT:

(i) There is very little difference between the starting levels (26.43/26.79 for the numerical tests; 27.95/27.16 for the spatial tests; 24.57/24.54 for the verbal tests, for the experimental and the control groups respectively).

(ii) Although the change in the averages is more pronounced in the EG than in the CG on the two numerical and spatial subtests, the Student's t shows only a tendency ($p = 0.10$) rather than real significance.

(iii) The verbal results, however, are identical in both groups and the progress is the same.

Discussion of the results

Despite the various drawbacks of the method using the paired groups, we obtained results using this technique which are more conclusive than with the analysis of covariance. The changes are in the same direction, with the most influential factors remaining the same.

The two statistical methods produced different results because our groups (experimental and control) were not totally comparable in level. An "IE effect" does, however, seem to exist, with greater improvement in the experimental group. This tendency can be seen in the overall results of the main tests and is most pronounced in the spatial tests. To be more precise, one should really make the comparison with a control group of identical standard.

Repeating in a structured and systematic way all the concepts and thinking activities found at each stage of IE makes it possible to refine thinking structures, if not to set them up. Thus, even if students have benefited from generally sufficient mediations, it would seem that they have much to gain from this organized repetition centred on the act of thinking. Immigrant adolescents with a disturbed past, who have experienced difficulties in adapting to a new culture, can be particularly helped by this method.

In fact, whatever one's personal views with regard to the belief that everyone should have the same chance at the start of the first year of secondary school, it is unrealistic to think that one can disregard what has taken place beforehand. The importance of the quality of first interactions with the mother on the development and construction of intelligence is there to remind us of that, just as is the first learning experience at primary school. From this perspective, the first year of secondary school constitutes an opportunity for a fresh start that can perhaps be seized by the student if the external conditions are favourable. This is precisely what the teachers responsible for the application of the IE experience can achieve.

Individual Development

There is much to be learnt from following the development of a child over two consecutive years, from the first to the second year of secondary school. I am particularly concerned to pick out what enriches and develops intellectual capacities, including the personality as a whole, and what, on the contrary, slows down or prevents the general opening out of the person.

The "objective" assessments (the results from the tests carried out before and after the IE treatment, the school reports from the first and second year of secondary school) and "subjective" ones (comments of different teachers, progress with the drawings) are valuable, even if in most cases the information about the child's past is very limited or even totally non-existent.

Sinbad's case

The IE teachers who worked with Sinbad, aged 12 years 1 month at the start of his first year in secondary school, spoke of a great step in maturity. This boy is one of five children. His father is a painter and decorator from the Comore Islands, his mother a housewife. His first year was very poor, particularly his second term in which he seemed to become undisciplined under the influence of restless classmates. It was his participation in IE sessions which gradually distanced him from them and allowed him to get back to work. His second year was good and he passed into his third year with encouragement from the staff meeting. He is a pupil who has become both responsible and mature. Sinbad is very ambitious since he wants to become a doctor, which his results in the test, as well as his progress in the past 18 months, should not prevent him from doing.

Willai's case

Willai, who is 14 years 2 months old, joined the IE programme during her second year in secondary school. The teachers responsible for the sessions said that it was an advantage for her, since it made her integration into the class all the easier. Willai, who came from South-East Asia, had been living in France for only four years and had not been doing well at school. Serious speech difficulties made her participation almost non-existent, but she gradually opened up, followed the sessions extremely well and finished the school year with acceptable results which were good enough for her to pass into the third year.

Xao's case

Aged 15 years 6 months in her first year of secondary school, Xao resembles Willai in many ways. Her father is a Cambodian labourer and her mother a housewife looking after her three children. At the beginning of the second year, Xao was described as lacking self-confidence, being extremely reserved, even very uncommunicative, and never smiling. She had difficulties in French, spelling and grammar, but was hardworking and good at mathematics and English. It was the IE sessions that taught her to relax and smile, much to the teachers' relief. She never participated much in the oral sessions but kept improving in the written ones. At the end of the second term of the second year, because of her age (nearly 17) she was guided towards a vocational *lycée*, but her progress meant that she was finally admitted into the third year. She made it perfectly clear to her IE teacher that she wanted to continue with the programme and complete the last three instruments which had as yet not been seen.

Lionel's case

Things are quite different in Lionel's case, since at the age of 12 years 1 month at the start of his first year, he was bad at all subjects and his teachers said that he was not interested in school. His results in the tests were poor at the beginning of IE (he was below average for his age in PMS 38) in many ways.

The IE sessions were the only classes where Lionel really joined in and his French teacher, who was carrying out the programme, noted with some surprise that "there, he could find the right words to talk about things", and she and her colleagues came to think more highly of him because of these contributions. She added that the French lessons had not allowed her to discover the "richness of his personality".

Lionel himself recognizes that IE has taught him to express himself. His school results, though still only mediocre, were good enough for him to pass into the third year. The posttests reveal an improvement (in PMS 38 his score rose from 29 to 39 points).

Conclusion

The extreme variation in individual situations as they can appear in the first year of secondary school is only partially illustrated in the five cases which we have just briefly looked at. In our low socioeconomic status school, the students could hardly be more heterogeneous: in one of the classes the ages ranged from 10 to 16 at the beginning of the first year!

In such circumstances, it seems that one of the best solutions to prevent teachers from becoming understandably discouraged when faced with an almost impossible task is to involve them in motivating educational projects.

The principal of the school achieved this remarkably well, not only with the introduction of IE but also with other educational projects, such as teaching the use of computers or giving individual attention in physical education and sport.

The teachers who used the IE programme felt that their general pedagogic approach had been radically modified. The "IE frame of mind" transformed their way of teaching their own subjects, since it threw light on what is involved in thinking and intelligence. The "cognitive modifiability" described by Feuerstein clearly also affects the teachers, perhaps above all. In addition, their attitude to the children themselves was altered: they no longer judge students simply on the basis of their success or failure in their subject, but are more concerned about a student's overall mental processes in some specific activity.

The nature of the IE sessions themselves has made the teachers sensitive to the fact that students who are considered shy or "not very bright" can come alive and show signs of intelligence when they are placed in a situation far removed from the usual school routine. That in itself is a very revitalizing realization for the teachers, since it is in complete contrast to the depressing feeling that there is nothing to be done and that despite all their efforts, school results do not improve. But there is more: if the teacher feels more hopeful, the students will almost certainly follow suit, in a similar way to mother–baby interactions in the first stages of life (Debray, 1987). The many studies of the role of teachers' expectations all point to the decisive influence on vulnerable students of their perceptions as to their teachers' belief that they can succeed. The more students have doubts about themselves—which is often the case for older pupils who have experienced a number of failures in the past—the more this factor will determine the final outcome. We have seen that the IE programme gives both teachers and students this kind of heightened awareness, and that the subsequent school career can thus be radically changed. The cases of Xao and Lionel each showed this in their different ways.

In order to adapt to the first year of secondary school, the student must be capable of organizing his or her work within the weekly schedule. This ability to organize one's timetable in advance takes a long time to master, and children from privileged backgrounds receive considerable help from their families. For children who come from so-called underprivileged environments there is no such assistance. Such children have, in addition to the handicap of having to cope on their own, the burden of overtaking their parents intellectually. Clinical psychologists and psychiatrists know only too well the strength of the subconscious failure mechanisms which are triggered off in order to minimize such "transgressions" (Malandin, 1988). The best way of preventing this from happening is through a teacher in whom the student can place his or her trust and who will open up the world of learning. This is precisely what the IE teacher can achieve through mediated learning. Learning systematically how to organize one's time can help the student to avoid the traps of the failure mechanisms.

In this context, the IE experience can provide an efficient way of giving new opportunities—if not equal chances—to children who come from underprivileged families, and thus significantly increase the number of students able to stay on at school. In addition, it helps children from different cultural backgrounds to integrate. This aspect, underlined by Feuerstein and his team, is confirmed by my own research (e.g. the examples of Sinbad from the Comore Islands, and Willai and Xao from South-East Asia). Interestingly, when such students are given a fresh start, it is their results in mathematics, physics and even English which improve first of all. This shows that intelligent students find it easier to deal with abstract logical reasoning through the language of mathematics than through a language. Indeed, the most insuperable cultural differences relate to the manipulation of the various nuances and subtleties of a language, because how well people find the words to express themselves is taken as an indication of the quality of their intellectual potential.

Thus, mediated learning as it is provided during the IE sessions by a well-trained teacher offers a wide range of stimuli: verbal, graphic, abstract, concrete, linked to daily life and to all branches of knowledge. Each member of the group will latch onto whatever suits his or her particular needs of the moment.

This notion of a stimulating external environment deserves our attention. A priori, this is what all teachers will be seeking to achieve, since they know from experience that lessons are better assimilated if they are taught in an atmosphere where the pleasure of learning and the desire to know more are the overriding factors. It is precisely this long-forgotten, perhaps unknown feeling that IE arouses when students realize that they can achieve something which they did not think they were capable of. This renewed self-confidence, fragile at first, will allow them to take the risks—often costly in terms of self-image—required for subsequent intelligent action. For this to occur, however, the students must be confronted with difficult and stimulating problems that they can solve. In France, both adolescents and adults who are assumed to be not very intelligent have very little chance of achieving this, since the mere recognition of an intellectual deficiency often leads to a dramatic fall in the expectation of success, as well as a similar reduction in stimulation from the external environment.

Notes

1. For a full description of Feuerstein's Instrumental Enrichment, see chapter by Link, this volume.
2. Bernard Douet was responsible for the statistical analysis.

References

Bacher, F. (1983). "Remarques sur quelques modèles utilisés dans l'étude des changements." *Psychologie et Pédagogie* (Bulletin du GPCO), Nos. 2–4.

Binet, A. and Simon, T. (1907). *Les enfants anormaux. Guide pour l'admission des enfants anormaux dans les classes de perfectionnement.* A. Colin, Paris.

Debray, R. (1982). "Qu'attendre d'un examen psychologique chez un adolescent?", *La pratique médicale*, **39**, pp. 55–58.

Debray, R. (1987). *Bébés/mères en révolte: Traitements psychanalytiques conjoints des déséquilibres psychosomatiques précoces.* Le Centurion, Paris.

Debray, R. (1989). *Apprendre à penser: Une issue à l'échec scolaire et professionel. A propos du Programme d'Enrichissement Instrumental de R. Feuerstein.* Eshel, Paris.

Esquirol, E. (1838). *Des maladies mentales considérées sous les rapports médical, hygiénique et médico-légal.* J. B. Baillière, Paris.

Eysenck, H. J. (1975). *The Inequality of Man.* Temple, London.

Malandin, C. (1988). *Scolarité et développement de la personnalité.* Ph.D. thesis, Université de Paris-V René Descartes.

Sanglade-Andronikov, A. and Verdier-Gibello, M. L. (1983). L'examen psychologique de l'enfant. Les tests d'intelligence, d'aptitude, de raisonnement. *Encyclopédie Médico-chirurgicale (Psyhchiatrie),* 37180 C 10, pp. 1–23.

II

Learning to Think:
The Infusion Approach

5

The Passion of Thoughtfulness: Arts, Humanities, and the Life of the Mind

MAXINE GREENE

*Teachers College,
Columbia University,
New York*

To link passion to thoughtfulness is to summon up images of incompleteness, of questions unanswered, of cravings unfulfilled. Thoughtfulness signifies care and attentiveness within the flux of things. It means awareness to the "claim on our thinking attention" made by events and facts by virtue of their existence (Arendt, 1978, p. 4). It seems a continuing "raid on the inarticulate" (Eliot, 1958, p. 128), a deliberate effort to form and express and inchoate. Passionless thinking too often slips into technical rationality, rule-governed, geared to closures and controls. Neutral, distanced, it solves problems, it calculates, it arrives at propositions, it concludes. Important though such thinking may be, it is not sufficient if we intend to provoke the young to be actively and humanely in the world, to become committed, to continue posing questions, and learning to learn. Thoughtfulness links thinking to desire, to reaching towards what is not yet; it ties it to imagining as well. For Mary Warnock, imagination is needed "for application of thoughts or concepts to things", and she speaks of how important it is to educate imagination viewed as part of intelligence, and how this entails education of the feelings as well. We must realize, she says: "that there is more in our experience of the world than can possibly meet the unreflecting eye . . . that there is always *more* to experience and more *in* what we experience than we can predict" (1978, p. 202).

Against this background, I want to argue for a central role to be played by the arts and humanities in the teaching of thinking. Such teaching, after all, ought to involve enabling students to make meanings, to use what they come to know in making sense of the lived world, the world they can see and hear and read. Their embeddedness in that world ought to be affirmed; so ought the networks of their relationships to one another and to the phenomena of what is called "reality". To say that is to suggest at the start that the teaching of thinking and the nurture of thoughtfulness ought to begin in a sceptical rejection of objectivism, in a recognition that "reality" must be understood as interpreted (variously interpreted) experience.

The life of the mind, then, is characterized by relationality and by the activities of interpreting and sense-making. John Dewey believed that "mind" should be thought of as a verb and not a noun. In its idiomatic use, "mind" refers to every kind of interest in and concern for things. It is not used to denote something self-contained or isolated, but always used in relation to situations, objects, persons and events. As Dewey says, "Mind is care, in the sense of solicitude, anxiety, as well as of active looking after things that need to be tended; we mind our step, our course of action, emotionally as well as thoughtfully" (1932, p. 263).

Rejecting the concept of mind as an interiority or an entity, Dewey was in the tradition of the post-Hegelians and of the existential-phenomenologists as well. Their philosophies of mind or consciousness posited a range of acts of consciousness, not a mere reception of data. Consciousness was regarded as intentional: it was always consciousness of something; and any act of consciousness (believing, conceiving, intuiting, judging, imagining, perceiving, analysing) was always directed towards something. Maurice Merleau-Ponty talked of a preconscious as well as a conscious intentionality. The preconscious gave to a landscape underlying later knowing, a landscape that became a text knowledge to translate (1967, p. xviii). Being a perceived landscape, the text was a configuration of perceived shapes, colours, sounds, which served as the substratum or foundation of the rational structures built up over time. Conscious or reflective intentionality, then, is concerned about the disclosure of what words and things mean, and about the understanding of our "effective involvement in the world" (ibid. p. xiv).

Involvement, understanding, perspectivism: all these are focal to a view of how informed engagements with the arts and humanities can enrich and intensify the life of the mind. It is necessary to add, however, that the acts of thematizing—representing and expressing—what is experienced, what is lived, are not the acts of isolated subjectivities. In the arts and humanities, as in the other spheres or provinces of meaning, the "raid on the inarticulate" can only take place with the aid of other human beings, past and present, who have developed schemes of interpretation or perspectives by means of which lived realities are disclosed. To learn to think, therefore, is to learn to enter certain of the culture's languages or symbol systems, or to participate in what Alfred Schutz called the various "provinces of meaning" (1967, p. 230) that give "accents of reality" to specific experiences. For Schutz, each of these provinces (that of the natural sciences, or the social sciences, or the arts, or the world of working, or the world of play) is characterized by a specific "cognitive style" and a certain way of directing attention to the common-sense world. The individuals who enter these provinces all come from distinct biographical backgrounds; they all move into the activity of sense-making from different locations in the social world. Thoughtfulness may have much to do with an awareness of the vantage points biography and location create. Such an awareness not only keeps alive a sense of agency or presentness to the activity under way, it also keeps alive the perspectival character of what is thought to be the "real"; since, situated as the person is and must be, she or he can only have a partial vision of surrounds. At most, the person can see facets, partial profiles of houses, trees, other human beings; a vision of wholeness is forever beyond the situated being's grasp. Some of the passion I have spoken of has to do with a craving for wholeness, for coherence, for totality. It is part of the sense that "there is more in our experience of the world than can possibly meet the unreflecting eye . . ."; and it is part of what keeps people trying to surpass what is, to reach beyond, or (as Martin Heidegger would put) "to unconceal" (1971, pp. 52–53).

For Heidegger, experiences with the arts were experiences of clearings or openings, where there were moments of "unconcealedness" and where there might be "the happening of truth" (ibid. p. 60). It is important to realize that the clearings would open in experience itself, that what was called "truth" had to be found in a work, and that truth usually became "in a thinker's questioning". This truth, however defined, is not to be confused with empirical truth or even truth in some metaphysical sense. Heidegger undoubtedly knew that those truths were contingent on particular modes of inquiry or belief, that they emerged from perspectives within spaces (apart from the arts) which other interpreters were trying to understand. John Gilmour (1986) has clarified some of Heidegger's meanings by reading "Portrait of an Old Man" by Rembrandt and Lievens in the light of "the happening of truth". Reminding us that Heidegger used people to focus on the works themselves and pay careful heed to the painted surfaces. Gilmour indicates that hand and palette are visible in the painting, that we are not looking through the painting into the artist's mind. It is evident too that we cannot use a correspondence theory of truth and assume that the painting objectively represents a physical model used by the artist. Heidegger would have us, rather, view the painting as a disclosure.

In asking what is being disclosed by the work, Gilmour suggests several of the ways in which such an encounter generates both thinking and thoughtfulness. For one thing, unique though the old man's face may be, the painting renders something universal about the human condition; and somehow it feeds—through a condensation of the image of an old man—into our own self-understanding. Yet because the image is so direct, we think of what hangs before us as the art work; and we forget that a long, perhaps dialectical, thought process lies behind the completed picture. Instead of looking at it as expressing a limited expressive stage, Gilmour tells us that we can see it now "as the product of a lengthy working process, which includes both the development of thoughts and their material manifestation in the artist's medium" (1986, p. 16).

There has been a kind of metamorphosis in time as the artist has interacted with the medium and the materials available to him, has modified, refined, until his images were transformed into what the painter believed at last to be an adequate expression. The meanings of it were not predefined and then embodied in the work; they did not exist, it might be said, until they emerged from what appeared on the canvas over time.

For learners to recognize this, to come in touch somehow with the "happening" marked by what lies before them, is to discover something about the dialectic, something about pictorial thinking, something about the nature of painting itself. If they are helped to stand and look questioningly, carefully at the portrait, to notice the particulars on the surface, to allow their imaginations to play over those particulars and integrate them gradually into a complex and palpitant whole, they may discover something new about thinking, feelings and imagining which they could not suspect before. In the case of certain paintings, they may feel themselves not only seeing more in the surrounding world as well as in the museum; they may find themselves abruptly released from what Richard Bell, writing about Giacometti's art, calls "the sterile, geometric cage of our scientific world" (1989, p. 17). Bell tells us that this is what happens when we come in touch with Giacometti's judgement on culture through his painting "The Nose". The painting itself renders a geometric frame, a constrained head, and a nose piercing the frame. Bell makes the point that he comes to the judgement he expresses from a beginning in non-cognitive sensory experience which later gives rise to the kind of cognitive leap out of which a judgement may come. Much depends, he says, upon reflection "on the manifold" given in our experience. The first judgement is an aesthetic one; but later judgements can be of diverse kinds.

> "The Nose" is a good example of the struggle of humanity to break out of the sterile frame we have built for ourselves through science and technology. Anxiety is apparent in the head caught in the frame, but the nose penetrates the surface of the frame. With "The Nose", Giacometti discerns the dominant underlying assumption of our culture—our scientific way of understanding—and awakens our consciousness to the *human anxiety* that has been created for us. The work embodies both the cultural assumption and the human passion. In it we can also become aware of our own alienation and of our passion to break out of structural moulds. Through it we, with Giacometti, struggle against brokenness. (1989, p. 18)

Bell's response may or may not be exemplary, although it provides a metaphor for the release made possible by encounters with works of art. Jerome Bruner once mentioned: "the construction and exploitation of the category of possibility, the formulated but empty category through which we search out new experience" (1962, p. 61).

Giacometti, whether by means of his solitary walkers in empty space, his attenuated men and women, his portraits, his abstract forms, somehow has made us see differently and, consequently, make rather different sense of our world. He knew, however, as do Bell and Gilmour, that what he created was in many senses within the aesthetic symbol system existing in the culture at the time, even as the judgement he made about constraint and loneliness and anxiety was itself consonant with existing modes of constructing social reality. Nonetheless, because of the power of his imagery, because the figures that are unlike living beings arouse in us responses like those aroused by desolate human beings, Giacometti makes us see differently and even feel differently. Engaging with his work, we find our taken-for-granted worlds defamiliarized. Defamiliarized, they become more visible in their wonder and in their deficiency: more thought-provoking, as Heidegger would say. This does not mean that the desolation that the paintings and sculptures express, the constriction and the loneliness are to be taken as more reliable, more valid diagnoses of the culture than others in the provinces of the arts or without. It simply means that the culture itself has been extended and that we have been enabled to look at it and its assumptions with fresh eyes. Looking at the work, we are part of that culture, even as the work is part of it; and to ponder the dynamics of our relationship to such work is to bring much more into the open about who we are as beings living in the world, even as it may bring into the open the need to think about what that world demands.

To be able to be fully present to works of visual art, to overcome the conviction that they are merely copies of representations, to live in the created world of formed content: all this takes education. The fact that what is required is a good deal more than "art appreciation" is testimony to the kind of thinking and, indeed, to the pluralist, expanded kind of knowing entailed by entry into pictorial spaces, by the grasping of depictions, abstractions, squares, coloured edges. Dewey wondered presciently in *Art as Experience* why aesthetic perception, unlike geology or chemistry, should be considered "an affair for odd moments"; and he spoke about the complexity of such perception in comparison with mere "seeing" or proper labelling or even recognition. There must be a deliberate ordering of the elements of the whole, an "extraction of what is significant". He wrote that:

> There is work to be done on the part of the percipient as there is on the part of the artist. The one who is too lazy, idle, or indurated in convention to perform

this work will not see or hear. His "appreciation" will be a mixture of scraps of learning with conformity to norms of conventional admiration and with a confused, even if genuine, emotional excitation. (1932, p. 54)

Dewey might well have agreed with Louis Arnaud Reid when he distinguished sharply between conceptual labelling and coming to know what we immediately perceive musically (or visually, or by means of words). Reid holds that art statements only take on aesthetic existence:

as experienced, as felt, as known, by a person or persons. A sonata, a poem, a picture, a dance, only fully exists . . . as it occurs in . . . aesthetic experience, or aesthetic experiences of it. The felt experience of a personal subject is, I suggest, organic to its existence. This by no means implies that art is "merely private, merely subjective", but only that subjective experience and cognitive feeling are part of its full existence, and centrally relevant. (1987, p. 42)

For Reid, all knowing, in addition to aesthetic knowing, was relational, whether it involved knowing people, knowing works of art, knowing in the ethical or deductive or empirical domains. This concern for a pluralist epistemology is evocative of Howard Gardner's theory of multiple intelligences (1983); and like Gardner's emphasis upon musical, spatial, bodily-kinesthetic and personal intelligences, it holds great relevance for making the arts central in curriculum.

Again, the argument here has to do with expansion of experience, with thoughtfulness and a critical attitude, not with the transfer of particular skills to other kinds of learning. I am not sure that there is evidence of transfer of training from any of the arts to other subject matters, and I believe the part played by the arts in human life is likely to be distorted if they are made mainly subsidiary in the schools, or instrumental or even "basic". I appreciate what Nelson Goodman has to say when he leaves open the question of the difference between fostering the aptitudes needed for the arts and the sciences, even as he makes so clear that the difference between them is:

not that between feeling and fact, intuition and inference, delight and deliberation, synthesis and analysis, sensation and cerebration, concreteness and abstraction, passion and action, mediacy and immediacy, or truth and beauty, but rather a difference in domination of certain specific characteristics of symbols. (1976, p. 264)

I take this to be the case with regard to the several "languages" of art—music, dance, literature, as well as painting—although I have only had the space to deal with painting.

Goodman also agrees with the various commentators already quoted on the matter of whether the aesthetic attitude can be understood as a merely passive contemplation of the immediately given, "uncontaminated by any conceptualization . . ." He goes on to say that:

we have to read the painting as well as the poem, and that aesthetic experience is dynamic rather than static. It involves making delicate discriminations and discerning subtle relationships, identifying symbol systems and characters within these systems and what these characters denote and exemplify, interpreting works and reorganizing the world in terms of works and works in terms of the world. Much of our experience and many of our skills are brought to bear and may be transformed by the encounter. The aesthetic "attitude" is restless, searching, testing—is less attitude than action; creation and re-creation. (1976, p. 242)

Turning to imaginative literature as emblematic of the humanities, I would argue in much the same way. Engagement with works of literature also makes possible "creation and recreation", as it provokes thoughtfulness and critique and a concerned being in the world. In this domain, however, the disagreements multiply, especially where meaning and referentiality are concerned. In presenting an argument for reconceiving the teaching of literature, within the contexts of teaching thinking, one has arbitrarily to set aside the debates about structuralism, deconstruction, textuality and even representation. There is no question but that English teaching and the teaching of the humanities generally are being affected by the post-modern challenges, most particularly those linked to pluralism, dialogism (Bakhtin, 1981), perspectivism, feminism and what Barbara Herrnstein Smith has called "contingencies of value" (1988); and attention to these concerns can make more meaningful and relevant the teaching of the humanities in troubled times. Here, too, the crucial point has to do with human consciousness in its relations to the lived world and to constructed social realities. It is to do with interpretive communities and subject–object connections and the life of language itself.

For Jean-Paul Sartre, a work of literature is an act of confidence in human freedom (1949, p. 51). Readers willing to break with the habitual, the mundane or the taken-for-granted in order to enter a fictional world might find themselves negating the social reality that conditioned them, seeking new ways of making sense. The unreal world of a novel is, of course, constituted by language and entered into by the release of imagination; and, as we have seen, imagination is the capacity to summon up what is not, to reach beyond the actual. We might consider for a moment the invented universe of Franz Kafka's *The Trial*, which begins in the most persuasive ordinariness: "Someone must have been telling lies about Joseph K., for without having done anything wrong, he was arrested one fine morning" (1962, p. 7).

Before long, the reader (looking through Joseph K.'s perspective) discovers that the ordinary rules and guarantees that anyone would assume to be normal have been set aside, and that no known tradition can account for K.'s position. Whatever the reader's situation, however he or she has constituted the novel as meaningful, that reader is bound to view

some dimension of his or her experience differently: the matter of institu-
tionalized power; the law; the authority of a dictatorial family or a
dictatorial state. Released, as it were, from whatever has seemed natural or
simply "given", readers may experience a fundamental questioning, may
think about their own thinking as seldom before.

What occurs in the course of reading imaginative literature can only
occur in the reader's consciousness as she or he succeeds in "disclosing in
creating... creating by disclosing" (Sartre, 1949, p. 43) under the guidance
of a writer whose work must be brought alive intentionally. Collaborating
in such a fashion, readers see more in their own lives, especially when the
novel at hand makes a demand: a demand that comes when gaps appear
that cry out for closing, when deficiencies reveal themselves that cry out for
repair. If a novel discloses injustices and abuses in the social world, as (for
example) Toni Morrison's recent novel *Beloved* so clearly does, that world
may well be animated by indignation when readers return from the
fictional reality of the novel to the lived, the mundane. Having attended
imaginatively to something they have brought alive in the manifold of their
own experience, something made possible through the re-ordering of the
stuff of memory and perception and understanding, they cannot but view
their own lives from a new vantage point. The woman, for instance, who
has been a mother, cannot but discover an aspect of mothering, of
mother-loving quite new when she reads *Beloved*. In this text, Baby Suggs,
her own slave days over, recalls how it was to have her children sold away
from her:

> The last of her children, whom she barely glanced at when he was born because
> it wasn't worth the trouble to learn features you would never see change into
> adulthood anyway. Seven times she had done that: held a little foot; examined
> the fat fingertips with her own—fingers she never saw become the male or female
> hands a mother would recognize anywhere. She didn't know to this day what
> their permanent teeth looked like; or how they held their heads when they
> walked. Did Patty lose her lisp? What color did Famous' skin finally take? Was
> that a cleft in Johnny's chin or just a dimple that would disappear soon's his
> jawbone changed? Four girls, and the last time she saw them there was no hair
> under their arms. Does Ardelia still love the burned bottom of bread? All seven
> were gone or dead. (1987, p. 189)

The details are familiar and they are thought-provoking. Grasping them
in a created context, readers may move from the well-remembered and the
cherished to what would be (for most) unthinkable. By the end of the
passage, many are likely to find what they have always considered natural
cruelly subverted. How could any human being take the responsibility for
selling children, for depriving a mother of the seven infants to whom she
had given birth? Memories of what it is like to fondle and raise and wonder
about little ones are likely to return. Along with that may come recollec-

tions of deeply repressed fears of losing them; and this is when outrage may flood in, retroactively with respect to slavery, in the present with regard to violated or abused or lost children. There may be outrage and passion and a longing for resolution, for repair.

But what does this have to do with knowing more about slavery in the southern United States before and after the Civil War? How does the fictional universe created by Toni Morrison relate to or shed light on the actualities the historical record presents? Recently, there have been a number of books appearing on slavery and what followed after abolition. Some are histories of various kinds; others are from the fields of economics or sociology. One of the social histories, Elizabeth Fox-Genovese's *Within the Plantation Household*, documents in scholarly detail the lives of slaveholding women and slave women, the communities they formed, the discrimination they suffered, the brutalities inflicted on the slaves. There are accounts of the shadow of the master or the overseer on various plantations, and descriptions of the ways in which the masters tried to present themselves as benevolent or superior beings, seldom duping those who suffered their domination:

> For as owner, the master embodied the power literally to dispose of their lives through the sale of them, their children, their husbands, or those who they held dear. Bitter resentment, fear, and the desire to placate combined in shifting and uneasy tension. The consequences of those complexities included the knowledge that power was no abstraction; it wore a white, male face. (1989, p. 190)

Dramatically rendered as it is, this constitutes what might be called "knowledge about". It is knowledge that can be validated through examination of the evidence and it may become cumulative knowledge, adding to and enriching what we already know about slavery, its economic aspects, its sexual or gender dimensions.

This text may be read interpretively, so that readers somehow manage to fuse the historical meanings they discover and the meanings they find in their present situations. A greater self-understanding may result, as well as a deeper understanding of a given moment in history. The historical account, unlike the novel, however, does not ask its readers to lend it their lives in order to bring the master and the slave women alive. Nor does it engage imagination and consciousness in the same way; it does not make the readers "see", as Joseph Conrad wrote. Conrad said that if an artist succeeded in that task, readers would find in a text "encouragement, consolation, fear, charm" and perhaps "also that glimpse of truth" for which they had forgotten to ask (1960, p. 31). Scholars and scientists, Conrad thought, addressed themselves to intelligence, to "credulity"; perhaps they goaded readers to think until they were better informed. The question of the relation between the "as-if" world and the historical "reality" remains open; and it would appear that teaching both kinds of text together might provoke thinking, even as it might deepen understanding of moments in the past.

Much the same might be said with respect to the many articles and books appearing on child abuse, some by social workers, others by psychologists or physicians, still others by students of the urban middle class and the poor. There are a number of novels and short stories on the subject; but one of the most compelling is still Fyodor Dostoyevsky's *The Brothers Karamasov*. There is a scene where Ivan Karamasov, the intellectual brother, is talking to Alyosha about how hard it is to love one's neighbours when one considers the widespread suffering of children: "There was a little girl of five," Ivan says, "who was hated by her father and mother, 'most worthy and respectable people of good education and breeding'. You see . . . it is a peculiar characteristic of many people, this love of torturing children and children only. To all other types of humanity these torturers behave mildly and benevolently, like cultivated and humane Europeans; but they are very fond of torturing children . . ." (1945, p. 286)

Ivan wants justice, it may be remembered, here on earth. He does not want to see forgiveness; he does not want harmony at the cost of unavenged suffering. Those reading cannot but experience a rupture and a demand. They cannot but be provoked to thoughtfulness, and to reaching with their questions beyond the known. Here, too, passion has a role.

Herbert Marcuse, stressing the importance of the "unreality" distinctive of such a work, wrote about the ways in which it might stand against "established reality" (1978, p. 58). In this case, it might "stand against" by provoking readers to reflection and critique, critique informed by passion, opening doors to repairs still to be understood. There are many novels, actually, that make established truths problematic for a length of time, sometimes throughout their lives: Melville's *Moby Dick*, Marquez's *One Hundred Years of Solitude*, Margaret Atwood's *Surfacing*, Ralph Ellison's *Invisible Man*, Milan Kundera's *The Unbearable Lightness of Being*. Teachers of thinking might well make their own authentic lists. If they do, if they continue to engage themselves with fictions of this kind, they are at least likely to keep in touch with the open question. If they can provide a sense of the open question to those they teach, they are more likely to present themselves as "reflective practitioners" (Schon, 1983), thinking in action rather than applying conclusions when problems arise.

Much has to do with their capacity (and, in time, their students' capacity) to achieve imaginative literature as meaningful rather than to seek within particular texts prefabricated nuggets of meaning. To do that is to look at what occurs in the course of reading from a range of perspectives: the narrators', the different characters', the outside voices, those of the readers choosing their roles as readers. If, say, it is *The Brothers Karamasov*, there are multiple standpoints to be taken upon the shifting ambiguous "world" waiting to be brought into being by the ones who read. That "world" can only come into being between the book lying on the table and the person decoding its pages; since it cannot be identified with what is printed on those pages, nor with what happens in the subjectivity or the consciousness of the one who reads. This, clearly, is the approach of those who have defined what is sometimes called "reader reception theory" (Eco, 1979; Fish, 1980; Iser, 1978). I chose it because the descriptions of the "act of reading" which it makes possible are in so many ways analogous to descriptions of reflective learning: learning as pattern-making, as "creation and recreation", as interpretation of lived experience in an expanding context of relationships.

Moreover, novels cannot be realized as novels or as works of art if readers do not engage with them in accord with norms that govern the reading of novels. At the very least, these norms have to do with the ability to recognize such works as fictional, to shape experience in accord with what is disclosed as the language is decoded, to attend to the figurative and the metaphorical, to perceive intertextual connections, to achieve meanings through imaginative movement through and around the work. There will never be total agreement on the standards of "good reading"; nor will there be total agreement on the criteria governing "good learning". Nonetheless, readers and learners must be aware of themselves inhabiting some normative community along with others, even as they develop expanding dialogue with regard to the existential and intellectual relevance of the standards according to which they choose to read and work and live.

The stress on action and the initiatives associated with the taking of action have significance for both acts of reading and acts of learning, I believe. There is something illuminating in the emphasis on collaboration; involving texts and readers willing to let their energy pour into particular works, striving dialectically to bring them to life. Wolfgang Iser writes that:

> the meaning of the text does not reside in the expectations, surprises, disappointments or frustrations that we experience in the process of gestalt-forming. These are simply the reactions that take place when the gestalten are disturbed. What this really means is that as we read, we react to what we ourselves have produced, and it is this mode of reaction that, in fact, enables us to experience the text as an actual event. (1978, pp. 128–129)

It is this mode of reaction that allows readers to animate the meanings of texts as realities. These events are not, of course, empirical or measurable. They occur in the feeling-structures, minds and imaginations of live social beings ready to relate dialogically to texts within diverse symbol systems. Most often, readers seek insistently for coherence, for resolutions of conflict and uncertainty. They cannot help but try to go beyond the partial and problematic, to totalize, to discover a sustaining unity. They exercise, if they can, imaginative ingenuity to bridge the gaps between the perspectives through which they have learned to attend: to reconcile Alyosha's vision of existence, say, with Dmitri's, or Ivan's tragic scepticism with Alyosha's enduring love. But no novelistic reality can ever be complete or harmonious, not so long as a plurality of perspectives is being rendered. Readers, like learners in the modern world, must discover how to live with contingency as they find out how to live with multiplicity. Clifford Geertz, reminding us that "multiplicity" is the hallmark of modern consciousness, finds illusory any hope of a general orientation or perspective: "The problem of the integration of cultural life becomes one of making it possible for people inhabiting different worlds to have a genuine, and reciprocal impact upon one another" (1983, p. 161).

This is consonant with Richard Rorty's view of solidarity or the "desire for as much intersubjective agreement as possible, the desire to extend the reference of 'us' as far as we can" (1985, p. 5).

The striving towards articulation, then, may become part of the striving towards reciprocity, towards something resembling what Hannah Arendt has called a "common world" (Arendt, 1958), so long as teaching is suffused with thoughtfulness and students are provoked to envisage possibility. There are no guarantees, just as there are no guarantees that the arts and humanities will enlighten or combat technicism or bring persons in touch with themselves. The alternative, however, may be an inhuman formalism and rigidity, the "frame" through which Giacometti was trying to break, the petrification that prevents learning and stifles critique. The poet Elizabeth Bishop (1983) began a poem called "Conversation" with these two lines:

> The tumult in the heart
> keeps asking questions

I would want to work towards a contextualized, perspectival curriculum beginning in tumult and warmed by passion. I would want to repair a thoughtless age by reaching out towards possibility.

References

Arendt, H. (1958). *The Human Condition*, University of Chicago Press, Chicago.
Arendt, H. (1978). *Thinking*, Harcourt Brace Jovanovich, New York.
Bakhtin, M. (1981). *The Dialogical Imagination*, University of Texas Press, Austin, TX.
Bell, R. H. (1989). Giacometti's art as a judgment on culture, *The Journal of Aesthetics and Art Criticism*, **47** (1), Winter.
Bishop, E. (1983). "Conversation", in *The Complete Poems*, Farrar, Straus, Giroux, New York.
Bruner, J. S. (1962). *On Knowing: Essays for the left hand*, Harvard University Press, Cambridge, MA.
Conrad, J. (1960). Preface to *The Nigger of the Narcissus*, in Miller J. E., Jr (ed.), *Myth and Method*, University of Nebraska Press, Lincoln, NE.
Dewey, J. (1932). *Art as Experience*, Minton, Balch & Co, New York.
Dostoyevsky, F. (1945). *The Brothers Karamasov*, Modern Library, New York.

Eco, U. (1979). *The Role of the Reader*, University of Indiana Press, Bloomington, IN.

Eliot, T. S. (1958). "Little Gidding", in *The Complete Poems and Plays*, Harcourt Brace, New York.

Fish, S. (1980). *Is There a Text in This Class?* Harvard University Press, Cambridge, MA.

Fox-Genovese, E. (1989). *Within the Plantation Household: Black and White Women in the Old South*, The University of North Carolina Press, Chapel Hill, NC.

Gardner, H. (1983). *Frames of Mind*, Basic Books, New York.

Geertz, C. (1983). *Local Knowledge*, Basic Books, New York.

Gilmour, J. C. (1986). *Picturing the World*, State University of New York Press, Albany, NY.

Goodman, N. (1976). *Languages of Art*, Hackett, Indianapolis, OH.

Heidegger, M. (1971). *Poetry, Language, and Thought*, Harper & Row, New York.

Iser, W. (1978). *The Act of Reading*, Johns Hopkins Press, Baltimore, MD.

Kafka, F. (1962). *The Trial*, Modern Library, New York.

Marcuse, H. (1978). *The Aesthetic Dimension*, Beacon Press, Boston.

Merleau-Ponty, M. (1967). *Phenomenology of Perception*, The Humanities Press, New York.

Morrison, T. (1987). *Beloved*, Alfred A. Knopf, New York.

Reid, L. A. (1987). *Ways of Understanding and Education*, Heinemann Books, London.

Rorty, R. (1985). "Solidarity or objectivity?" in Rajchman J. and West C. (eds.), *Post-Analytic Philosophy*, Columbia University Press, New York.

Sartre, J.-P. (1949). *Literature and Existentialism*, The Citadel Press, New York.

Schon, D. A. (1983). *The Reflective Practitioner*, Basic Books, New York.

Schutz, A. (1967). "On multiple realities", in *Collected Papers*. Vol. 1, Martinus Nijhoff, The Hague.

Smith, B. H. (1988). *Contingencies of Value*, Harvard University Press, Cambridge, MA.

Warnock, M. (1978). *Imagination*, University of California Press, Berkeley, CA.

6

Cognitive Acceleration through Science Education

PHILIP ADEY

*King's College,
London University*

Throughout the history of education debate there has been a dialectic concerning education as an opportunity to learn things directly useful for survival (in a modern society, this is related to employment), and education as a way of transmitting culture and developing the mind, in a rather general sense. Explicitly or implicitly, all elementary, secondary and higher education curricula include a proportion of the latter type of objective. We do not send children to school just to learn facts and skills to fit them for work, and we do expect education to develop their intelligence such that it can be applied in novel and unspecified situations.

From time to time claims are made for different subjects within the school curriculum as being particularly well suited to develop logical thinking. Traditionally, this was a justification for the teaching of Latin, centuries after it had been of any practical use. Mathematics is a slightly more recent claimant, but today it is science educators who are most vociferous in their assurances that their subject is in a unique position to develop clear, rational thinking in pupils of all ages and abilities. For example, "An introduction to science method contributes to the preparation of young people for working life as well as to *their intellectual development* [my italics]" (DES, 1985, p. 3); and "Throughout their science education pupils should be encouraged to develop their powers of reasoning by reflecting on their own understanding, and by appreciating that learning may involve a change in the way they think about, explain and do things" (DES, 1988, p. 6).

There is, of course, no evidence whatsoever to support any of these claims, an omission for which scientists, of all people, should be most ashamed since a belief in the need for evidence is central to their philosophy. Moreover, it seems futile to make such claims for any subject *qua* subject. If there are aspects of formal education which do promote the development of general intelligence in children, and I believe that there are, they are likely to be embedded in particular forms of teaching and learning across the curriculum. Nevertheless, because of my own background, and because funding agencies tend to see science and technology as attractive (for all the wrong reasons of course; they think that science has more vocational value than social studies), we have set our investigations in the context of science lessons. In my description of the Cognitive Acceleration through Science Education (CASE) project I will try to highlight particular aspects of pedagogy which do seem to have contributed to such success as can be shown, and then you may decide whether and how such a pedagogy can be applied within other subject areas[1].

A Psychological Model

Cognitive Acceleration through Science Education has some characteristics of a curriculum development project: we have, after all, developed and published curriculum materials for teachers and pupils (Adey, Shayer and Yates, 1989). But primarily it is a research project investigating the question of whether it is possible, within the context of normal (in Britain) mixed-ability schools with normal teachers, to raise the general level of thinking of adolescent students.

As with a research project, any teaching strategies that are to be proposed may be expected to be rooted in a psychological model providing a set of propositions about the mechanism of cognitive development, which might be manipulated by educators to the advantage of pupils. The model of cognitive development and learning originating with Piaget and elaborated and operationalized by Case, Lawson, Longeot, Pascual–Leone, Shayer and many others has been through cycles of fashion in the education world. In the 1960s, Piaget was discovered in the United States, and for a while pupils and topics were categorized as "concrete" or "formal operational", often with the implication that this was all one needed to know. Inevitably, and properly, reaction set in and those of us working with the Piagetian model would often be met with after-the-presentation comments such as "I thought Piaget had been disproved".

The current position could be described as bimodal: on the one hand there are those (pragmatists) who use concrete and formal operations as useful descriptions of general types of thinking of which different pupils seem to be capable. Pupils can be reliably assessed for their type of thinking, and such assessments used as one of the input variables into various correlational and predicative experiments on learning and instruction, or even just to match materials to children's thinking. At the same time, more theoretical researchers continue to test and develop the model, to elaborate it and to try its limits. Whatever one's view about the validity or usefulness of the Piagetian model of cognitive development, it remains a force in educational research and practice, perhaps especially in science education.

In devising an intervention programme to be used by teachers, aspects of the model on which we concentrated were the schemata of formal operations and the mechanism by which the development of the central cognitive processor develops the capability for formal operations. Particular features of this mechanism which were of interest were the need for cognitive engagement with a problem, cognitive conflict, metacognition and (from Feuerstein) bridging. We also learned from Feuerstein's experience that little of permanence would be likely to be achieved by a programme lasting less than two years. I will illustrate briefly how these principles were used in the development of *Thinking Science* and in the design of the experiment to test its effectiveness.

Thinking Science (ThiSci) consists of 30 activities defined by teachers' notes and pupils' work sheets. Each one is designed to replace one regular 70-minute science lesson. Each activity concentrates on one of the schemata of formal operations shown in the list of activities (Figure 6.1), although no attempt is made directly to teach the schema. The experience

1 What varies?	Variables
2 Two variables	Variables
3 The 'fair' test	Variables
4 What sort of relationship?	Variables
5 Roller ball	Variables
6 Gears and ratios	Proportionality
7 Scaling: pictures and microscopes	Proportionality
8 The wheelbarrow	Proportionality
9 Trunks and twigs	Proportionality
10 The balance beam	Compensation
11 Current, length and thickness	Compensation
12 Voltage, amps and watts	Compensation
13 Spinning coins	Probability
14 Combinations	Combinations
15 Tea tasting	Probability
16 Interaction	Variables
17 The behaviour of wood lice	Correlation
18 Treatments and effects	Correlation
19 Sampling: fish in a pond	Probability
20 Throwing dice	Probability
21 Making groups	Classification
22 More classifying: birds	Classification
23 Explaining states of matter	Models
24 Explaining solutions	Models
25 Explaining chemical reactions	Models
26 Pressure	Compound variables
27 Floating and sinking	Compound variables
28 Uphill and down dale	Equilibrium
29 Equilibrium in the balance	Equilibrium
30 Divers	Compound variables

FIG. 6.1   List of Activities and Schemata in *Thinking Science*

of many shows that such attempts are usually futile. The application of "cognitive conflict" and the encouragement given to "metacognition" through ThiSci activities are illustrated by two examples in the appendix. The process of "bridging" was embodied in the in-service training associated with the materials in the project. During one-day meetings held every term during the two years of the project, teachers engaged in exercises to show how links could be made between the ThiSci activities and their regular science curriculum. During on-service visits by the project team, further opportunities for bridging were explored in the context of each school's curriculum.

Testing the Intervention

The design of the CASE experiment in which the ThiSci methodology was tested is illustrated in Figure 6.2. Experimental classes were chosen in eight secondary schools, some of them first year (age in the United Kingdom about $11 +$) and others starting in the second year (age about $12 +$). Control classes were identified in the same schools, some taught by the same teacher who took the experimental classes, and some by different teachers. All schools were mixed-gender. ThiSci intervention activities were used in experimental classes at the rate of about one every two weeks over the two-year period.

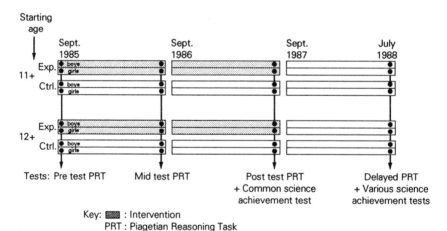

Fig. 6.2   CASE Experimental Design: Scheme of Interventions and Tests

The "testing programme" consisted of:

(i) Piagetian Reasoning Tasks (PRTs) (Shayer, Wylam, *et al.*, 1978), which provide a measure of level of cognitive development (Shayer, Adey and Wylam, 1980);

(ii) science achievement tests which assess directly students' knowledge and understandings of concepts.

The PRTs were given to all experimental and control classes as pretests, after one year, after two years (the end of the intervention programme), and then finally one year later again as delayed posttests. On each occasion all students performed the same tasks.

Science achievement measures were obtained at the end of the two-year intervention period, and one year later. The test at the end of two years was given to all of the participating schools, devised in co-operation with the teachers and covering a range of concepts that were common in all of the schools' curricula for that year. One year later it was not possible to devise a common science test for all of the students, since they had dispersed to different classes, and some to different schools. Altogether, the students who had been experimental or control CASE subjects probably took about 14 different science examinations around July 1988. This did at least mean that we were looking at the students' achievement of the science objectives which had been set for them by the schools themselves, and not ones imposed from outside. The procedure enabling comparisons to be made between students who took different science tests is detailed elsewhere (Shayer and Adey, 1989), but in summary what we did was to use the regression of "control" groups' delayed science scores on pre-PRT scores for each science examination as a basis for predicting what science score each "experimental" student should get, given his or her pre-PRT score. The difference between the predicted science score and that obtained is a measure of the extent to which experimentals were different from controls three years after they started out together and one year after the end of any intervention. The difference obtained for each student is the "residualized gain score" (r.g. score).

Results

In presenting the results of a longitudinal study in which various tests were given at intervals over a three-year period to school students, there is some problem in deciding on which particular sample the results are to be presented. Inevitably, over the period of the experiment students change schools and classes, are sick sometimes, or play away football matches on Wednesday afternoons. The exact sample that completes any one of the tests therefore varies from time to time. Table 6.1 shows the tests in which we are particularly interested.

In order to provide a final picture which is as uniform and as informative as possible, we will consider the sample of students who have all taken the prePRT test as well as the DelSciAch test. Results based on other tests will

TABLE 6.1   *Summary of Tests over the Two-year Intervention Period and One Subsequent Year*

Type	Sept. 1985	July 1986	July 1987	July 1988
Piagetian	Pretest PrePRT	Midtest (MidPRT)	Posttest (PosPTR)	Delayed test (DelPRT)
Science			Common science achievement (PosSciAch)	School's science achievement (DelSciAch)

be given for the subsamples from this main sample of students who have also done the other tests. The essential data is presented in Table 6.2. Each of the sets of test data will be considered in turn, and we will look separately at boys and girls and at students who started at 11 + and those who started at 12 +.

TABLE 6.2   *Summary of Piagetian Score Gains and Post-Science Achievement Scores after Two Years of Intervention and One Subsequent Year*

		12+ Boys		12+ Girls		11+ Boys		11+ Girls	
		Ctrl.	Exp.	Ctrl.	Exp.	Ctrl.	Exp.	Ctrl.	Exp.
PrePRT	N	44	36	26	34	47	35	32	30
PosPRT	M	0.22	1.32	0.77	0.80	1.04	0.73	0.79	0.87
gains	σ	1.48	0.98	1.10	1.01	1.14	1.00	0.77	1.13
(levels)	sig.		< .001		n.s.		n.s.		n.s.
PosSciAch	N	15	17	12	17	28	16	19	17
(%)	M	57.60	47.35	43.83	38.47	50.21	44.43	41.79	45.82
	σ	14.24	14.00	16.73	12.03	15.60	9.39	11.82	10.43
	sig.		< .05[1]		n.s.		n.s.		n.s.
PrePRT	N	35	40	19	34	39	33	30	29
DelPRT	M	1.32	1.22	1.14	1.12	1.52	1.33	1.16	0.71
gains	σ	1.04	1.56	1.13	0.98	1.02	1.44	0.84	0.85
(levels)	sig.		n.s.		n.s.		n.s.		< .05[1]
DelSciAch	N	49	43	29	36	47	37	32	31
(residual-	M	0.64	10.63	0.00	4.18	0.43	2.73	−0.11	7.02
ized gain	σ	13.68	16.32	11.26	14.41	13.16	15.45	11.81	12.76
scores)	sig.		< .005		n.s.[2]		n.s.		< .05

1. Larger samples, including those who did not do delayed science achievement, show no significant difference.
2. The proportion of experimental subjects with positive residualized gain scores is significantly greater than the proportion of controls with positive scores: $z = 1.70$, $p < .05$.

PosPRT

What is interesting is the gain in level of cognitive development as measured by the Piagetian Reasoning Tasks from the beginning of the experiment until the conclusion of the two-year intervention programme. This is given by the pre- to postgain scores on the Piagetian tests. If one takes all students together, regardless of age and gender, one finds a significantly greater mean gain by the experimental group as compared with the controls. However, as is clear from the first section of Table 6.2, this effect is in reality all concentrated in the group of boys who started the programme aged 12 +. No overall effect is apparent in the other groups. To consider the groups as wholes, however, can hide an interesting feature. Figures 6.3a, 6.4a, 6.5a and 6.6a show the distribution of pre- to postPRT gains for the four groups. For the 12 + boys and the 11 + girls, the distributions appear to be bimodal, and this can be shown statistically to be the case. For these groups at least, it appears that some students were affected significantly by the intervention, while others were not. Bimodal

a. Distribution of pre -post PRT gain scores

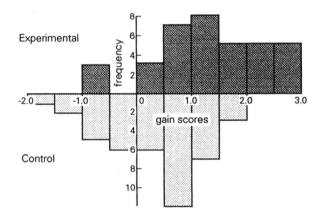

b. Distribution of delayed science achievement residualized gain scores

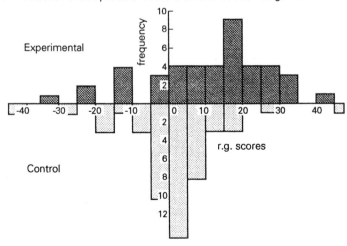

FIG. 6.3   Boys, 12+

distributions will occur again, when possible interpretation will be discussed.

PosSciAch

The common science achievement test given immediately after the intervention programme was not administered by all of the schools in the project, and so the sample number is quite small. Even, however, if one looks at the larger sample of all those who did both the prePRT and this posSciAch, no significant differences emerge between experimental and control groups. It seems that, even where levels of cognitive development are enhanced, there is no concurrent effect on students' ability to process science learning. One might note in passing that the intervention lessons did replace about one quarter of the regular science lessons, so that the experimental group had significantly less time than the controls to cover the science content of the two-year period.

DelPRT

The Piagetian test given one year after the end of the intervention provides information about the stability of any differential gains in cognitive development made by the experimental group. It is clear from Table 6.2 that one year later there are no significant differences on measures of cognitive development between the two groups. Any greater gains made by experimentals that may have been apparent immediately after the intervention have withered away during a year of ordinary teaching.

DelSciAch

It is when one looks at the students' success in learning the science of their regular curriculum during the year following the intervention programme that one sees a real effect. Two of the four age/gender groups show significantly higher mean scores by those who had previously been experimentals than those who had been controls, and for a third (the 12 + girls), evidence from the proportion with positive residualized gain scores points in the same direction. Figures 6.3b, 6.4b, 6.5b and 6.6b show the distribution of r.g. scores of experimentals compared with controls of the four groups, and once again it is apparent that in the three groups for which we have an effect, the experimental groups' distributions are positively skewed or even bimodal. In fact, the evidence obtained from the cumulative X^2 sums comparing the actual distribution of frequencies obtained with that expected on the basis of the same mean and standard deviation as the control group, suggests that all three groups (12+ boys, 12+ girls and 11+ girls) are bimodal. In all of them, some students have been very

a. Distribution of pre -post PRT gain scores

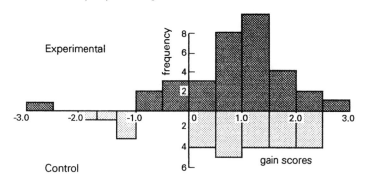

b. Distribution of delayed science achievement residualized gain scores

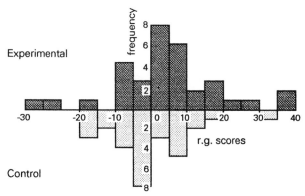

FIG. 6.4   Girls, 12+

significantly affected by the interventions, whilst others have been affected little or not at all. In every case where a bimodal distribution is found, there is no relationship between the starting level of the student at a pretest and the extent to which he or she benefited from the interventions. One can say neither that those who started low made the greatest gains, nor that those who started high were in the best position to gain from the demands of the ThiSci activities.

Discussion

These results can be crudely summarized as follows: at the end of the two-year intervention period, there are some real gains in the levels of cognitive development of experimental students but no measurable improvement in their science achievement. One year later, the gains in

Why the Lag in Science Achievement?

If one supposes that the interventions have in fact had a real effect on students' ability to process new information, then it is not until this processing ability has been improved that it can be brought to bear on new learning. On the basis of this argument, the experimental students start the academic year following the intervention in a condition in which they find learning science easier, and so the high-level concepts that may previously have caused them problems are not now a major obstacle. Students who, through the interventions, have had an accelerated development of their deep-level processing capability are able to learn better, and tests of their learning which take place subsequently will show them to be performing better than those who have not experienced the accelerating interventions.

Applying this argument to the results we obtained at the delayed posttest, and noting the absence of any difference in levels of cognitive development at this point between those who had previously been experimentals and those who had been controls, one might predict that science learning in the next year—1988–89—will be the same for both groups. We will be testing this by looking at the results of the externally set GCSE examination which all of our subjects who started in the 12 + group will be taking at the end of the 1988–89 academic year.

What about Gender and Age Differences?

We have previously suggested explanations for these differences in terms of the brain growth spurts which occur at different times in boys and girls (Adey and Shayer, 1989). An alternative, or perhaps parallel, explanation might be sought in differences in learning styles, which I will discuss further below.

Why are Some Affected Much More than Others?

There was no difference in the teaching style and school ethos experienced by experimentals who benefited from the intervention and those who did not. Differences may therefore be attributed to different learning styles, and we propose to investigate further the influence of learning styles, as described for instance by Cohen (1986), in response to the ThiSci style of promoting cognitive engagement.

What Next?

We have used Piagetian notions of cognitive development to posit ways of enhancing the development of thinking in schools and to design curriculum materials on this basis, and have had results which are sufficiently encouraging to persuade us to continue to work with the model. Apart from the investigation of learning styles, some of the issues which we wish to pursue further include:

(i) the nature and extent of in-service training which would be necessary, or sufficient, for the reliable transfer of the effective pedagogy developed in the CASE project to a wider audience of teachers and trainers;

(ii) the effect of gains in cognitive development achieved through activities set in a science context on achievement in other areas of the curriculum; we have, in fact, some raw data on achievement in mathematics and second-language learning, but it has not yet been processed.

Finally, in considering the broad forms of our engagement, what are the implications of our results for the redefinition of the curriculum? I think I can best answer by describing the reaction of students to the pink work sheets whose appearance came immediately to be recognized as heralding a *Thinking Science* lesson. The students groaned! They groaned because they knew that the next hour was going to require them to think harder than perhaps in the rest of the week, and humankind is such that it does not generally relish the prospect of hard work. And yet within a few minutes of the groaning, those same students would be involved in the activity with enthusiasm. The prospect of work may have been conventionally distasteful, but the practice of active engagement in a problem proved, in fact, to be attractive and motivating. There is a deep-rooted desire within people to exercise their minds. What we need in the whole school curriculum, for all abilities, is to release and capitalize on this desire, rather than to bottle, channel and eventually to kill it.

Note

1. The CASE project was based at King's College, London University. It was funded by the Economic and Social Research Council from 1984–87. The director of the project was Dr Michael Shayer.

References

Adey, P. S. and Shayer, M. (1989). "Accelerating the development of formal thinking in middle- and high-school students." *Journal of Research in Science Teaching.*

Adey, P. S., Shayer, M. and Yates C. (1989). *Thinking Science: The Curriculum Materials of the CASE Project*, Macmillan Education, London.

Cohen, R. (1986). *Conceptual Styles and Social Change*. Copely, Acton, MA.

Department of Education and Science (DES) (1985). *Science 5–16: A Statement of Policy*, HMSO, London.

Department of Education and Science (DES) (1988). *Science for Ages 5–16: Proposals of the Secretary of State for Education*, HMSO, London.

Shayer, M. and Adey, P. S. (1989) *Long-term effects of an intervention programme in high-school science classes.* King's College, London.

Shayer, M., Adey, P. S. and Wylam, H. (1980) *"Group tests of cognitive development . . . ideals and a realization". Journals of Research in Science Teaching,* **18.** pp. 157–168.

Shayer, M., Wylam, H. *et al.* (1978). *CSMS Science Reasoning Tasks.* NFER, Slough, United Kingdom: (available from Science Reasoning, Room 5215, King's College. London Centre for Education Studies).

Appendix

Floating and Sinking Jars (Figure 6.1)

Five jars (A–E) are the same size but increase in mass from 400 g to 1200 g.

Six jars (1–6) are the same mass but increase in size (Jar A and jar 6 are the same jar).

For each jar, students note the mass and size, then put it in water. They have a chart like that shown, on which they mark whether the jar floats or sinks.

From this experience, they establish two concrete, 2-variable, models: "small things sink, big things float" (from 1–6); and "heavy things sink, light things float" (from A–E). Each of these is adequate itself.

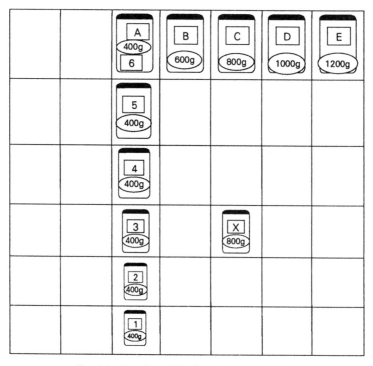

FIG. 6.1   Samples of *Thinking Science* Activities

Now Jar X is produced. It is the same mass as Jar C (which floats), and the same size as Jar 3 (which floats). Pupils are asked to predict whether it will float or sink. Predictions made on the basis of the concrete models already established are that it will float. It is put in the water, and sinks. To accommodate this, a new model involving three variables—mass, size and buoyancy—must be constructed.

Making Groups and Thinking Back

Students engage in a number of classification exercises such as:

... ticking the living things in a list of living and non-living things;
... spotting characteristics shared by, and different between, "creepy crawlies" shown in pictures;
... classifying chemicals according to characteristics such as colour and solubility, and then making a 2 × 2 table of the four possibilities;
... sorting vertebrates into groups;
... arranging foods on the shelves of a larder.

They are then given the following exercise:

... Put a tick by the classification activity you found easiest.
... Put a cross by the one you found most difficult.
... Why was the one you ticked the easiest?
... Why was the one you crossed the most difficult?
... Has everyone ticked and crossed the same ones as you?
... Write a sentence about a friend, using the word "characteristic".
... Why do you think that it is useful to be able to classify things?

7

Learning Thinking through the New Technologies

MICHEL CAILLOT

Laboratoire interuniversitaire de recherche sur
l'éducation scientfique et technologique,
Université de Paris VII,
Paris, France

The Backround Report at the end of this volume draws our attention to two approaches to learning to think: by teaching general thinking skills which can then be applied across the curriculum; or by "infusion" through teaching specific disciplines, an approach supported particularly by teachers of mathematics and science. As someone professionally interested in the link between research on teaching science subjects and the new educational techniques, I am more in agreement with the second point of view. But there are other reasons which cause me to give serious consideration to the teaching of thinking through the disciplines: the results of research into the cognitive sciences.

Firstly, learning should be seen as the process of constructing knowledge. The student does not come to the teacher as an empty vessel which merely has to be filled with knowledge. In actual fact, students arrive at school with a lot of knowledge that they have already constructed for themselves. This knowledge is often erroneous, incomplete and contradictory. But it exists and therefore has to be taken into consideration. Thus learning consists in a real conceptual change achieved by the construction of knowledge by students, starting from their own existing framework.

Secondly, all the research done on the differences between novices and experts has shown that experts organize knowledge, often hierarchically, around general unifying principles linked to the area of their expertise. Moreover, in solving problems, they use methods specific to their subject. It is the novices who use general strategies, usually inefficient, such as the analysis of ends and means. The latter depend heavily on the context, interpreting the tasks in terms of their superficial characteristics rather than their deep structure. Hence, the importance of contextualized knowledge. Brown, Collins and Duguid (1988) use the term "situated cognition".

All consideration of the teaching of thinking should take these factors into account. In France, a commission has been established to look at the content of teaching, made up of a dozen well-known social scientists (presided over by Bourdieu and Gros). One of their recommendations is that "particular stress should be laid on teaching intended to ensure considered and critical assimilation of the fundamental ways of thinking (i.e. deductive, experimental and historical), as well as critical and reflective thinking".

What, then, can the new educational techniques bring to developing deductive, experimental or historical modes of thinking?

Three ways of using computers in schools have been distinguished by Taylor (1980, cited in OECD, 1989):

(i) as tutor (exercises, tutorials, simulations and model building, problem solving, educational games);
(ii) as tool (information retrieval, word processing, laboratories, and application programmes);
(iii) as tutee (exploration and discovery, microworlds).

In fact, these categories are not as mutually exclusive as they might seem, and one can find software which covers two of them. However, the categories are useful in order to see to what extent the different software packages can help in stimulating thought and in developing new thinking skills.

The Computer as Tool

Research and Information Retrieval

The advent of a large number of data banks is a major feature of the modern world. There are thousands of them and they are easily accessible. Even though they are often confined to the use of the experts in specific disciplines, some of them can be used in schools. Software packages exist which incorporate a selection of raw data that can be used in history, geography and economics. This information is generally most useful for problem solving, and it can also be the starting point for model building, to describe, for example, change over time. Having access to data in significant amounts, and then having to interpret it, means that students practise such intellectual skills as classifying, sequencing, analysis, or indeed using different methods of presentation (tables, graphics or histograms) which are the end product of active thinking in context.

A French project conducted by the Institut National de la Recherche Pédagogique (INRP) involves a tool which can be used in several different disciplines: satellite photographs. The pictures are, in fact, digital images whereby the computer visualizes different phenomena. These can be used in teaching geography or in courses on the environment: students find themselves actually in the position of a specialist faced with a mass of results that have to be processed in order to develop a hypothesis. Over and above the multidisciplinary aspect, always valuable in itself, the student's activities are made possible thanks to the computer, and a variety of cognitive processes are involved.

Word Processing and Writing Skills

By word processing, I do not mean the standard software packages such as Word or MacWrite, but rather those which provide aids to written expression, developing and organizing ideas (text plans) and changing or rearranging them. These packages represent a significant improvement in helping students to organize their thoughts. Riel, Levin and Miller–Souviney (1987) have developed an interactive programme for creative writing for 10-year-olds. They follow a sequence, guided first by the computer, then by the computer and the student together, and finally by the student alone:

(i) choice of words or phrases from a given menu;
(ii) writing of own words or phrases with a choice of options;
(iii) an imposed structure of paragraphs with free text within this framework;
(iv) free text (with some guidance about the structure of the story).

Underlying this example is the notion that written expression is a cognitive process like any other, and that narratives have a structure which must be respected.

Aids to Mathematical Reasoning

Mathematics teaching can now draw on tools to help the development of reasoning in, for example, geometry. This subject is recognized by mathematicians as being very hard for students of 14 years of age since it involves pure deductive reasoning, based on inferences gained from theorems and axioms, and students have difficulties in understanding the rules of the deductive "game". In fact, this approach is quite unlike the way people normally try to solve a problem: in daily life, we consider the data and the goal simultaneously, and try to reach a solution by finding the route between them.

Anderson *et al.* (1986) have developed a program called *Geometry Tutor*, based on artificial intelligence techniques, to help students to construct a proof. Students have to work through the process of deduction. They have at their disposal a screen with the starting hypotheses shown at the bottom and the conclusions at the top: when they have made a tree joining the two on the screen, they have proved the hypothesis. Students can construct the tree starting either at the bottom (the hypotheses) or the top (the conclusion). They advance step by step, using theorems or premises; they may reach dead-ends and it may even be necessary to retrace their steps, so that the proof looks like a tree with broken branches. But at least it is no longer a linear process, as may happen when the proof is shown in the classroom. The screen becomes an external record of the work, where students can see the state and path of their reasoning, that is, their thought processes. This tool therefore allows students to keep track of their thinking while it is going on.

Still in the field of geometry, there are software packages which allow the student to construct hypotheses. This is a highly mathematical activity which can be carried out by students if they have the tools to do it. One such tool is the French software developed at the University of Grenoble (Baulac, 1988), Cabri-Géometre (Cahier de Brouillon Informatique), which teaches the construction and use of geometrical figures. The figure constructed on the screen is always accurate (to the degree of screen resolution), unlike drawings of the same figure on paper, frequently awkward when done by beginners. What is important is that the student can make small changes to the figure or explore other values (length of segments, angles, radius) to test whether the premise is always proven in other circumstances. This system allows the student to make and test hypotheses: mental activities typical of mathematics and of other disciplines as well. Students do not undertake a proof at this stage, but they are engaged in a process of thinking and of induction that can easily be transferred to other domains.

Model Building and Simulation

The computer can put students in situations which launch them on a process of exploration with minimal guidance. This is the philosophy behind the microworlds created by Papert (1987). The interesting fact about microworlds is that exploration can lead directly to model building.

We understand the world we live in by building up mental pictures for ourselves. I do not need to be a mechanic to have a mental picture of how my car works: I have constructed a qualitative model which is adequate for me in my daily life. Scientists, too, have always constructed models to explain the phenomena around us. They are still building models, and this capacity is perhaps an essential aspect of human intellectual activity. It is therefore important to learn how to build models, something which rarely happens in the classroom.

Once the model has been built, it needs to be made to function so that forecasts can be made, which are then compared with actual experience. The computer can help both in building the model and in testing it (model simulation). Obviously, such software is found for science subjects, but it also exists in economics.

Through the Smithtown program (Shute and Glaser, 1986), for instance, students become familiar with the laws of supply and demand. By altering various parameters, they see the effect which these have on the market of an imaginary town. For example, they can study what happens to the demand for cars during a period when local incomes are rising. The aim of this package is not really to teach economics, but rather to help students to improve their ability to create models. The microworld can show up effective (or ineffective) strategies, by comparing the student's performance with optimal activity sequences. If the student, for example, changes several variables at the same time, the tutor will intervene to advise a more systematic method of research. This type of explicit teaching of the methodologies of discovery models is highly contextualized.

In our laboratory, Durey (1987) has shown how students of mechanics (in schools and universities), by studying the trajectories of balls in sport, are able to select and use increasingly sophisticated models:

- model of a ball: point→rigid sphere→flexible sphere;
- environment: airless→in air;
- bounce: high→low.

The computer is used as by engineers in a real-life situation: it does calculations which are impossible to do by hand. It enables the students to solve the problem posed: find the best model to explain the trajectory of a ball in a photograph. Students have to plan their research, choose which model to use, test and compare the results of the experiment against the model. This project has shown that it is possible to create a new curriculum based on real-life situations, where learning happens in a specific context. The students have used their knowledge in a subject-based situation and their expertise has increased.

Models can also be constructed with the aid of a computer. In our laboratory, for instance, software was devised to introduce a simple particule model of matter to 13- and 14-year-olds (Méhuet, 1988). It does not involve atoms or molecules, but uses mobile square symbols of varying number and average speed. The aim is to help students understand phenomena such as how the odour of perfume spreads or the pressure is brought into balance between two linked bottles of compressed air. The students are asked to use the properties of the model to explain or forecast new phenomena.

In the United States, diSessa (1982) has shown how students can, through computers, express their pre-Newtonian views and modify them. Students find themselves faced with a contradiction between their expectations of a trajectory and the actual movement. They are led to develop a qualitative Newtonian model of forces to describe what appears on the screen, and correct their errors.

Finally, different models can be constructed and tested in the same program; this is the explicit aim of Roschelle's Envisioning Machine (1988). In the software, the screen is divided in two. On the right, students "throw" a ball and the movement is shown. On the left, they can construct a model with several tools at their disposal: a grid allows them to locate the position of the ball, there is a device for replacing the ball by a point, different speeds and acceleration can be displayed, and so on. The idea is that, by judicious choices, the student will be able to replicate the movement shown on the right side of the screen.

If I have emphasized the role of computers in model building, it is because it seems to be that they form an integral part of human intellectual activity. Thinking takes place in context, and the computer is a good way of simulating important practices in our technical world. The knowledge involved is simultaneously declaratory, procedural and heuristic, linked to a specific content. With such an approach, the computer can be an aid to practical intellectual activities and assist learning in complex domains. But in order for this to happen, the activities offered to learners must be of good quality and appropriate to the aims.

References

Anderson, J. R., Boyle, C. F., Corbett, A. and Lewis, M. (1986). *Cognitive Modeling and Intelligent Tutoring*, Technical report. Carnegie Mellon University, Pittsburgh, PA.

Baulac, Y. (1988). "Cabri-Géométre, un système d'EIAO pour la géométrie élémentaire", *Actes d'Applica* 88. 1st Congrès européen sur l'Intelligence artificielle et formation, Lille, October, pp. 349–362.

Brown, J. S., Collins, A. and Duguid, P. (1988). *Situated Cognition and the Culture of Learning, Report No. IRL* 88–008. Institute for Research on Learning, Palo Alto, CA.

diSessa, A. A. (1982). "Unlearning Aristotelian physics: A study of knowledge-based learning", *Cognitive Science*, 6, pp. 37–75.

Durey, A. (1987). "Vers des activités didactiques de mise au point de modèles physiques avec des micro-ordinateurs. Exemples: trajectoires et rebonds de balle en rotation". B.Sc. thesis, Université de Paris VII.

Méhuet, M. (1988). Internal document, Laboratoire interuniversitaire de recherche sur l'enseignement de sciences physiques et technologique, Université de Paris VII.

OECD (1989). *Information Technologies in Education: The Quest for Quality Software.* OECD/CERI, Paris.

Papert, S. (1987). "Microworlds: Transforming education", in Lawler R. W. and Yazdani M. (eds.). *Artificial Intelligence and Education.* Vol. 1. Ablex, Norwood, NJ. pp. 79–94.

Riel, M. M., Levin, J. A. and Miller-Souviney, B. (1987). "Learning with interactive media:

Dynamic support for students and teachers", in Lawler, R. W. and Yazdani, M. (eds.), *Artificial Intelligence and Education*, Vol. 1, Ablex, Norwood, NJ. pp. 117–134.

Roschelle, J. (1988). Personal communication, Institute for Research on Learning, Palo Alto, CA.

Shute, V. and Glaser, R. (1986). *An Intelligent Tutoring System for Exploring Principles of Economics*. Technical report. Learning Research and Development Center, University of Pittsburgh, Pittsburgh, PA.

Taylor, R. (ed.) (1980). *The Computer in the School: Tutor, tool, tutee*. Teachers College Press, Columbia, OR.

8

Strengthening Reasoning and Judgement through Philosophy

MATTHEW LIPMAN

*Montclair State College,
Upper Montclaire,
New Jersey, United States*

Traditionally, the aim of education has been the passing on of knowledge. The educated person has been conceived of as the knowledgeable person. And one becomes knowledgeable through the process of learning.

This concentration upon learning and knowledge is no longer acceptable. We are all aware how rapidly any given bit of knowledge can become obsolete. Consequently, even if we were to agree that educated persons must be knowledgeable, we must also stipulate that they be reasonable and judicious. This means that the educational process must be one that cultivates reasoning and judgement. And even if we were to agree that learning is an important aspect of education, I think we must now be prepared to acknowledge that education is initiation into the process of inquiry.

We should not leap to the conclusion that by inquiry one means only scientific inquiry. There are non-scientific forms of inquiry as well as scientific forms. One example is philosophy. Philosophy is inquiry into the generic characteristics of good thinking. It is concerned with the general problems of definition, of classification, of inference, of truth and of meaning, and not just these problems as they manifest themselves in specific disciplines like history, psychology or physics. Since it is best to approach these problems in terms of broad outlines first and then move on to more precise examples in the special fields of study, philosophy is *par excellence* the discipline that raises the generic questions that can introduce us to other disciplines and prepare us to think in those other disciplines. Practitioners who perform with distinction in their special fields of study are those, I suggest, who have not forgotten the logical, epistemological and ethical questions they were taught to raise in philosophy.

Good scholarship, however, is not the sole justification for incorporating philosophy into the educational process. There is also the need for good citizenship in a democratic society. Such a society cannot do without reasonable and judicious voters, jurors, parents, administrators and consumers. Free and just societies are made up of rational, equitable and participatory institutions, and of individual citizens who deliberate critically and creatively. But all of these features require reasoning and judgement, and to try to foster reasoning and judgement without involving philosophy is like putting on a performance of *Hamlet* without involving the Prince of Denmark.

I have been attempting to make the case that cognitive education without philosophy cannot be successful. Let me now turn 180 degrees and argue that cognitive education *with* philosophy, at the elementary school level, must be equally unsuccessful. I am speaking here of philosophy in its traditional, academic guise: the philosophy of the universities. Children would reject it as arid and irrelevant.

We seem to be left with a deadlock: cognitive education is impossible without philosophy and is equally impossible with it. We are in a dilemma, to be sure, but there is a way out of it. Philosophy can be—and already has been—redesigned so as to be welcomed by children enthusiastically. What remains now is to redesign the curriculum so as to welcome philosophy. I should like, however, to address my remaining remarks to the reconstruction that has taken place in philosophy, and to defer until some other occasion consideration of the problem of reconstructing the curriculum. I shall begin by noting the presuppositions guiding the construction of an elementary/secondary philosophy curriculum:

Presupposition 1: Such a curriculum must be impartial with regard to different philosophical positions, yet representative of philosophy as a whole.

Presupposition 2: Such a curriculum must be taught in a non-indoctrinational manner. This requires that teachers be pedagogically strong but philosophically self-effacing.

Presupposition 3: Children wonder about the world and so do philosophers. Children can entertain philosophical ideas when these are phrased in language they can understand, and they can invent philosophical ideas of their own. In brief, children have a natural affinity for philosophy.

Presupposition 4: The logical moves children make in conversation are not materially different from the moves philosophers make. Both are to be found making assumptions, drawing inferences, defining terms, building on one another's ideas, constructing classifications, analysing ambiguities, and so on.

Presupposition 5: Many of the most important terms employed by or analysed by philosophers are also to be found in the vocabularies of young children. For example, *good, right* and *fair* (in ethics); *true, possible* and *correct* (in epistemology); *beautiful* and *art* (in aesthetics); *reason* and *means* (in logic); and *person, life* and *world* (in metaphysics).

Presupposition 6: The questions children ask often resemble those asked by philosophers, in that both groups put in question what is otherwise taken for granted. Thus children, like philosophers, will enjoy appearance/reality puzzles, one/many puzzles, body/mind puzzles and so on.

Presupposition 7: The notion that children are too immersed in "concrete" experience to be interested in and to discuss abstract ideas is simply erroneous. Indeed, this is an adult prejudice that has caused countless children to grow up "abstraction-deprived".

Presupposition 8: Children think better when they are surrounded by models of good thinking. These models may be their teachers, their texts and their peers. It is particularly important that their texts present them with models of children deliberating together and forming classroom communities of inquiry.

Presuppositon 9: Children are more likely to learn when their texts are in narrative form—as short stories or novels—or in other literary forms such as poetry, because this enables them to grasp the contextual meanings which are more elusive in expository texts, and to grasp these meanings as part of an organized whole.

Presupposition 10: Although intelligence is capable of being expressed in many ways, the fact remains that written and verbal language is the currency of the classroom. Children need help in reasoning verbally in ordinary language; symbolic reasoning is for them of secondary importance insofar as what we are considering is the educational system as presently organized.

Presupposition 11: Children want meanings, and it is the possibility of finding such meanings that is a major motivation for them. Consequently, content-free exercises, which are likely to seem meaningless to children, should be utilized sparingly.

Presupposition 12: For effective cognitive education, instructional manuals are necessary so as to provide exercises for the strengthening of cognitive skills and discussion plans for the fostering of concept formation.

Presupposition 13: To preserve the quality and integrity of the discipline, exercises should be written by curriculum experts in the discipline, not by teachers. Likewise, teachers should be taught by discipline specialists, not by other teachers.

Presupposition 14: Effective cognitive education focuses upon the strengthening of four clusters of skills: reasoning skills, inquiry skills, concept-formation skills and translation skills.

Presupposition 15: Reasoning is a craft and can best be taught through cognitive apprenticeship, which involves modelling, coaching and much practical deliberation. Judgement is an art and cannot be taught as such to others. Yet it is something thinkers may be able to teach themselves to do. This will most likely happen if we provide children with an intellectually stimulating environment and encourage them to form communities of inquiry. Individuals reason better when they internalize the disciplined dialogue of a reasoning community, and they arrive at individual judgements after having thoroughly participated in the group's deliberations. To draw the conclusion of a deductive argument takes reasoning; to form a hypothesis or generalization or analogy—or to criticize a hypothesis or generalization or analogy—takes judgement. A sound education must cultivate both reasoning and judgement since, like body and mind, both are necessary for the constitution of a complete person.

I would like to turn now to a closer consideration of the content and composition of the curriculum. With regard to the content, perhaps the best I can do is to quote a portion of an episode from a children's novel, so that you can draw your own conclusions about the way the philosophy is inserted, just beneath the surface of the prose, where the students can readily discover it for themselves.

Suki is about 14 years of age in this story, and her brother Kio is about six. Their father, Mr Tong, is a furniture maker of Oriental descent. Their mother died several years ago. The children, with their father and Suki's friend Anne, have been invited to visit the farm of their grandparents, whom they have never met. When we meet them, they have been exploring the apple cellar, the egg cellar and the henhouses, and they have seen the charred remains of a great barn that had burnt to the ground.

> Finally, they wound their way back up the path to the house. In the living room, the great stone fireplace had been lit, and Suki, Anne and Kio stood warming themselves in front of it, slowly rotating as if on individual spits. They were hungry, and the food, when it came, was so delicious they almost couldn't recognize it. The bread, the milk, the eggs, the butter, the vegetables—every taste was fresh, distinct and intense.
>
> "It's as if the food we usually eat is just a pale copy of this food," Suki remarked. "Compared to the milk we get at home, this is real milk! And these eggs taste like eggs ought to taste—like real eggs!"
>
> Her grandfather permitted himself a slight smile, although it threatened for a moment to fracture his face. Then he lit his pipe and relaxed. "Well, son, what do you think?" he asked, addressing Kio. "Would you like to be a farmer some day?"

Kio's mouth was full of blueberry muffin, and his "I don't know" came out sounding like "ow-no".

"Are you going to rebuild the barn?" Mr Tong asked.

Suki saw her grandfather redden, but he merely remarked, "I don't think so."

Her grandmother leaned over to Mr Tong and said, "It's just about killed him—that fire."

Suki watched the flames in the fireplace. In her imagination she saw the great barn ablaze, and her grandmother restraining her grandfather. "Fire," she said to herself. Other images thronged into her mind, the pump, the bracing autumn air, the soft turn of the meadow. "Earth, air, fire and water," she thought.

"It went up like tinder," said Suki's grandfather. "That's wood for you. Can't trust it. You can only trust stone. I'll use stone, if I ever build another one."

"Ah," mused Mr Tong, "wood never betrays us, although sometimes perhaps we betray it. When I'm planing a piece of oak or walnut, or while I'm sanding them, or rubbing them down with steel wool, I remember that they were once parts of living trees. Any piece of wood you pick up, like this table top here, or these chairs—it's wood that was once alive. Even now it has a warmth to it that stone never has. Wood is live, but stone is—stone is—" he paused, unsure about completing his thought.

"Even wood petrifies," the farmer responded. "Sooner or later, everything turns to stone."

"Suki," said Kio, "you know that sea shell you have at home? It's stone, and it was once alive."

"Well, it's not exactly stone, Kio. But Daddy, how about that coral necklace you once gave me? How about coral reefs? Weren't they once alive?"

Before Mr Tong could answer, his mother-in-law commented, "Of course everything changes. That's nature. But what's this about everything turning to stone? Nonsense! Everything changes—vegetation turns into mulch, and mulch turns back into plants again. Only change is constant."

Her husband responded: "I sawed and planed every board in that barn. Now it's all ashes, and those ashes are not going to turn back into a barn. Use stone, I say. Build things to last forever."

The room fell quiet. Anne had felt somewhat like an eavesdropper during the entire conversation. She found the silence almost unbearable. She became aware that a clock was ticking in a nearby room. Silently, she counted the beats, hoping that a chime would mark the quarter-hour.

Suki's grandmother spoke up again, a flash of fire in her eyes, "What will be, will be. But don't confuse our job and nature's. Nature's job is change—forever turning one thing into another, never knowing or asking why. But our job's turning the world into poetry!"

Startled, Suki looked up and found her grandmother looking at her.

"Your father tells me you write poetry, Suki."

Suki tried to say something, but she only murmured something unintelligible.

"I did too, when I was your age, and for a good many years afterwards." Suki's grandmother glanced at her husband and sighed. "It's funny, though. I have a photo album full of snapshots, but I can't stand to look at them. When I see them, I shake my head and say, 'That's not me!' But I still go over the poetry—I read it and re-read it. It's just as fresh as when I first wrote it. And I say to myself, 'If I'm anywhere, it's here in these words.' "

"Maybe you didn't know it, but your mother wrote poetry too," Suki's grandfather added.

Suddenly Suki has a very clear image of her mother.

"I didn't much approve of it, but she went on writing anyhow," he added.

Suki's grandfather and grandmother exchanged glances. Suki's grandmother got up, went to the chest of drawers in the corner, and got out a sheaf of papers in a folder. "We want you to have them," she said, handing the poems to Suki. Suki's grandfather nodded his approval.

Suki hugged the poems. She rose, silently kissed and hugged each of her grandparents, then returned to hugging the poems. She knew she didn't want to read them until she was safely alone, at home.

Later, as they were leaving, she tried to tell her grandparents how much their gift meant to her. They nodded and replied, "Just don't be so long about coming back."

Mr Tong shook his mother-in-law's hand warmly. "I'm going to think about what you said, that our job's turning the world into poetry."

"Oh," she replied with a smile, looking at Suki and Kio. "You seem to be off to a pretty good start already." (Lipman, 1978, Chapter 5).

The 14-year-olds who read and discuss this episode quickly spot the controversial philosophical issues that are strewn throughout its length, and their questions, written on the chalkboard, become the agenda for the group's deliberations. They generally ask such questions as, "Is reality the way things are or the way they ought to be? Is the difference between appearance and reality like the difference between stale and fresh? What does it mean to say that "our job's turning the world into poetry"? Is the grandmother really in her body or in her words? What did the grandmother

TABLE 8.1   *Structure and Rationale of the Philosophy for Children Programmes*

Grade Levels	Philosophy for Children Programmes	Skills Emphasized
6		*Immediate inference*
		Symmetrical and transitive inference
	Harry	Translation
		Generalization
5		Categorical syllogism
		Hypothetical syllogism
		Reason giving
		Concept formation
		Classification
	Kio and Gus	Exemplifying
4		Part–whole relationships
		Means–end relationships
3	*Pixie*	Ambiguity and vagueness detection
		Seriation
		Similes, metaphors, analogies
		Concept formation
2		Comparing
		Distinction making
		Connection making
		Formulating questions
1	*Elfie*	Giving reasons
		Telling stories
K		

give Suki?" When augmented by exercises and discussion plans from the instructional manual for the *Suki* programme, the classroom dialogue soon becomes an intensive investigation of such traditional aesthetic and metaphysical themes as art versus nature, stability versus change, life and mind, mind and body and appearance versus reality. Conversations about inviting, profoundly contestable topics like these are ideal for sharpening and strengthening children's reasoning skills and judgement.

Having provided you with a specimen of the fictional content of a children's reader, let me turn now to the structure and rationale of the curriculum as a whole, as shown in Table 8.1.

The four earliest programmes strengthen lower-order but foundational skills such as comparing, distinguishing and connecting; middle-order skills such as classification, seriation, analogical reasoning and immediate inference; and higher-order cognitive skills such as syllogistic reasoning, using criteria and making judgements. (These "orders" are logical rather than chronological in character. Middle-order skills presuppose lower-order skills, and higher-order skills presuppose both. But at any age, children are to be found using skills of all three orders, although some more awkwardly than others.) The curriculum stresses the logical sequence on the assumption that this is the sequence to which psychological development conforms in any case. The curriculum at each grade level provides instances which call for lower-level, middle-level and higher-level skills, on the assumption that children of any age are to be found sharpening and strengthening skills belonging to all three logical strata.

To transform the classroom into a community of inquiry that is both cognitively and affectively interactive, one needs to see the thinking skills as emerging from specific disciplinary sources, and as connected with specific mental acts and psychological dispositions (see Figure 8.1).

These skills and dispositions are not isolated constructs: they emanate in force, collectively, from the employment of the Philosophy for Children Programme (see Figure 8.2).

Since Philosophy for Children is a "whole language" educational approach, it emphasizes the basic skills of reading, writing, speaking and listening. That is, it seeks to permeate these basic skills with strengthened reasoning and judgement. Once this is done, the students themselves will carry their heightened reflectiveness over into their regular school disciplines (See Figure 8.3).

At the same time, it must be understood that the subcategories of philosophy provide precisely the normative and criteriological considerations which the present-day school curriculum notoriously lacks. To teach the disciplines critically and reflectively, one must explore their logical, ethical, epistemological, aesthetic and metaphysical presuppositions. Once this is done, students find that the subjects they study have

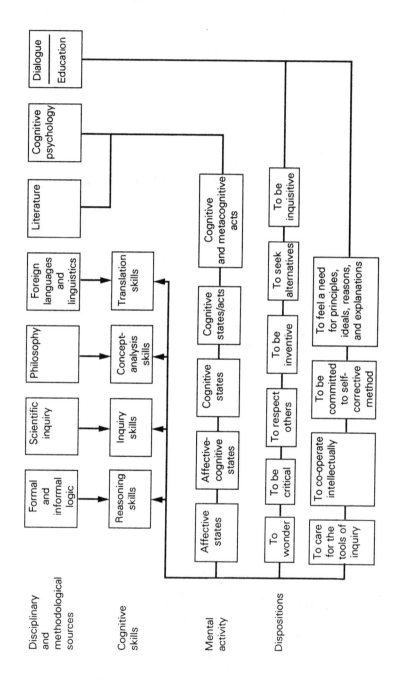

FIG. 8.1   Thinking skills connected to disciplines and dispositions

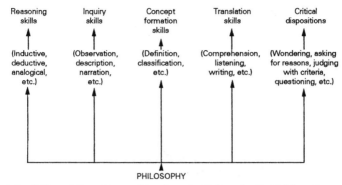

FIG. 8.2   Skills and dispositions arising from the Philosophy for Children Programme

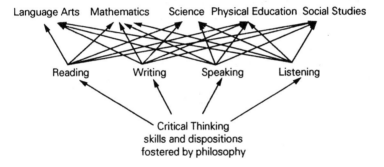

FIG. 8.3   Transfer of reasoning and judgement skills to school disciplines

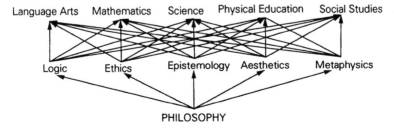

Fig. 8.4   Philosophical subcategories linked to school disciplines

far greater unity and continuity than had previously been the case (see Figure 8.4).

Here I must leave the analysis of the role of philosophy in education, and turn to a brief consideration of its academic impact. Approximately two dozen experiments have now been performed, including, most recently, an impressive study in Austria. Several of these experiments have been conducted by the Educational Testing Service (ETS), and I shall cite the results of two of these. One involved 2,300 5th, 6th and 7th grade students of diverse ethnic backgrounds, with a smaller number of comparison students. At the end of a year of exposure to *Harry*, which was implemented two and a half hours a week in the programme classes, the experimental group did significantly better than the controls in eight of eleven grade-level comparisons ($P = 0.015$). And in another ETS study of an inner-city population, the 100 experimental students did significantly better than the 100 controls ($P = 0.00$), with a 36 per cent greater gain in mathematics proficiency, a 66 per cent greater gain in reading comprehension, and an 80 per cent greater gain in reasoning, after one year of exposure to *Harry*. Still other studies show significant gains in creativity.

I have tried to show that philosophy has a content that is essential to education, that it works well in the classroom, and that it produces highly desirable academic consequences. But I must return to the fact that our theme is thinking in education, and so I feel I should say a few words about the way philosophy fulfils this requirement.

Calls for thinking in education generally and rightly specify "critical thinking", since it cannot be denied that ordinary, uncritical thinking is plentifully present in the average classroom. Now, just what is critical thinking? There are a number of available definitions, but school teachers and administrators complain that current definitions provide too little guidance. I shall therefore offer my own definition. If it is acceptable, the only question remaining would be whether grade-school philosophy conforms to it satisfactorily.

First, I maintain that critical thinking must be a form of inquiry, and I take inquiry to be a self-correcting practice. I therefore assume that one essential feature of critical thinking must be that it is self-correcting. Secondly, I maintain that critical thinking is thinking that takes special circumstances into account when applying rules to cases or theory to practice. A second essential feature of critical thinking is therefore that it is sensitive to context. Thirdly, critical thinking is reasoned thinking. But, more than that, it relies heavily upon that special class of highly reliable reasons known as criteria. Thus, a third aspect of critical thinking is that it relies upon criteria for its practical applications. Skills, for example, are performances appraised by criteria. (Need I add that the discipline that studies the normative, descriptive and methodological functions of criteria is philosophy?) Fourthly, critical thinking, being practical, or applied reasoning, is aimed at the production of judgements. Thus, being conducive to judgements is the fourth essential feature of critical thinking.

We can now collect these four points into a single definition: *critical thinking is thinking that is self-corrective, sensitive to context, and relies upon criteria for the formation of judgements.*

Let us go back to the little story about Suki, her brother Kio, her friend Anne, her father and her grandparents. Consider it as a possible model. Was the thinking it portrayed self-corrective, sensitive to context, reliant upon criteria and formative of judgements? And was your thinking, on deliberating a little upon the story, likewise encouraged with regard to these very same characteristics of critical thinking? My hope would be that you would agree on both counts, for I could then rest my case.

A final word. I have argued that knowledge is inadequate as a goal of education, and that reasonableness and judiciousness are more important. The ancients knew this too, but the word they were inclined to use—*wisdom*—has connotations that may make some of us feel uncomfortable. And yet, how else could they expect wisdom to have been implemented and revealed, except through reasonableness and good judgement?

Education, on the way to us from the Greeks, chose the easy, obvious path. It was manifest that children lacked knowledge: education would therefore supply it to them. What was less clear was whether children were any more lacking in wisdom than we ourselves were. It is something we both could use more of, children and adults alike. Let us hope that this new emphasis upon thinking in education will turn our inquiries in the direction of strengthening reasoning and judgement. From my point of view, this would entail nothing less than accepting philosophy as a required subject in the primary and secondary-school curriculum.

Reference

Lipman, M. (1978). *Suki*. IAPC, Upper Montclair, NJ.

9

From Practice to Theory: Improving the Thinking Process

BRITT-MARI BARTH

Institut supérieur de pédagogie de l'Institut catholique de Paris, France

As a researcher and teacher educator, my main concern is how to convey conceptual understanding of the learning process to future teachers so that they can enhance children's higher-order thinking and help them become aware of their own thinking capacities.

There is now general agreement that it is important for learners to construct their own knowledge. No one else can do it for them. But this consensus poses major pedagogical problems: it means that teachers must assist learners in their personal construction of knowledge rather than giving it to them ready made. When one considers how this can best be done, many questions arise:

(i) What does it mean to construct one's knowledge? How does a symbol come to carry meaning?

(ii) How can we describe the cognitive processes by which individuals construct their knowledge in a way that permits the teacher:

... to recognize it when it occurs;

... to make it occur by providing adequate learning situations;

... to make the learners themselves aware of what occurs so that they can learn to regulate their own thought processes?

My own research project—motivated by observation of the destructive effect school failure has on children—started out in the early 1970s from these kinds of questions. Observation of children's misconceptions in learning situations at school led me to identify three main difficulties, independent of age and subject matter:

(i) confusion between the word and the meaning;

(ii) confusion between relevant and non-relevant factors;
(iii) inadequate reasoning, since rote learning is inappropriate.

This analysis made me aware of the close relationship between the thought process itself and what one thinks about: the two cannot be separated. Knowledge, then, could not be an accumulation of facts passively received from the outside, but must be more like a complex system of connections actively constructed from within. If the first approach comes closer to the way teachers tend to think of knowledge, it is little wonder that learning problems arise. Piaget was no doubt right when he said that it is not the subject matter that the children do not understand, but the lessons they are given.

At this point in my questioning I discovered *A Study of Thinking* (Bruner, Goodnow and Austin, 1956). It was a revelation to me. It described perception as information processing, showing what happens when individuals try to make order in their environment, by which mental strategies they come to consider different things as similar. Bruner insists on the importance of conceptualization: almost all cognitive activity depends on it.

I started building upon a conceptual framework of psychological theory (enlarged over the years to include recent theories in psychology as well as in other cognitive sciences), as I moved between theory and practice. This background led me to develop "models" to illustrate these abstract cognitive processes in a concrete form in order to observe them and to gain a deeper understanding of what we actually do when we think and learn.

These models take the form of learning–teaching strategies which are elaborated in such a way as to put the processes concerned into action. Some of the models focus separately on each of these processes (like comparison, for example), others on the integrated process of concept formation. One model examines the structure of knowledge itself. They are all conceived to be used within the school curriculum or for teachers' education.

The difficulty in constructing models which put abstract processes into action lies in the need first to identify these processes. My own observation and understanding of children's conceptions and misconceptions, gained through developing and trying out the models with them, made me choose and explore the following processes as being essential parts of the conceptualization process:

   . . . discrimination;
   . . . comparison (analogical and analytical);
   . . . inference (inductive and deductive), testing it;
   . . . hypothesis (testing it: considering evidence, detecting inconsistency, arguments).

Even if these processes can be applied in different ways, it seems necessary to start by being aware of the conceptualization process as a universal form of thought.

The proposed models (in their present form) can be used as teaching methods that enhance conceptual learning. They have been experimented with for this purpose and are presently being used in many classrooms as an alternative to expository methods, still common in France. But their main benefit lies perhaps in using them in order to study the link between action and thought, to understand how pedagogical procedures enhance cognitive procedures. In other words, by offering a live experience of a modelled thought process to learners (at their level, independent of age), they enable learners to return to it, to separate the process from its content, identify the process, understand which factors favour its appearance and which ones hinder it.

In many ways, the difficulties in teacher education are similar to those encountered in school; how to convey complex, abstract knowledge in such a way that the learners integrate it, with transfer. Transfer is the central problem. An individual has to derive a conceptual understanding of abstract knowledge (permitting transfer) from multiple, concrete experiences and then compare them in order to transform his or her initial conceptions. If thinking is the most important area of the curriculum, then thinking is what the learner needs experience in. But thinking cannot occur without a content. In my view, thinking is best developed by an in-depth study of a particular subject (which is not to say that introductory exercises across the curriculum could not be useful). This is why it is essential (through initial teacher education) to provide all teachers with the necessary tools to enable them to develop their students' thinking capacities through the study of their subjects and then, further, to make their students aware of these capacities. Transfer of thinking skills from one area to another does not always happen spontaneously.

My own experience in teacher training has confirmed this conviction: a thorough study of thought processes by teachers develops their capacities of analysis and critical judgement, as well as creative solutions to learning difficulties. I have seen teachers of all levels, well versed in their disciplines, transform their expository methods so as to guide their students to acquire an essential understanding of their subjects. When teachers are capable of recognizing and inducing higher-order thinking processes, making students aware of them as they proceed, they no longer need models; they can create their own, knowing for what purpose. The value of a model does not lie in its degree of truth, but rather in its capacity for improving our understanding, and thus our actions. Our improved actions will then further increase our understanding, and that will enable us to create new, more accurate models.

So far I have been discussing the proposed models in a general way. Let me now give some details of how two of them function: first a model to examine knowledge itself and then one to examine the process of concept formation. What difficulties in the learning process do they try to illustrate? What solutions do they suggest? What conditions affecting the learning process do they imply?

The following discussion will be easier to follow with some specific examples in mind. *Knowledge*, a vast general term, is used here to cover specific knowledge, as it appears within any subject in the curriculum. In biology, it could be the study of how the heart functions or what a microbe is. In physics, it could be understanding the difference between solids, liquids and gases or knowing what energy is. In history, it could be the study of different political systems or understanding what characterizes a revolution. Knowledge could be a grammatical rule, a mathematical theorem or an economic theory. Knowledge could also be very subjective and personal, like "beauty" or "people in whom I have confidence". In order to visualize the progression of examples (or model cases) of some specific piece of knowledge, it may be helpful to keep a visual concept in mind, such as the style of painting called "Impressionism".

One obstacle to the learning process is inherent in the nature of knowledge itself: traditionally we treat knowledge as a preconstructed truth and present it as a linear accumulation of facts to our student. This way of proceeding can only work if teachers' and learners' knowledge is similar, which is rarely the case. It then becomes important for teachers to explore the "school knowledge", not in order to mirror their own expert knowledge but in order to adapt it to the students' novice knowledge. This is why a first model is proposed in order to reflect upon the knowledge to be taught and make it "accessible" to the learner who is to explore its meaning.

This model, shown in Figure 9.1, is based on the structure of a concept, which can be applied to any knowledge. Knowledge is thus formalized as a complex structure of relationships. This structure is not the same, however, for every individual; the knowledge of the "expert" is organized in a more complex way than that of the "novice". Experts situate the elements in relation to a whole conceptual network they have worked out through their experience. But the novices' organization is not yet very solid; it often consists of isolated elements which they relate to a few disparate experiences that they cannot yet generalize. Alternatively, they may create a false organization that is too solid. If the latter is not modified in time, the students will find themselves in trouble later. Hence, the way "what we know" as organized should be a subject for teachers' reflection, for the way we perceive and conceive new knowledge depends on this organization. In other words, the organization of our old knowledge determines the way we integrate new knowledge. It is the gap between the expert's knowledge and the novice's knowledge that makes the exchange difficult. So the problem is how to make them adjust to each other in order to bring out the same meaning.

With this goal in mind, the model of the concept is proposed as a pedagogical tool for examining the teacher-expert's "knowledgeable knowledge" in terms of the student-novice's construction of knowledge. The model makes it possible to formulate general questions about knowledge.[2]

Other general categories of attributes—for example,—purpose, process, cause and effect can be useful in order to examine and reflect upon knowledge. Most disciplines also have their own specific categories of questions that enhance appropriate thinking skills.

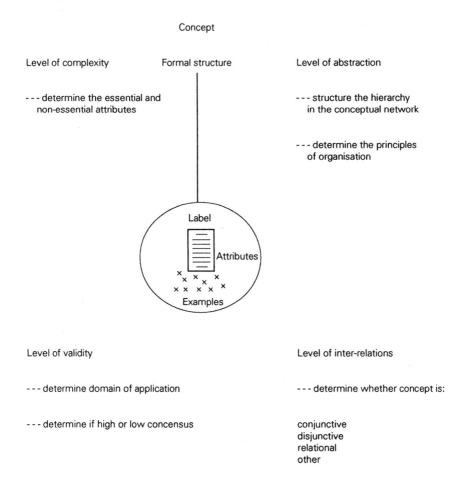

FIG. 9.1 The concept as a model to examine the structure of knowledge

... What is essential for the learner? (level of complexity).
... For what purpose? What transfer? For what fields of application?
(level of validity).
... Where is this knowledge situated in a conceptual hierarchy? (level
of abstraction).
... What is the relationship between the specific elements? (level of
inter-relationship).

In the case of impressionism it could apply as in Figure 9.2.

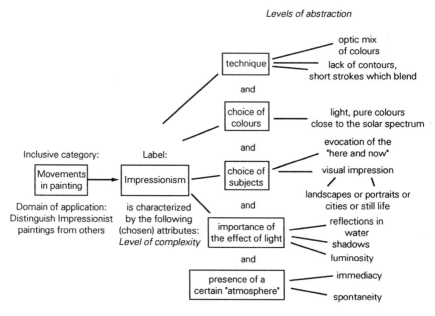

FIG. 9.2   The Example of Impressionism

There is a dual advantage in analysing knowledge in this way. On the one
hand, the analysis allows the teacher to examine knowledge and to define
it in terms of the person who is then to construct it. Experience shows that
teachers have great difficulty in formalizing knowledge and in verbalizing
essential attributes, even if they master them implicitly (which is true for all
experts). On the other hand, it allows the learner to discover that it is
possible to approach all knowledge in a formal way. This realization
completely transforms the cognitive behaviour of the learner: he or she
understands what to look for. This is the first step towards cognitive
autonomy, which will then allow the learner knowingly to set up a strategy
for constructing meaning.

This first reflection on the structure of knowledge itself already contains
a portion of the answer to an essential question that shapes the whole

process of learning: the intellectual receptivity of the learner. What can be done to make the learner want to think and be attentive? That requires a considerable cognitive effort. Constructing knowledge in a school setting is not a spontaneous act.

Wishing to be attentive is not always sufficient to make one so, especially if the content is of no particular interest to students. But it is easier to get their attention if they have something specific to do, hence the idea of creating anticipation of a goal through the task itself: a task which is structured, with a beginning and an end, a task that can be mastered by the student while it presents some sort of intellectual challenge. Thus we create an anticipation of the goal to be attained—without which there is no attention—by proposing a task which is conceived so as to set off a process of conceptualization. It is important for the students to understand what they have to do, and to be capable of doing it, for them to expect success from the start. Discouragement is the greatest enemy of any intellectual activity.

A well-conceived task can thus stimulate different types of motivation, according to the individual—an interest for the activity itself, an intellectual challenge, the genuine possibility of success, the need for self-esteem—while at the same time it provokes thought and stimulates reasoning. The intellect and the emotions are inseparable. The pedagogical procedure itself must involve the student affectively. It is the teacher's responsibility to accomplish this.

If the choice of the task is important for all these reasons, it is also strictly linked to another factor that conditions learning: the way learners come in contact with the new knowledge. Are they going to listen to a definition? Look at diagrams? Handle objects? The task-procedure proposed to the students in this pedagogical model consists in getting them to construct the concept gradually from very precise, concrete examples and counter-examples. Knowing what a concept is, they are asked to compare the examples in order to discover what they have in common. All suggestions are written down, then crossed out when no longer relevant.

The function of the examples is to multiply experiences with the knowledge in its concrete form. Abstraction grows out of real experience; if the student has not yet had any experience (consciously, in a specific context), he or she must be supplied with it. Counter-examples, by their contrast, allow the students to be guided towards a finer perception, to make them aware of relevant similarities and differences of concepts within a given field of application. A wise choice of these examples is essential to broaden and transform the initial perception of the learners. They have to be tested with them to see whether they have the desired effect, which is to allow abstraction to be constructed by a continuous alternation between concrete examples (model cases) and formulations of what they have in common.

Impressionism, as defined earlier, could be illustrated by slides representing paintings by typical Impressionist painters, like Renoir, Monet, Pisarro, clearly exhibiting the chosen attributes. Non-essential attributes, also present, like the kind of subjects (landscape, portraits, cities, still life) or the season, would have to be varied in order not to cause confusion. The counter-examples could be, to start with, abstract paintings in strong colours, like Picasso, Kandinsky or Braque, where no common attributes are to be found. If the technique of the Impressionist painters is not well distinguished, a counter-example showing the opposite kind of technique could be shown, such as certain of Matisse's paintings. Observations like "it looks blurred", or "there are no lines" could be linked to comparisons of techniques: others, like "I would prefer to be in that painting", could be linked to comparisons of different atmospheres. "It's soft" could lead to an observation of colours, as compared to other paintings. To show the natural "here and now" kind of subjects typical of the Impressionists, counter-examples with a historical or mythical theme, painted in a studio, could be contrasted with "the impression" a real landscape offers. To show the importance of the effect of natural light, reflections in the water, coloured shadows and general luminosity, could be compared to plain surfaces. To put the perception of subtle distinctions to a test, counter-examples which come very close, like pre-, post- and neoimpressionists could be compared (but only at the end): how are a Turner, a Signac, a Seurat or a van Gogh different? Alike? What conclusion do we draw?

The examples must be sufficient in number and variety for their comparison to involve the student in a real epistemological search. (A prior understanding, by the student, of the structure of the concept-knowledge is the condition for this.) The variety of examples and counter-examples encourages the learner to make multiple comparisons and to put the concept in its conceptual framework. A concept does not exist alone but always in a conceptual framework, and it is important for the student to be able to distinguish subtle differences between similar concepts so as not to confuse them.

The order of the examples is also important. It allows the teacher to make sure that temporary knowledge can settle in before it is upset by the introduction of an example that causes amazement or doubt. Before a learner is able to modify a conception, he or she must be aware of it.

The dialogue that accompanies the confrontation of examples and counter-examples allows the students to clarify and rectify the models they are constructing. This confrontation appears at different levels. First, new knowledge is confronted with the learners' existing knowledge. This is expressed through their verbal observations and thus permits the teacher to find out what their initial perceptions are. Then there is a confrontation between the students' different perceptions, as expressed in their verbal interaction and argumentation. Finally, there is a confrontation between the students and the teacher, generated by the latter's questions, which lead to analysis and critical judgement, as well as to the search for precise formulations.

This dialogue also allows reasoning to be revealed. When the teacher thinks aloud with the learners he or she gives them the actual experience of an abstract process: this experience will then make it possible for them, not to imitate it, but to become aware of it and make it their own. Thus it is the students who are led to think and reason; the teacher's role is to guide this reasoning and help the students go further in the development of their knowledge than they could have done on their own. Verbal formulation is part of the learning process itself: language becomes a tool for thinking that allows experience to be transformed and assimilated.

The cognitive process is thus set in motion by a cognitive procedure (Figure 9.3) conveyed by the instructions for the task and the choice of examples. This choice can create astonishment, questions, hypothetical

TIME to represent the task

	TIME to perceive, absorb, the new	perception:
I	information	distinguish differences
N		
S	TIME to compare the new information	comparison:
T	with what one already knows	analogical or analytical
R		
U	TIME to explain, account for, one's	first inferences:
C	intuitive perceptions	inductive or deductive
T	(memory support)	
I		
O	TIME to explore (the right to errors,	verification
N	crossing out what is no longer	
S	relevant)	
	TIME to perceive links, make new	new inferences
	connections, restructure	

Beginning of synthesis

A	TIME to compare the new connections	
S	with other people's	
S		
E	TIME to rectify and reformulate	
S		
S	TIME to verify and transform	new verifications
M		
E	TIME to make final formulations	generalization, hypothesis
N		
T	TIME to consolidate and memorize	

The *procedure* can be varied: time, task,   The *process* is directed
modes of presentation or of grouping, etc.   (but not necessarily linear)

Fig. 9.3   Guiding the process: Co-construction

answers, argumentation. The teacher's role is to help students to perceive links and encourage formulation, verification and reformulation. This mediation allows the learner to establish a connection with the teacher's empirical knowledge and, progressively, to transform it; it limits the separation of empirical knowledge and declarative knowledge, which prevents the transfer from taking place. It stimulates the relating of various mental images to each other, whether they be visual, auditory, or kinesthetic.

Learners build their abstract knowledge from direct confrontation with real examples (chosen for them) of this knowledge, helped by the person who is guiding them, somehow negotiating the meaning with them. The teacher becomes the "co-constructor" of meaning. The procedure is flexible and may vary but this process of constructing meaning—a close alternation between intuition and analysis, between hypothesis and verification—should always be set in motion by the learner. Individual differences may be taken into consideration within this universal process. The role of the mediator may also be taken by a more experienced peer, but it is insufficient to put students into a group for interactions to be of high quality. On the other hand, with the rules of the game well defined and understood (which are actually rules for thinking) and with training to act as a member of a group, students profit by learning together.

The assessment of learning is a part of the process and starts at the outset. It is formative, allowing for constant correcting along the way. A mistake has a positive role, for it leads to the analysis and transformation of initial and intermediary conceptions. Counter-examples can function as a set of "mistakes" which, when well chosen, surprise students and induce them to ask questions, reflecting a genuine interrogation on their part.

Admittedly this approach takes time: this is the prerequisite for reflection, which one tends to overlook. But this time is saved in the long run, for the student learns how to regulate his or her thinking and is thus prepared for cognitive autonomy. This type of evaluation in which students are led to analyse new examples by justifying their conclusions is an efficient way to break them of the habit of always wanting to give the "right" answer, which defeats real learning. Justification leads to critical judgement, argumentation and self-evaluation. The students participate in the assessment of their learning; once they have understood the essential criteria, present in the model cases, they can easily check themselves: "*If* such and such an element (attribute) is present, *then* I am looking at such and such a phenomenon (concept)." This is hypothetical reasoning, verified during the thinking process and concluded by a generalization. This active exploration is indispensable for memorization and transfer. It also lays the foundation for a later realization of the nature of reasoning itself.

The final evaluation is to be found at three levels: meaning (attributes), symbol (the word), and production of personal examples (transfer). This evaluation makes sure that acquisition has not remained on the level of verbal association (recognition of a few examples in response to a stimulus) but has moved up to the level of *conceptulization* (ability to generalize, to extend the criteria observed to a whole category).

In this way, a higher level of reflection (induced in the students through the teacher's mediation) allows students to acquire knowledge on the level of conceptualization; but it is possible for them to go further: consciously mobilizing their minds for future learning tasks. To bring about transfer of cognitive processes, the teacher must be able to recognize them. Before practising metacognition with one's pupils, one needs to have a clear idea of what cognition is. One must be able to separate the teaching content from the cognitive processes used to assimilate it, in order to have children think about the process itself. It would be worthwhile to pursue the question of metacognitive teaching, not only in learning situations provided and guided by the teacher, but also when using a good computer programme. If the use of the computer is to enhance transfer of thinking skills in the learner, one would need to elicit reflection on why it was good, and what it helped the learner to do.

The teacher's role in this approach is essential and specific: as the mediator between the learner and knowledge, he or she is responsible for putting the students in a position from which to construct knowledge rather than supplying them with ready-made knowledge. The teacher does this by providing an adequate learning task and by modelling higher-order thinking while guiding the students' thinking. Further, by teaching in a metacognitive way, he or she makes it possible for the learners to become aware of, and later integrate the thinking process itself.

My research lies within a Vygotskian and Brunerian theoretical framework. The following quotation from Bruner, interpreting the "zone of proximal development", as defined by Vygotsky, makes this apparent:

> If the child is enabled to advance by being under the tutelage of an adult or a more competent peer, then the tutor or the peer serves the learner as a vicarious form of consciousness until such a time as the learner is able to master his own action through his own consciousness and control . . . it is then he is able to use it as a tool. (Bruner, 1985)

With this background, my own work with children and teachers has added a theoretical and operational understanding of the thinking processes and the conditions under which these can be better developed. There is much work needed to gain a deeper knowledge in this field of study. In the meantime we must use the knowledge we already have to create the best conditions for teachers and pupils to succeed in their respective tasks.

Howard Gardner's theories of multiple intelligences (Gardner, 1983) are certainly among those which can permit us to draw further conclusions on how these universal thinking processes can be applied in different ways, depending on how various symbol systems shape them. Today's transdisciplinary research in cognitive sciences should help to give further clues to the eternal philosophical question: how does the mind work?

In the meantime, we have to use the knowledge we possess in order to create the optimum conditions under which teachers and learners can best fulfil their tasks. Helping teachers to acquire a conceptual understanding of what understanding is, as well as to be good thinkers themselves, promises to produce a qualitative change in the way we teach. This change might best come about through a kind of a partnership between researchers and teachers in a common search for how our current knowledge can be applied to the greatest benefit of our schoolchildren.

Notes

1. For a detailed description, see Barth (1987, Chapter 6).
2. This formal approach to knowledge, as a structure of connections could be further developed. See Perkins (1986).

References

Barth, B.-M. (1987). *L'apprentissage de l'abstraction, méthodes pour une meilleure réussite de l'école*. RETZ, Paris.
Bruner, J. S. (1985). Vygotsky: A historical and conceptual perspective, in Wertsch J. V., *Culture, Communication and Cognition: Vygotskian Perspectives*. Cambridge University Press, Cambridge.
Bruner, J. S., Goodnow, J. J. and Austin, G. A. (1956). *A Study of Thinking*. Wiley, New York.
Gardner, H. (1983), *Frames of Mind: The Theory of Multiple Intelligences*. Basic Books, New York.
Perkins, D. N. (1986). *Knowledge as Design*. Erlbaum, Hillsdale, NJ.

10

Thought Processes in Learning

ANTOINE DE LA GARANDERIE

Director of Research,
Université de Lyon II, France

In his *Experimental Study of Intelligence*, published in 1903, Alfred Binet recounts observations of his two teenage daughters. His method was to set them an intellectual task, such as to define something, memorize some words or describe an object, and then to ask them what was going through their heads while they were carrying out that task. This procedure has been called *experimental introspection*. During the same period, psychologists Watt, Messer and Bühler at the Würzburg school used the same procedure when questioning their students and members of their research team.

As this is not a historical study, there is no need to discuss the details of their findings here. However, it may be helpful to indicate the sources the author studied under the psychologist Albert Burloud at Rennes University. Burloud's work combines the methodological principles of the Würzburg psychologists with those he identified from the work of Maine de Biran into an original synthesis. The author stands squarely in this current of thought.

Being attentive, memorizing, understanding, reflecting, reasoning, discovering and inventing are all essentially intellectual acts which need to be specified clearly. By placing students, colleagues and myself in situations requiring such acts to be performed so as to find out afterwards what was going on in the mind at the time, I have sought to identify the patterns which account for their effectiveness.

My questions were systematically intended to:

(i) try to elicit everything which the respondent might have more or less implicitly experienced;
(ii) identify the factors determining successful performance of the intellectual act under consideration.

This aim combined pedagogical need with psychological intent. Obviously, people as a rule remain unaware of all the processes going on through their heads when performing any task, whether manual or intellectual. Some kind of assumption is therefore required to imagine what mental processes and content may be involved.

It is of course easy to complain that any such approach is bound to be arbitrary, since we can only discuss the mind subjectively, and the pitfalls of bias, illusion or suggestion are therefore obvious enough. But I decided to disregard these as based only on prejudice and to let the facts speak for themselves in the end. In *Défense et illustration de l'introspection* (1989b) I explain why. Everyone has experienced the way in which a thought process can be modified to adapt it more closely to a situation. This straightforward practical observation can usefully be applied on a systematic basis, as the following account will now show.

Seeking impressions, including my own, from many different kinds of people, I found that being attentive, memorizing, understanding, reflecting, reasoning, discovering and inventing were perceived as formal, imperative exercises, when not strictly operational. Respondents reported or imagined being in a physical attitude illustrating an expression of their awareness that "I must pay attention", "I mustn't let myself be distracted", "I must concentrate". They saw themselves with knitted brows, arms crossed, lips pursed. "I must try to learn this", "I must memorize this", "I must know this by heart", and the picture is of a head bent over a book, studying the lesson, eyes scanning the text. "I must make an effort to understand", "I must understand", "I can see my face lit up by understanding" and so on.

These terms of the cognitive vocabulary presented pedagogically in the form of educational injunctions open up no avenue for their effective management. They lock the individual into verbal or visual patterns which congeal into anxiety. On this point, introspection provides a wealth of entirely objective information. Practically all respondents say that that is indeed how they experience or have experienced these educational imperatives. They report that their formulation by the teacher yields no practical meaning. At most, they derive a negative meaning: don't let yourself be distracted, don't neglect to learn the lesson, don't repeat parrot-fashion, don't let your mind drift, don't give any old answer. This led them to believe that apart from the effort they made to stop counterproductive thoughts, they could only hope to receive that gift which is never described and which the individual either does or doesn't possess. At best, the attempt to maintain these formal principles in one's head and to ward off irrelevant instincts or wishes might create the most favourable conditions for understanding to dawn. Is this not indeed corroborated by unexpected breakthroughs after years of dry slogging?

But we can do better than that. I consider that we can perfectly well manage to apply descriptive definitions to these fundamental concepts of cognitive psychology and should therefore include them in general pedagogical theory. If so, the concepts are bound to show a characteristic pattern that needs to be retrieved, not invented. For although pedagogical theory has so far failed to identify this pattern, for thousands of years people have known how to be attentive, memorize, understand, reflect, reason, discover and invent, doubtless following the pattern without realizing it. This is enough to indicate an approach in terms of trying to answer the following question: what are the conditions which the mind has to satisfy so as to ensure that it performs these cognitive acts or "thought processes" successfully?

We may now try to construct a theory explaining how the favourable conditions can be substantiated. Putting myself in the various situations involving these different types of "thought process", I started with the first—attention, without which cognition is impossible—but soon found that the cognitive imperative instructing me to be attentive closed me in on myself, like the serpent biting its own tail. At last the only thing I could be aware of was my own desire to be attentive and I was not open to the object to which I was supposed to be paying attention. What, in any case, does "being open to the object" mean? I tried to find out what it was that made my cognitive act of attention effective, and realized that success came when I evoked the object concerned. I describe to myself the object to which I am to be visually attentive, and if I am asked to pay attention by listening to something being said, it is still by inwardly commenting[1] that I perform the mental act of attention. Similarly, if I am being asked to attend to some object which is to be touched, smelled, manipulated, it is still through *verbal evocation* that my cognitive act of attention becomes effective.

How can I be sure of this?

In the first place, the decision to evoke the object of attention by commenting on it introspectively almost completely eliminates any inclinations towards being distracted; secondly, I realize that my introspective commenting on the object to be attended to allows me to integrate it; and lastly, if anyone asks me about a matter to which I have been attending in this way, I always feel that I am in a position to give an answer. Looking back on my academic past, I realize that I was praised for attentiveness every time I had set about attending by commenting introspectively, but was called inattentive when all I had made was "a great effort" to pay attention but without the mental commentary.

Respondents were able to confirm the validity of this theory: a person is being genuinely attentive when deliberately evoking the object of attention. Going no further than a formal desire to be attentive gets us nowhere. However, one essential distinction must be made.

Many respondents, though I can give no precise statistic, said that to achieve an effective cognitive act of attention, they did not use words to describe or comment on the object but expressed it in visual images reproducing it in some more or less original way, or translated it into visual terms if the object was some kind of sound. A few people said that they evoked the object of attention visually if it was visual, and verbally if it was auditory. Another small number said that they evoked a visual object of attention verbally, and vice versa in order to derive a means of "understanding" from the translation. Only a few people said that they applied all these different strategies, depending on the occasion.

Several consequences of psychological or pedagogical interest can be drawn from these observations:

First, respondents were able to indicate that had I not pointed out that the act of attention did not derive its effectiveness from obedience to some formal instruction, they would never have noticed the fact. They would have been even further from realizing that evocation of the object of attention by comment or image was the inherently essential condition for attention to be effectively given. Nor would they have realized that in order to bring about such an evocation, one must have an intention to do so. In short, all accepted that the inquiry they had agreed to undergo had enabled them to realize the existence of internal processes of which previously they had not been directly aware. They concluded that they would henceforth possess mastery over the attention process and that it would be up to them to put it to work whenever they so wished, no longer having to wait for happy inspiration and, most important of all, for matters in which they had supposed themselves untalented and had been experiencing setbacks. One might object to this by asking how a person could ever intend anything implicitly?

Psychologists know that people can, without realizing what they are doing, make their minds evoke whatever they are perceiving and can even get into the habit of doing so. The habit is self-reinforcing when rewarded with success, even though it might never occur to the person to think about it. Because of the fact that the cultural climate overestimates the idea that in intellectual life, success derives mainly from giftedness, the person is distracted from any need for introspection as to the source of these fortunate outcomes, since they can be regarded as God-given.

Next, when we look closely we can see that certain conditions have to be satisfied for cognition to proceed successfully. These conditions must be sought inside the cognitive processes themselves. The idea here is as follows: when the mind succeeds in being attentive, in memorizing, in understanding or in reflecting, the processes involved are not the same as when it fails to do so. What, then, makes them efficient? The clue lies within the processes themselves. I have already pointed out the difference between an act of attention in response to a straightforward formal instruction, and one regulated by the unconscious intention of evoking, by visual images or words or indeed comments, the subject to which attention is to be paid. Introspection reveals the inherent benefit when an act of attention is accompanied by an unintentional evocation of its subject.

Lastly, being able to show how the mind operates successfully has pedagogical consequences. All teachers ought to be aware of these processes and to teach all their students how to apply them, using language suitable to their age. This would release the students from the shackles of the formal injunctions they have endured for centuries. Needless to say, years of experience have enabled me to verify the benefit of teaching my students this technique. They now know how to proceed mentally in order to perform schoolroom tasks, from the simplest to the most complex.

Having presented the method recommended here and the benefits it offers in connection with the act of paying attention, we may now proceed further in the same direction.

Let us take the act of memorizing. Here also, effectiveness is associated with evocation. Memorizing can be described in terms of its own meaning as the cognitive act by which one brings into existence, in an imaginary future, whatever it is one intends to retain. So I may picture in my mind the diagram I shall be having to reproduce during the lesson and imagine that I am in the process of drawing it for the class. If it is for the purpose of a future examination in some unknown location, I invent the surroundings. The main thing is the mental training I practise because it is that which fixes what I intend to retain in the future. If I am proceeding verbally, I do not picture the diagram but try to describe it by commenting on it introspectively in precise detail, so as to be able to repeat it while at the same time imagining myself to be in the future. In short, memorizing adds to the act of attention the pattern of an imaginary future surrounding the thing to be remembered and actively used to recall it.

Here I have merely described the act of memorizing in terms of its general structure, without going into detail. Learning something by heart, learning something that has to be understood, finding a way of solving problems or developing some theory, are all identifiable memorization methods. It is not possible to describe them in detail here, but see *La pédagogie des moyens d'apprendre* (The Teaching of Ways of Learning) (de la Garanderie, 1984), in which I devote a chapter to the cognitive act of memorizing. These few lines on the subject will, I hope, be enough to bring out the difference between formally instructing a student to learn some material or other (even if accompanied by such advice as: read this, re-read that, copy that, say it out loud) and the definition of the cognitive act of evocation consisting in incorporation of the thing to be evoked in an imaginary future in which the student tries to retrieve it.

How does the mind understand something? In reading a book, a novel or scientific or philosophical work, the cognitive process leading to understanding is always the same. I comment inwardly on what I am reading, then I compare that comment with the text itself to test its validity. When the book is easy, my comment flows freely and I have no need to re-read the text to check the validity of my comment. Critical comparison between the evocation constituted by the comment and the text itself is made during the first reading.

When the book is difficult, it requires several readings and the comment may alter considerably, sometimes being discarded for a new one. The critical comparison between comment and text produces judgements which may prompt an understanding of what the text means. If the intention is only to evoke the text literally, I may memorize it, especially if I am training myself to include the repetition in an imaginary future, but I will not understand it. Therefore, I need to comment inwardly on it, that is, endeavour to express it in other words. This calls for a different intention from when only straightforward memorization is intended (leaving aside the pedagogical problem of whether this is really advisable). That is of no concern here. I am seeking to show that in the act of understanding, another structure is added to attention and memorization, that of imagining evocations for comparison with the matter to be understood, from which understanding of its meaning may spring.

As well as respondents who reported proceeding in much the same way as I do, there were others who, instead of commenting introspectively on what they were seeking to understand, evoked visual, concrete or symbolic images according to the kind of material they were dealing with. These are the pictures they use when making a critical comparison with the material they are trying to understand, leading on to comparative judgements from which understanding may arise. Their procedure is therefore much the same as mine: evocations are formed for the purpose of setting up a critical comparison. But the difference lies in the content of the evocations. Mine are verbal, theirs are visual. I have met respondents who will use both kinds of evocation to improve their chances of obtaining a comparison which will lead them to understand something.

Some respondents report that if what they are trying to understand is a visual form, such as a problem in geometry or the machinery of a complex physical apparatus, they do not hesitate to describe what they are looking at in words, because translating their subject provides them with an easier comparison than they would get from a picture, which might lock them into a crude memorization. Conversely, if they are dealing with some historical, philosophical or literary material, they will contrive some schematic view of it in order to identify its essential features. Others experience a need to evoke words which they can go on to define.

It is the definitions they obtain which they will critically compare with the material concerned, always in the hope that these will yield understanding of what it means. All these different ways make no difference to what seems to be the essence of the act of understanding, which is the outcome of an impact between evocations deployed for comparison with the material to be understood, but deployment of these evocations stems from the intention of thereby equipping oneself to make the comparison.

The difference will be clear between this analysis of the act of understanding and the pedagogical advice which may result from it on the one hand, and the advice usually given on the other: try to find the general idea, what the author wanted to say, the meaning of the demonstration; underline words or key phrases. This is not to say that it is wrong to try to identify the general idea or to discover the meaning of a demonstration, nor to bring out the main features, but that the mind cannot perform these until the act of understanding as defined above has taken place because they presuppose it, since they can only be based on evoking meaning.

For me, to reflect is merely systematically to evoke experiences to relate with the matter in hand, whether it be literary, scientific or technical. Sometimes I will come back to a situation posing a problem, to what I already know, mainly to knowledge I consider to be involved. In order to do this effectively I have found that I need to begin by evoking the situation or the problem, because if I were merely to picture the topic I would induce only a very limited range of my experiences. I have also found that I need to explore systematically the field of my experiences related to the matter in hand. Some respondents recognized my method of reflecting as being like theirs. Others differed because their evocations were in visual form, whereas for me those who operate as I do, they took a verbal form. We need not consider the way in which one may wish to organize the evocations in order to solve the situation or the problem in hand by utilizing them in a particular order, or grouping some of them into more serviceable representations. In other words, a complex cognitive mechanism is involved in reflection. This can be described and it relates to the type of situation or problem in hand.

When I am reasoning, I mentally start by establishing a programme for thought, depending on what kind of reasoning I have chosen. If it is to be inductive, I prepare to sustain it by deliberately bringing together those facts which may lend themselves to comparison, with the aim of arriving at some law. For instance, this was how I looked for what there was in common in all the cognitive processes that I proposed to describe. To do this, I mentally defined each of them and observed that they all contained two concepts: intention and evocation. But in order to arrive at that generalization, it was not sufficient to review the characteristics of the facts. It was necessary to have the intention of comparing them, with the view to identifying any similarities or identical properties they might contain. It is that intention which determines a mental representation in which such similarities or identities will fit together, and from which sudden understanding of a possible law will arise. For a deductive reasoning process, I verbally evoke the principles or laws which will govern it. Since every operation of the mind necessarily involves some goal, every time I describe an operation of the mind it is not enough to identify the effective cause of that operation; the goal to which it is directed must also be specified. That is why attention cannot be defined as an effort of concentration. We need to be able to say what the goal of that effort is. It was this that enabled me to posit the hypothesis that the purpose of attention was to bring out the subject of attention by an act of evocation.

For me, all this is the outcome of verbal evocation, inductive and deductive introspection. While some people also reason in this way, using exclusively verbal language, others need visual evocations in concrete or symbolic forms. In the latter case the visual symbol can of course vary, either taking abstract forms such as outlines, initials, vectors or representational forms containing some general meaning. It is by relying on these symbols that respondents in this category can use these evocations to verbalize the meaning and articulate it in an argument. Apart from what the evocations contain, I find two basic concepts: the intention and the evocation.

I have come to realize that creative imagination needs to be cultivated while attending to perceived objects. It is not when one is in the process of seeking some problem, writing a poem, composing a piece of music, that one should begin to worry about having imagination. That would be a lost cause. The source of creative imagination lies in the relationship with the world of perception. We need to look at the world, listen to it with the intention of evoking whatever riches it may have which are waiting to be discovered or invented. In this way we will be evoking not just the object itself but, more imaginatively, what latent presences or absences it may enclose which will be tomorrow's intuitions. Without going into detail, it seems undeniable that when discoverers like Pasteur, Claude Bernard, Einstein, Freud, and inventors such as Denis Papin, Edison, the Lumière brothers, set out to evoke the world, they were anxious to safeguard its latent presences and absences. That is how their work brought to light the latencies which they had so usefully garnered with their earlier, raw evocations.

In this rapid overview I have sought only to give some glimpses of the pedagogy that can be drawn from an effort to approach cognitive processes by the method of experimental introspection (see de la Garanderie 1989a, 1989b).

The descriptive definitions of the main concepts of cognitive psychology which I have just presented lead on directly to the teaching of how the mind works, and should enable pupils to teach themselves how to think, especially since the concepts can perfectly well be explained in simple words that a child can understand.

Note

1. Binet used this expression (*un discours parlant*) (Binet, 1903, p. 57).

References

Binet, A. (1903) *Etude expérimentales de l'intelligence*, pp. 311. Schleicher, Pans.
Garanderie, A. de la (1984). *La pédagogie des moyens d'apprendre*, Le Centurium, Paidoguides, Paris.
Garanderie, A. de la (1989a). *Comprendre et imaginer*, Le Centurion, Paidoguides, Paris.
Garanderie, A. de la (1989b). *Défense et illustration de l'introspection*, Le Centurion, Paidoguides, Paris.

11

The Project FACE
(Formal Aims of Cognitive Education)

TOUKO VOUTILAINEN

Institute for Educational Research,
University of Jyväskylä, Helsinki, Finland

Introduction

In a sense, the beginning of the project FACE[1] can be traced back to the late 1960s, when a state curriculum committee was preparing a proposal for a comprehensive school curriculum. The committee also maintained that the general, formal characteristics of knowledge should be given an important place in school education. It devoted a special chapter of its report to the main features of the matter, but failed to present a detailed plan or any practical suggestions.

The need for such guidance was felt throughout the implementation of the changes in the Finnish school system, especially because of the ever-increasing load of teaching/learning matter. Finally, in 1985 a project (FACE) was started that aimed, by means of research and experimentation, to develop a list of formal targets for cognitive education which—considered to be content-free—could then be used as guidelines, not only for many practical decisions taken in schools but also for ways to improve the learner's thinking skills.

The FACE project is an initiative of the Finnish National Board of General Education (NBGE). Amongst other things, the NBGE's duty is to help and encourage development work in schools and municipalities.

The research activities will be completed by the end of 1992. Only then can the results be fully evaluated and published. Because of the nature and complexity of the project's target, however, the results cannot even then be considered as final. Research on the formal aims of teaching and on their practical adjustment will obviously continue in other fields. In the project group it is believed that if the formal aims can be introduced and disseminated widely in school education—especially by means of teachers' basic training—they could provide a general and, at the same time, realistic basis for a purposeful development of students' thinking skills.

It is worth mentioning here the recent public debate in Finland on the need for an updating of the concept of knowledge. The discussion, primarily initiated by the NBGE, was taken forward by the work of the FACE project, whose researchers wrote a special pamphlet on the "developing" concept of knowledge seen from the viewpoint of schools. These discussions have already shown that significant changes in school practices would be welcome, affecting all the essential elements of everyday school life, for example, the form and amount of curricular and textbook content, the teaching/learning methods, the modes of measuring students' and teachers' success, and so on. Eventually, they would aim to improve the learners' thinking skills; this goal is beginning to be regarded as the real purpose of schools in an "information society".

How Can Thinking be Developed in Practice?

The Form and Contents of Knowledge

Even though the threshold and techniques for data storage and processing have expanded and changed, the concept of knowledge itself has not altered. Using concepts, drawing conclusions, avoiding contradictions, applying the criteria of truth as well as other essential cognitive activities, still take place in our thinking as before. The way in which this knowledge can be exploited in teaching is the most essential question in the FACE project.

All knowledge can justifiably be divided into two integral parts: its form and its content. Form has no significance without content, and content without form cannot be an object of thinking.

In practice, the form and content of knowledge differ from each other: the form of knowledge may and often does remain essentially the same, even if the content changes substantially. The form of knowledge is bound to the concept of knowledge, which can in fact be defined only in terms of the formal qualities of knowledge.

The formal aims of cognitive education in this paper mean those goals set for teaching that are independent of content, that is, matters related to actual knowing. For FACE, the most important forms of knowledge are: concept formation, thinking (deduction and induction), explaining, truth and perceiving wholes. It is our belief that most of the formal aims which can be consciously emphasized in school instruction can be summarized under these five headings. The formal aims have been presented as specific goal statements, which are closely related to instruction. There are also some aims that influence the affective aspect of thinking.

Can Thinking be Developed by Teaching Logic?

To what extent can we consciously exploit information about knowledge in our own thinking? For instance, propositional logic, which is perhaps the most comprehensively studied field of logic, can consciously be used to a limited extent to help thinking. Even then, it would presuppose a thorough knowledge on the part of the teacher, and consciously applicable logic is usually mastered by only a few teachers.

Even though the starting points for the development of thinking lie in epistemology and logic, they do not form part of our project's curriculum. We feel that it is impossible to teach logic with sufficient precision and to such an extent that students could exploit it in their thinking. The "demands" of logic can be taken only indirectly into consideration in teaching when content is dealt with. The principal question is: what are those constituents and qualities of thinking which can be identified so that development of thinking occurs?

The answer to this question is that there are many. Reason, of course, is the foundation of all thinking, but many of the constituents of thinking (in the broader sense of the word) are not able to be found in logic textbooks.

The Formal Aims and Thinking

The formal aims deal with those qualities of cognitive activity that can be influenced in a way which makes it possible to call the consequent permanent effect "the development of thinking".

In thinking, we are always faced with situations which presuppose awareness of the logical structure of thinking processes. Events like this occur *i*) in connection with concepts, and particularly when abstract concepts are used; *ii*) in separating premises and inferences from each other; *iii*) in checking whether the error is in the premises or in the deduction itself; *iv*) when contradiction arises; *v*) in checking the prerequisites for causal and final explanation; and *vi*) in applying the criteria for truth of some propositions, and so on. These situations can of course also be identified and classified in other ways.

When new things are studied, these situations related to the formal aspect of knowledge occur even more frequently than usual. In teaching, they cannot be avoided as easily as in other circumstances. In order to solve problems most effectively, someone in the classroom must master the formal structure of knowledge. This is, of course, the teacher.

It does not, however, suffice that teachers somehow "manage" the situation. They must tutor their students in understanding the solution to the formal problem. They should orient their thinking in such a way that corresponding problems could be avoided or that students would frequently be able to manage them themselves. This aim can be achieved by setting unambiguous, formal objectives to cognitive education in addition to contextual ones.

How the Formal Aims are Applied

The formal aims are deduced from the concepts of knowledge and thinking. They are formulated into goal statements which guide the treatment of knowledge in textbooks and in the classroom. Some of these goal statements deal with the thinking processes of students in teaching situations, some with textbook analysis, and some with the motives and attitudes connected with study, that is, its affective aspect.

Which goals are applied in each situation remains at the discretion of the teacher. Similarly, the teacher decides which methods he or she uses to promote the attainment of the goal in question. The teacher can and should plan in advance the goals and methods to be applied, but the final decision must be made in the actual teaching situation.

In principle, it is perhaps possible to follow plans and timetables, but this is not the case in thinking. Exact and detailed planning in advance is not feasible in the teaching of formal knowledge. Where and how in the teaching process the critical elements are introduced during a given lesson cannot be stated with certainty beforehand.

We are not talking here about methodological tricks to encourage memory but a continuous and persevering work with the critical aspects of knowledge taught in accordance with the formal aims of the project. So far, teachers have not been extensively trained for this task, and only those teachers who have taken part in the experiment have received the necessary training.

Of course, there have been skilled and clear-thinking teachers throughout the ages who have applied formal aims in their teaching. This has, however, occurred unconsciously, unsystematically and fragmentarily. One of the most essential purposes of the FACE project is to define the formal aims in a way such that teachers can adopt them generally. Because the development of thinking primarily takes place in the communication of teaching content between the teacher and the student, the aims have to be mastered using almost the same application as a professional football player needs to master his technique.

The Use of Questions in Teaching

The focus of attention on the critical aspects of thinking takes place mostly in the same way as in everyday life, that is, with questions. For this purpose we have developed forms of questions that correspond to the formal aims. When the variables in the form of questions are given a content, they become actual questions. First, teachers put these questions to the students. Then the students are gradually trained to put similar questions to themselves, the teachers and to each other. These question formulae are also translated into the foreign languages taught.

It is not necessary for the students to be familiar with the epistemological background of these question formulae. It is more important for them to perceive the questions as justified, sensible, often necessary and always clarifying. Students' interest in the question formulae is expected to increase with age. We do not yet know how far we can proceed in the teaching of the rationale for questions.

One general characteristic of this project is that it does not offer many detailed and exact methodological instructions; the main emphasis is on the aims, which we feel is the most important aspect of an activity as diverse and complex as thinking.

How Can the Development of Thinking be Studied?

The Initial Phases of the Experiment

Whether setting the formal aims as conscious goals of teaching promotes the development of thinking and other cognitive activities is of course a question that has to be asked. Mere belief in the fact that things will happen that way is no proof that they really will happen. Even though this programme includes inferences drawn directly from epistemological facts which do not have to be—and often cannot be—empirically tested, the final result has to be checked with the help of experience. Experiments carried out in schools constitute the second phase of the FACE project.

The project was officially approved as a part of the development programmes of the National Board of General Education in 1985. The experiment was started in three schools, and 25 teachers participated in it. Students were between 13 and 15 years of age.

While the formal aims were developed theoretically, lectures were given to teachers, and experiments were carried out with them. Teachers made decisions with the supervisor of the experiment on some limited subject matter, and attempted to realize the formal aims in their teaching, later reporting their experiments in writing.

This initial phase has primarily consisted of teacher training and experimentation. Despite numerous lectures and about 400 pages of text on the formal aims at their disposal, teachers have found the task difficult. We feel that the main reason for this is that they have not had the required epistemological training to prepare them for absorbing such topics. Teachers' interest has nevertheless been maintained, and they have observed progress in their thinking themselves.

Further Experimentation

The second phase constitutes experiments in certain classrooms which were initiated in the spring of 1989. Three experimental classes (students of 13–17 years old) have been formed in the participating schools. In these classes, attempts are made to follow the formal aims of cognitive education in almost all teaching. There will of course be differences in emphasis in the various school subjects, but as a whole the system of formal aims will be the same for all teachers. The experimental teaching will be continued for three years.

In the development of thinking, it is not feasible to restrict the activity to any given school subject: it must be carried out in all subjects. The youngest students in the experimental classes are at present 13 years old, but the experiment will reveal whether it is possible to extend it to younger age-groups.

It is not possible to attain fast results with a system following the formal aims. Progress can be achieved only by many years of work.

Aims of the Experiment

The aim of the experiment is to obtain a clear and reliable answer to at least the following questions:

(i) How should the formal goal statements be presented in order that they be explicit and easy to adopt?

(ii) How well can teachers learn the formal aims and apply them in their teaching?

(iii) How do teachers use question formulae corresponding to the formal aims in their teaching?

(iv) How well do students learn to use the same question formulae?

(v) How do the different aspects of students' thinking change when the formal aims are applied in almost all teaching?

(vi) What demands does the development of thinking make on teaching materials and methods?

(vii) What effect does the development of thinking have on learning outcomes? (The improvement in learning outcomes and the development of thinking are not the same thing in today's schools.)

It is obvious that the study will produce even more information besides that considered so far.

Research Method

Certain parts of the lessons in the experimental classes will be videotaped for three years. The teachers will not generally know which of their lessons are to be videotaped. It is our intention that all the teaching given under the project's auspices will be experimental. The teachers will not be given any methodological advice beforehand, but they are expected to achieve the formal aims at their own discretion.

The video material will be analysed as soon as it reaches the researchers, according to a programme that has been planned in advance. The purpose is to find out how the teaching of the formal aims takes place in practice. Teachers are also given immediate feedback so that they can change their teaching methods by themselves. Follow-up is of course focused on students' reactions as well as observations of changes in their thinking.

Expected Outcomes of the Study

The outcome of the FACE project will include the following:

> (i) the epistemological fundamentals for the formal aims of cognitive education; a mimeographed tentative draft of these has already been made available to teachers.
> (ii) goal statements presenting the formal aims of knowledge. At present there are about 80 statements presented in the mimeograph; this number may seem large, but the statements are closely connected to each other and in fact constitute subcategories.
> (iii) question formulae dealing with the structure, rationale and other formal factors of knowledge. These have proved difficult for teachers and will have to be reformulated.
> (iv) application instructions for each subject. The formal aims are in principle content-free and emphasis differs when the formal aims are studied in the context of different content-knowledge areas.

Once the results of the project have been evaluated, they could have a positive effect on teacher training, curricula and teaching materials. The experiment is extensive and will take many years, but we feel that a comprehensive and reliable picture of the development of thinking by formal aims cannot be obtained without considerable time and effort.

Note

1. The FACE project is guided and assisted by a group chaired by Veikko Lepistö, Head of Department at the NBGE.

   The author, formerly headmaster of a Helsinki experimental secondary school, was responsible for establishing the principles of the project, contained in seven volumes in Finnish, comprising more than 400 pages. These have been used as the basis for the teachers' in-service training programme which he has planned and supervised.

The principal academic authority on the project was Ilkka Niiniluoto, Professor of Theoretical Philosophy at the University of Helsinki, assisted by two researchers, Patrick Scheinin from the University's Department of Teacher Education, and Jouko Mehtäläinen.

III

The Application of Cognitive Knowledge to the Teaching of Thinking

Critical Thinking Across Multiple Intelligences

MINDY L. KORNHABER and HOWARD GARDNER

Project Zero, Harvard University,
Cambridge, Massachusetts, United States

A Glance at Three Critical Thinkers

When the American historian Barbara Tuchman began *The Guns of August*, her account of the beginning of World War I, she recognized she had "a spectacular subject" (Tuchman, 1981, p. 21). She eagerly delved into primary source materials, among them soldiers' memoirs, generals' accounts, and documents in government archives. Although she knew that most of these materials reflected some degree of bias and that some were even untrue, this, too, was data for her: "Even an untrustworthy source is valuable for what it reveals about the personality of the author, especially if he is an actor in the events" (*ibid.*, p. 19). In addition to extracting facts from primary sources, the historian rented a Renault and drove over the battlegrounds of Belgium, Luxembourg and Northern France. This helped her to get a sense of the terrain, how it looked to the soldiers and generals who had fought there, and how it might have affected the course of events.

By the end of this process, Tuchman hadn't compiled a book but had only accumulated thousands of details, each recorded on its own index card. And, "to offer a mass of undigested facts, of names not identified and places not located is of no use to the reader and is simple laziness on the part of the author" (*ibid.*, p. 18). For Tuchman, the first task was to reconstruct the chronology, which she regarded as "the spine of history" (*ibid.*, p. 9) and essential for understanding cause and effect in her discipline. Still, this ordering of facts, however exact, did not dictate which details to present. According to Tuchman, the crucial task was choosing among them: "Selection is everything; it is the test of the historian" (*ibid.*, p. 73).

By what method did this selection occur? Tuchman did not work from hypotheses. As she put it, "Prefabricated systems make me suspicious, and science applied to history makes me wince" (*ibid.*, p. 22). In her view, history could not adhere to systems or patterns, since "one of its basic data is the human soul". Therefore, to select the details, "the conventional historian, at least one concerned with truth, not propaganda, will try honestly to let his 'data' speak for themselves, but data which are shut up in prearranged boxes are helpless. Their nuances have no voice" (*ibid.*, p. 248).

Thus, Tuchman's work required resourcefulness in collecting facts. Yet it also demanded skill in interpreting the thoughts and actions of history's often unpredictable players and rendering these into an accurate, coherent and convincing narrative.

While Robert Bakker, an unorthodox palaeontologist, is also a resourceful fact-gatherer, he goes about making meaning from facts in a way fundamentally different from Tuchman. As a scientist, his data and inquiries are shaped by theories. That is, he begins with the current understanding of dinosaur evolution, puts forth an alternative integrated account of what might have happened, and then uses a variety of empirical, experimental and argumentative evidence to support his theory. According to Bakker, a good theory does not distort the facts. Instead, "it's a verbal picture of how things might work, how a system in nature might organize things—atoms and molecules, species and ecosystems" (Bakker, 1986, p. 27).

Much of Bakker's work has developed from his doubts about a traditional theory that dinosaurs were "dimwitted", maladapted, "swamp-bound monsters of sluggish disposition" (*ibid.*, p. 15). Given that there were hundreds of species of dinosaurs and that these comprised the predominant large land animals for at least 130 million years, Bakker thought the extinct beasts should be viewed not as symbols of obsolescence but as an evolutionary success story. Using both new and existing evidence, he has been able to generate original theories to justify this claim.

The traditional notions about dinosaurs arise in part from their classification as cold-blooded reptiles. However, according to Bakker, "No one, either in the nineteenth century or the twentieth, has ever built a persuasive case proving that dinosaurs as a whole were more like reptilian crocodiles than warm-blooded birds" (*ibid.*, p. 27). Bakker believes the cold-blooded label stuck so long only because "there are just not enough sceptical minds to . . . ask the embarrassing question, 'How do you know the label is right?'" (*ibid.*).

Armed with his doubt about dinosaurs' cold-bloodedness, the paleontologist began to investigate differences between cold- and warm-blooded animals. He knew that—with the notable exception of human beings—warm-blooded animals mature much more quickly than cold-blooded ones. Using evidence from the rings found in fossil bones and teeth, similar to those found in trees, he saw that dinosaurs often exhibited quick, warm-blooded growth. Bakker and Armand de Ricqles, a French paleontologist, independently found that thin sections of dinosaur bone, when viewed through a microscope, revealed a spongy texture that cold-blooded creatures lack (*ibid.*, p. 347).

Bakker knew as well that cold-blooded creatures cannot sustain any degree of speed, and their slow metabolisms result in gaits that are proportionately small for the size of their body. This led him to investigate fossilized dinosaur footprints. Using a mathematical formula, Bakker could calculate the speed of a dinosaur from its size and the length of its strides. These calculations indicated that *Tyrannosaurus rex* may have travelled as fast as 45 miles per hour, far too fast for any chilly-blooded beast.

Paleontologists conduct research not only in the field and the laboratory but also in museums. While searching through specimen bins in a museum's basement, Bakker found a skull of a small cousin of *Tyrannosaurus rex* that had never really been studied. It looked very similar to those of birds, a class of animal known to be quite ancient, and in which the same sort of hollows are needed to cool the brain in these high-metabolism, warm-blooded creatures. Based on this and his other findings, Bakker has made a persuasive case that dinosaurs should be reclassified as warm-blooded. He and his colleague, Peter Galton, have also argued that birds should be grouped together with dinosaurs, from which they appear to have descended, into an entirely new class of vertebrates (Bakker and Galton, 1974).

Unlike historians or paleontologists, composers have no written or physical records to which they must adhere. They are not bound by the historian's actors. They do not build or rebut scientific theories. And yet, despite this lack of "evidence" and method, composers can also make their thoughts cohere and can create messages which bear meanings for themselves and others. They do so by organizing pitch, rhythm and the timbre of various instruments, which constitute the "medium" or "symbol system" in which they work.

In composing *Les Noces* (*Svadebka*), Igor Stravinsky had to devise a unique instrumental ensemble to accompany a new stage form with which he planned to represent a Russian village wedding. *Les Noces* was not a ballet or an opera. Instead, it was "an amalgam of ballet and dramatic cantata that he was himself unable to describe" other than as "Russian Choreographic Scenes" (Craft and Harkins, 1972, p. 23).

Stravinsky travelled from Switzerland to Kiev in 1914 to locate a collection of Russian folk songs from which he could cull a libretto. By the end of that year, he had composed a musical sketch for the first of the piece's four tableaux. Within three years, all of the music for *Les Noces* was completed. However, orchestrating the music—establishing the sonority of the work—was a problem that the composer would return to again and again for nearly a decade.

At first, Stravinsky planned to use voices and a large orchestra, though one largely devoid of percussion. However, in early January 1915 the composer had scored the piece for voices, woodwinds, brass, percussion, and bowed and plucked instruments including balalaikas and guitars. Soon after, he replaced these plucked instruments with other plucked instruments: a harpsichord and a string quintet playing pizzicato. Then, at the end of January 1915, Stravinsky first heard the cimbalom, the sound of which compelled him to rescore *Les Noces* to include this large, hammered string instrument (*ibid.*)

By 1919, the composer still faced problems of staging and sonority. At that time, Stravinsky wrote to his friend, the conductor Ernest Ansermet, "I do not know what to do with the '*Noces*' " (*ibid.*, p. 25). He wondered if it could be staged without scenery, but with "pianola, harmonium, two cimbaloms, percussion, singers and conductor on the stage, together with the dancers". Nor was the orchestration settled in 1921, when he wrote to a music publisher, "I am in effect completely reworking the instrumentation for a new ensemble of winds, percussion, and one or two parts for piano" (*ibid.*, pp. 25–26).

Only in April 1923 was the orchestration to *Les Noces* finalized. The composition had crystallized around the sound of hammered instruments: four pianos and an array of pitched and unpitched percussion instruments. With this ensemble, Stravinsky had arrived at a sonority that Robert Craft described as reminiscent of the "pots and pans as well as drums, tambourines, cymbals [that] were bashed, hammered, clapped together, rattled and rung throughout the ceremony and celebration in order to drive away evil spirits" (*ibid.*, p. 26). Stravinsky noted that this solution "would fulfil all my conditions. It would be at the same time perfectly homogeneous, perfectly impersonal and perfectly mechanical" (Stravinsky and Craft, 1962, p. 118). These qualities suited the "roleless", symbolic nature of the ritual that was being portrayed.

Critical Thinking: One Form or Many?

In these examples, we have observed highly professional experts thinking in a deep way about their subject matter. In that each expert made analyses, judgements and evaluations all the time, it seems legitimate to speak of his or her engagement in critical thinking. Yet, is the thinking that has been sketched here all of a piece? Is Tuchman's selection of detail and her attention to the nuance of human written expression somehow equivalent to Bakker's hypotheses and interpretation of fossil evidence? If the thinking is different, is it just a matter of inductive versus deductive logic?

Would either of these forms of logic, or some combination thereof, have been adequate—or even appropriate—in Stravinsky's quest for the apposite instrumentation?

In Western societies, a long tradition posits a single form of logic and, by extension, a single form of thinking. This tradition begins with Plato. We see in his writings the elevation of abstract reasoning processes; mathematics was regarded as the gateway to all "higher" understanding. Likewise, Descartes held arithmetic and geometry in a privileged rank because the thinking involved in these disciplines was at least subject to doubt and most independent of external influences. The supremacy of abstract thought may have reached its apogee in the early twentieth century with the work of Bertrand Russell and Alfred North Whitehead. Russell attempted to express and solve philosophical issues in terms of symbolic logic, and thereby render them independent from experience. He noted that "People have discovered how to make reasoning symbolic as it is in Algebra, so that deductions can be effected by mathematical rules" (Russell, 1917/1963, p. 60).

> (i) Pure mathematics consists entirely of assertions to the effect that if such and such a proposition is true of anything, then such and such another proposition is true of that thing. It is essential not to discuss whether the first proposition is really true, and not to mention what the anything is of which it is supposed to be true. (*ibid.*, p. 59)

The weight of this long tradition is apparent in the predominant role that logical-mathematical thinking continues to play in our schools. Most schools emphasize the development of mathematical logic and those forms of language which conform to propositional arguments. Most standardized tests administered by schools attempt to document precisely this range of thought.

However, we strongly disagree with those who maintain that genuine thinking inheres only within this narrow range. While the utility of logical-mathematical thinking is evident in Bakker's work, all too often it is used as a paradigm for thought in all domains, media, and symbol systems. It is the burden of this paper to show that logical-mathematical intelligence represents but one of the ways of thinking, though perhaps one which has had special importance in the recent history of Western thought.

In our view, there are different forms of thought and reasoning. These forms are associated with different symbol systems (language v. pictures), purposes (aesthetic v. scientific) or different cultural values (to understand or prove; to demonstrate or inspire). The perspective we maintain also has a respectably long historical tradition. Less than a century after Descartes, Vico criticized the elder philosopher for focusing on mathematics and science to the exclusion of art, history, law and other areas of knowledge.

He also disputed Descartes' notion that only one form of inquiry was valid for every discipline of study. The German philosopher, Wilhelm Dilthey, rejected Platonic ideals as well as Cartesian notions of absolute standards built on mental speculations. He held that knowledge was grasped through life's rich and varied experiences, including the arts, legal and religious codes, and interactions with other people. Ernst Cassirer, roughly a contemporary of Bertrand Russell, believed that the symbols of logic and mathematics did foster precise and generative thought. However, he maintained that thought also functioned through the symbols of religion, myth, the arts, language and history. Cassirer held that human beings required a wealth of diverse symbols to capture and communicate experience.

When we look again at our three experts, it is true that cause and effect, and even propositional thinking, might be at work in all of these cases. For example, it is possible to imagine Stravinsky saying, "Aha! If I use percussion and four pianos, then I can achieve the impersonal effect I'm after!" However, we do not conclude from this that such propositions are framed by one overarching form of thought. Though the insights of composers may be expressed in verbal terms—many articulate musicians (and their biographers) have given us written accounts of their efforts— their skill cannot be obtained or executed via words. It must come through the grasp of relationships and extensions implicit in particular arrangements of pitch, rhythm and timbre.

We assert that an analogous situation obtains for other disciplines. The use of logical-mathematical thinking is generally but one (and not necessarily the most important one) of the ways people conceptualize and carry out their work. Certainly, in roles as diverse as the historian, the paleontologist and the composer, it is an oversimplification to search for only one form of thinking.

In this paper we put forth a quite different approach to issues of thought and cognition. We propose that all unimpaired individuals have the capacity to pose questions and seek solutions, using several intelligences. Each of these intelligences has its own characteristic way of processing information and ideas, and addressing the possibilities generated by different kinds of problems. In short, each has its own form of thought. These forms of thought are rigorous, but they do not necessarily have interesting affinities with induction and deduction in numerical or propositional form. Instead, each exhibits its own characteristic "logic" of implications: a logic derived from understanding the principles and applications of different symbol systems as they are used within a given culture. We believe that these varieties of thinking, as well as the contexts in which they are likely to be expressed or developed, must be taken into account in discussions of intelligence, education and their assessment.

The Conventional View

Though we do not hold to only one form of "intelligence", it is the belief in just such a single entity that has guided traditional thinking about intelligence for much of this century. This tradition began innocently enough. In 1904, at the request of France's Minister of Public Education, Alfred Binet and his associate Théodore Simon, compiled a series of short problems to be used as psychological tests of intelligence for children of different ages. The purpose of these first intelligence tests was to identify schoolchildren who were mildly retarded or otherwise learning-disabled, and to provide them with appropriate remediation. In these tests, trained administrators asked the children brief "practical" questions (e.g. "which is the prettier face?", "which colour is this?") and had them carry out a few ordinary tasks (counting backwards from 20, counting coins). Though a single numerical score was derived from a child's performance, Binet warned against allowing this score to reify an issue as complex as human intelligence. Binet also warned against using the scores to establish a mental ranking of all students. Furthermore, he made no conjectures about a score's origins and believed they could be improved with education (Binet and Simon, 1905; Gould, 1981).

However, Stanford University's Lewis Terman soon revised the test and put it to uses its originator never intended. In an effort to standardize scoring, Terman added new test items and reassigned many of the original questions—which Binet had determined were appropriate for a particular age level—to older or younger children. Terman also helped to devise tests that could be given in mass administrations. Unlike Binet, he called for the universal testing of schoolchildren and declared that children's intelligence test scores were largely immutable (Terman, 1916, 1923). Thus, soon after Binet's death in 1911, intelligence tests, in a standardized American guise, regularly served not as a means just to identify and help the disabled but as a label, a point at which both normal and learning-disabled children's abilities and potential could be fixed (Gould, 1981).

Considering the importance that such tests have had in determining "intelligence", it is well worth noting that intelligence as manifested by an IQ score differs markedly from intelligence as it is ordinarily described in lay language and as it is embodied in active adult experts. An IQ test presents questions requiring the test to supply a short answer within a very limited space of time. However, we say that Stravinsky, Bakker and Tuchman, our "real thinkers", carved out their own projects and then pursued these over an extended period. While these same individuals worked within a discipline they found compelling, an IQ test does not necessarily engage the test taker in any issues of interest (Gardner, 1983; Sternberg, 1984, 1988). Furthermore, in an intelligence test, the test taker needs little in the way of in-depth knowledge, which at times may even interfere with the kind of glib facility rewarded by these instruments. In contrast, we saw that the thinking evinced by Tuchman, Bakker and Stravinsky employed and expanded upon information and techniques that had evolved over centuries in their respective disciplines.

The divorce between thinking (assumed to be very general) and content (assumed to be an interfering variable) was supported early on in the development of intelligence testing. Alfred Binet's measures employed a "shotgun" method: "It matters very little what the tests are, so long as they are numerous" (Gould, 1981, p. 149). His assessment of intelligence was based on a variety of questions and tests whose content had little relevance to formal school subjects. A dozen years later, Charles Spearman, the British psychologist and inventor of factor analysis, formalized this separation between content and thinking with his idea of "the indifference of the indicator" (Spearman, 1923). He asserted that one general intelligence, or "g", existed. To Spearman, "g" represented the ability to recognize relationships and correlations. Though he allowed that a variety of symbolic media might be used to identify "g", most developers of intelligence tests tacitly assumed the centrality of (in our terms) linguistic and logical-mathematical forms of thinking, with a touch of spatial reasoning tossed in. And, it was these forms of thinking that they sought to measure. This limited conception of thinking and disregard for content are still prevalent features within the intelligence testing industry, though several psychologists have offered statistical analyses of intelligence tests that indicate that thinking is neither content-free, nor is it adequately represented as a single entity (Guilford, 1967; Thurstone, 1935, 1938).

The Theory of Multiple Intelligences

One characteristic of statistically based claims concerning the nature of intelligence, and the form or forms of thinking which underlie it, is that they are founded on correlations within and between results of intelligence tests. Test developers generally try to establish these high correlations in order to give credibility (in more technical terms, reliability and validity) to their instruments. However, given a multitude of tests and test takers, it is possible to establish different kinds of correlations, depending upon how the results are analysed. One analysis can yield a single underlying correlation, justifying the existence of "g". Yet another statistically valid approach to the same scores may result in two or more clusters of correlations, or group factors, indicating that more than one thinking process (or "vector of mind") may be operating (Thurstone, 1935).

It is possible to take a very different tack. Rather than rely significantly on tests and their intercorrelations, Gardner decided to examine empirical information concerning human cognition from a number of disparate sources. These encompassed biological, psychological and cross-cultural data. In particular, he looked at what is known about the development of symbol-using capacities in normal children and gifted children. He also studied the breakdown of cognitive capacities in brain-damaged individuals.

Based upon these investigations, Gardner formulated his theory of multiple intelligences. This theory, discussed in detail in *Frames of Mind* (1983), proposes seven relatively autonomous areas of human cognition, or "intelligences". In the theory, an intelligence is defined as an ability, or set of abilities, that enables an individual to solve problems and fashion products that are of consequence on one or more cultural contexts. Intelligence is conceptualized not as a "thing", but rather as a potential, the presence of which allows an individual access to forms of thinking appropriate to specific kinds of content.

In order for an ability to qualify as an intelligence, it must meet at least several of the following criteria. These include its possible isolation by virtue of brain damage; its presence in special populations such as *idiots savants* or prodigies; its rootedness in evolutionary history; the existence of one or more core information-processing operations or mechanisms; evidence from psychometric findings; evidence from experimental psychological tasks; a distinctive developmental path including one or more definable "expert" end-states; susceptibility to encoding within a symbol system, and cross-cultural usage.

Using this definition and set of criteria, it is possible to speak of at least seven different intelligences: linguistic, logical-mathematical, musical, spatial, bodily kinesthetic, interpersonal and intrapersonal. While we will describe each of these seven separately, it is rare to find any of them operating in isolation, except in cases of gross pathology. It is only through the combination of these intelligences that we can account for a relatively complete range of abilities and end-states exhibited across human cultures. Furthermore, though we will describe seven intelligences, it may well be that a persuasive case can be made for others. This list is not meant to be exclusive or exhaustive. Rather, it simply represents the evidence (and arguments) that we have marshalled up to this point.

Of the seven intelligences, *linguistic intelligence* is the most widely studied. Neurobiological evidence for its existence includes studies of normal language processing, as well as studies of language impairment in brain-damaged individuals. The core, information-processing operations of this intelligence encompass semantic, phonological, syntactic and pragmatic competences. Within a short span of years, all normal children develop competence in these core functions, though the degree of sophistication and the applications to which individuals ultimately put this intelligence vary greatly.

We see linguistic intelligence manifested in the work of, among others, poets, lawyers and writers. For example, when Barbara Tuchman combined words, coined phrases, and added rhetorical flourishes to weave together historical narratives, she exploited various aspects of her linguistic intelligence; she was thinking and problem solving in the medium of natural language.

Musical intelligence, through its core operations of pitch, rhythm and timbre, enables an individual to make and derive meaning from the organization of sound. Like linguistic intelligence, there is broad neurological support for the autonomy of this "frame of mind", as witnessed in musical prodigies, autistic individuals, and studies of the brain which reveal that the processing centres for music are distinct from the auditory channels of language. Unlike linguistic intelligence, in which all normal individuals develop serviceable skills, musical development is more variable. In Western societies, fewer individuals use this intelligence for "making sense", and this ability rarely reaches high levels without some degree of formal instruction.

Musical intelligence plays a central role in the work of instrumentalists, singers, conductors, composers and audio engineers. We see it in action in Stravinsky's understanding of rhythm and pitch, which made it possible for him to compose the music for *Les Noces* as well as several other works within a three-year period. The problem unique to *Les Noces* concerned sonority. Only in thinking through the possibilities afforded by a large orchestra, a small ensemble with plucked instruments, and other combinations, was Stravinsky able to establish a felicitous instrumentation for *Les Noces*.

Musical ability is often linked to mathematical and logical skills. However, there is ample evidence among prodigies and other special populations to justify it as a separate intelligence. Further, unlike music, *logical-mathematical* ability has no particular link to the auditory/oral realm. From Piaget, we know that the development of logical-mathematical intelligence begins in explorations and orderings of the world of objects. By the age of four or five, children understand that an object in a series can correspond to a numeral one two or three, and have begun acquiring the core operation of numbering. Eventually, they can take the concept of number and the operations performed on numerals out of the realm of objects and represent them by a variety of symbols (Piaget, 1965; Piaget and Inhelder, 1969).

In its higher reaches, mathematics and logic are little concerned with objects or numbers; as we saw in the case of Bertrand Russell, both explore chains of reasoning and the links between them on a purely abstract plane. Unlike mathematicians and logicians, scientists, financial analysts, accountants, engineers and most computer programmers use these abstract forms of logical-mathematical intelligence as tools for work which ultimately relates back to some physical reality.

The core operations of *spatial intelligence* include accurate perception of forms or objects, the ability to recreate these without reference to their physical stimuli, and the ability to manipulate or modify such images in space. Though logical-mathematical and spatial knowledge both grow from perception of objects, neurological studies have shown that the brain is more "dedicated" in spatial intelligence; this form of thought is largely dependent on the functioning of the right posterior region of the cortex. We also find evidence to support its existence through its isolation in Nadia, an autistic individual who could nonetheless draw with great accuracy; in prodigies, such as Picasso; and in a large number of child chess wizards for whom powerful and flexible spatial representation is essential. Many intelligence tests have noted the extent to which spatial abilities are quite independent of abilities to deal with language or with other conventional symbol systems.

Though we most typically associate this intelligence with artistic skills, in Western cultures growth in drawing ability for most individuals ceases at about the age of 12 (Gardner, 1980; Lowenfeld and Brittain, 1982) unless external support and tutoring is provided. Yet, we should also appreciate the diverse uses of spatial intelligence exhibited by aeroplane pilots, architects, navigators, engineers and surgeons. Such thinking was at work as well in Bakker's ability to recognize the similarity between a bird's and a dinosaur's skull.

Bodily kinesthetic intelligence is the ability to solve problems or to fashion products, using part or all of one's body. This form of intelligence features as its core operations the skilful control of one's own body and of objects in the world. Though movement involves a complex co-ordination of neural, muscular and perceptual systems, the neurobiological focus in most humans is the left hemisphere, and the corresponding, dominant right side of the body. We see support for the autonomy of this intelligence in *apraxias*—injuries or disorders in the left hemisphere that impede bodily kinesthetic activities—even though an individual remains largely unimpaired in cognitive and physical skills.

The bodily kinesthetic category clashes with traditional Western notions of intelligence. However, in juggling, gymnastics, ballet, or building machines, there is an intricate sequence of action that requires problem solving, planning and practice no less than that demanded by other kinds of human endeavours. We witness this intelligence in dancers and choreographers whose work entails thinking in the medium of their bodies, imagining what is feasible, expressive and appropriate with regard to a specific problem. The American choreographer, Merce Cunningham, provides us with an example of such thinking:

> The basis for the dances is movement, that is, the human body moving in time-space. The scale for this movement ranges from being quiescent to the

maximum amount of movement (physical activity) a person can produce at any given moment. The ideas of the dance come both from the movement, and are in the movement. (John-Steiner, 1985, p. 20)

Last in our inventory are two personal intelligences:

Intrapersonal intelligence consists of a core capacity permitting individuals to access their own feelings, and alongside this to distinguish among different feelings, This intelligence also enables people to comprehend their wishes, desires, goals, strengths, weaknesses and even their own particular profile of intelligences. When fully developed, it comes to play an organizing or executive role *vis-à-vis* one's other intelligences: a sort of "central intelligence agency". It allows people to understand their feelings and the profile of their own intelligences, and enables them to use such knowledge effectively.

Interpersonal intelligence involves a core capacity to notice and make distinctions among the feelings, behaviours, motivations and related attributes of other individuals. In developed form, interpersonal intelligence features a sensitivity to the full gamut of traits and understandings displayed by all the individuals with whom one comes into contact.

Though interpersonal and intrapersonal intelligences are clearly linked in everyday life, each has its own distinctive development and pathology. Essential to the neurobiology of personal intelligences are the frontal lobes. Damage to this area of the brain will not necessarily hinder a person's performance in an IQ test, though it can radically depress a person's sense of purpose, motivation and his or her responses to other people. We see isolation of interpersonal intelligence in its absence in some autistic children. Intrapersonal pathology is exhibited in some psychopathic disorders in which people may show great awareness of others' motivations and intentions, without being able to sort out their own.

Keen interpersonal intelligence is one mark of gifted teachers and parents. It is also essential to political and religious leaders. Ronald Reagan's popularity as president of the United States was dependent on his ability to understand the importance of, and to some extent exemplify, widespread American sentiments. The work of Mother Theresa is achieved in part through her ability to appreciate—and get others to appreciate—the dignity and the humanity of the poor.

Intrapersonal intelligence was evinced by Freud's self-understanding and in the way he marshalled his personal, linguistic and logical-mathematical capacities to establish the new discipline of psychoanalysis. It is evident, too, among certain artists and writers, such as Marcel Proust and Virginia Woolf, here describing her feelings before and after receiving the inheritance that enabled her to work steadily on her own writing:

... always to be doing work that one did not wish to do, and to do it like a slave, flattering and fawning, not always necessarily perhaps, but it seemed necessary and the stakes were too great to run risks; and then the thought of that one gift which it was death to hide—a small one but dear to the possessor—perishing and with it myself, my soul—all this became like a rust eating away the bloom of the spring . . . However, as I say, my aunt died; and whenever I change a ten-shilling note a little of that rust and corrosion is rubbed off; fear and bitterness go . . . So imperceptibly I found myself adopting a new attitude towards the other half of the human race. It was absurd to blame any class or any sex, as a whole. Great bodies of people are never responsible for what they do. They are driven by instincts which are not within their control. They too, the patriarchs, the professors, had endless difficulties, terrible drawbacks to contend with. (Woolf, 1929, p. 38)

Education and the Development of Intelligences

We have shown that there exist different forms of intelligence, each apparently exhibiting its own characteristic kinds of development, breakdown, and expert forms of thinking. It might nonetheless be the case that these forms of thought are closely linked to one another, as Piaget maintained, with sophistication in one intelligence being tightly yoked to sophistication in the remaining intelligences.

In fact, however, empirical work presents a different picture. The newer lessons of child development indicate that, though people do progress through stages in their understanding and ability to employ their cognitive skills, this progress is not as synchronous as Piaget believed; instead, it varies across the intelligences (Damon, 1989; Gardner and Wolf, 1983). Moreover, the existence of a particular strength in one intelligence simply does not predict comparable strength (or weakness) in other domains (Feldman, 1986; Gardner, 1983). While language development proceeds to a rather high level in nearly all normal individuals, and the regular demands of social interaction enable most people to achieve workmanlike responses from their interpersonal intelligence, the degree to which individuals can exploit their other intelligences is more variable, and more dependent on study, tutoring, or other external supports.

The extent to which such support exists no doubt reflects, at least in part, the values of the surrounding culture and the presence of adult states which require or foster the use of an intelligence (Feldman, 1980). Different cultures highlight different intelligences and combinations of intelligence. We see examples of this among certain African tribes in which virtually every member is expected to sing well and be able to dance (Messenger, 1958). And, in pre-revolutionary China, not only were the scholarly classes adept at calligraphy, poetry and a Chinese form of chess but, in keeping with traditional Confucian values, there was widespread achievement in painting, and playing a musical instrument (Lowry, Wolf and Gardner, 1988).

Given these examples, one could still ask why should we consider devoting our energies to developing those intelligences upon which Western culture seems to place relatively limited demands? Why should we consider expanding the roles they play in our schools?

One reason to broaden our approach is the great number of children who never "connect" to school. Education that is largely limited to linguistic and logical-mathematical thinking ignores the fact that many students find problematic those subjects traditionally embraced by these two intelligences. By restricting education to logical-mathematical and linguistic thinking, we limit opportunities to engage students' minds and to foster student achievement. For example, among youngsters who may not excel in traditional school subjects are those who might be intrigued by subjects rich with spatial thinking such as architecture, painting or paleontology. Those with a forte in the personal intelligences might establish stronger ties to learning if they could have regular access to drama, writing and other disciplines that drew upon their strengths (Gulbenkian, 1982; Sarason, 1983).

A second reason for schools to expand their approach is that the intelligences we have sketched represent not just contents but ways of thinking. If we allow opportunities for students to learn through other channels—for example, if we could call upon their spatial intelligences, via architecture, painting and paleontology to teach history and biology—we might foster more widespread learning in traditional school disciplines (Gardner, in preparation; Gulbenkian Foundation, 1982; Walters and Gardner, 1985).

We should also keep in mind that, in the West, the hegemony of linguistic and logical-mathematical thinking over conceptions of intelligence and schooling has clouded the reality that these two forms of thought, alone or in combination, cannot meet the variety of tasks and challenges that human beings confront. This is especially true for problems that occur outside school walls (Gardner, 1990; Sarason, 1983; Sternberg, 1988; Walters and Gardner, 1985). Therefore, not only does the two-pronged method fail to equip many students for academic success, it also falls short of fulfilling schools' oft-stated mission: "preparation for life". Such a narrow form of education hinders not just "average" or disadvantaged" students, but may even alienate those very few students who are preparing for academic or highly intellectual careers (Jackson, 1968). Our opening sketches illustrate that critical thinkers at work in the real world often require a wide array of thinking capacities.

In Barbara Tuchman's work as a historian, it is clear that linguistic intelligence, though essential, would have been insufficient. In her reflections on history, we see the importance of interpersonal intelligence in interpreting the often conflicting written records. Tuchman wrote, "Sympathy is essential to the understanding of motive. Without sympathy and imagination the historian can copy figures from a tax roll forever . . . but he will never know or be able to portray the people who paid the taxes" (Tuchman, 1981, p. 47). Furthermore, to comprehend accounts of battles and portray them more clearly, Tuchman employed spatial intelligence:

> [By driving] I learned the discomfort of the Belgian *pavé* and discovered, in the course of losing my way almost permanently in a tangle of country roads . . . why a British motorcycle dispatch rider in 1914 had taken three hours to cover twenty-five miles. Clearly, owing to the British officers' preference for country houses, he had not been able to find Headquarters either. (*ibid.*, p. 20)

In Robert Bakker's work, logical-mathematical thinking is used in the service of interpreting dinosaur strides and extrapolating from this the possibility that these creatures were warm-blooded. It is possible his hypothesis might have resulted only from reading about dinosaur tracks, and that his own thinking could be presented through linguistic and logical-mathematical means. However, Bakker is an exceptional anatomist. He relied on his spatial thinking to see the implications of certain skeletal features on the musculature and potential speed of various species. This intelligence also enables him to illustrate his ideas with drawings of charging and jumping dinosaurs. Occasionally, he uses scale models of dinosaurs and, calling upon bodily kinesthetic intelligence, trudges them through boxes of damp sand to demonstrate his findings.

In order to compose *Les Noces*, Stravinsky engaged more than just his extraordinary musical intelligence. His sensitivity to language and to how its accents and those of music needed to fit together, are partly responsible for the piece's ability to communicate. For this particular work, Stravinsky called upon spatial intelligence to arrive at a proposed staging of the piece. His ability to realize the music relied heavily on bodily kinesthetic skills necessary to playing the piano, without which he claimed he could not compose at all.

In each of these cases we have seen how several intelligences in combination made possible these three individuals' achievements. However, we also saw that each person exploited his or her intelligences in different ways for different ends. Thus, for example, Tuchman used spatial intelligence to get a grasp of battlefields and to understand the impact they had on historical events; Bakker's spatial intelligence helped him to visualize the structure of dinosaur anatomy and to hypothesize about their metabolic rates; Stravinsky engaged this same form of intelligence to imagine which placement of musicians, singers and dancers might best express the pageant of a traditional peasant wedding.

These examples help to illustrate that, outside of school, individuals call upon various forms and applications of thinking. We believe that similar opportunities for diverse and flexibly used thinking ought to be encouraged in education, both to foster more links between children and schools, as well as to prepare children for the world beyond school. Yet, it appears that the decontextualized settings in which most education takes place may frustrate such opportunities.

Thinking in Context

Unlike most modern school-bound learners, our three critical thinkers not only engaged more than their linguistic and logical-mathematical intelligences, each of them also worked within rich contexts. They were deeply interested in their subject matter; they were free to "enter the field" to get information about it, and they could also consult with colleagues. In addition, they were able to determine their own tactics, organize their materials and present their work in a manner they found congenial.

It is worth noting here that, prior to the advent of mass formal education, most youngsters learned in highly contextualized settings. Often, they were apprenticed in some trade or skill where they observed and had ready access to useful adult roles. Apprenticeships incorporated regular and often well-defined stages of hands-on learning through which the apprentice achieved mastery. They also provided frequent and informal feedback on the learner's progress. We regard these features as highly useful, and believe they should become part of the education of every child. At present, however, one is likely to encounter vestiges of apprentice methods only in progressive schools, vocational education, and (paradoxically) graduate training.

For those few youngsters who attended school before the era of mass education, their studies encompassed disciplines that were often central to the life of the surrounding community. With the possible exception of religious communities, such meaningful contexts are rarely afforded to schoolchildren today. While neither schools nor apprenticeships were likely to be particularly pleasant, their relevance to the wider world was usually evident.

Alas, the situation for most students in schools today could not be more different. Modern schools often view their primary task as presenting, on a mass scale, disciplines that derive from those formerly available only to the privileged élite, for whom careers in law, the ministry or the university were likely choices. This is not at all meant to denigrate mathematics, foreign languages, philosophy or biology (or the capacities of our young people). It is simply intended to call attention to how decontextualized such content is to the majority of students in our schools. Furthermore, unlike apprentices, these schooled children will rarely benefit from continuing interactions with community members who deploy knowledge or skills in a meaningful way (Adams, 1986; Burgess, 1986b; Gardner, 1990; Polanyi, 1958, pp. 49–65).

Just as the unusually decontextualized setting of school renders its subjects of little interest or consequence to many students, so, too, are the methods by which the lessons are imparted. A classroom "discussion" rarely resembles the communication of ordinary speech (Jackson, 1986); the pace and variety of a lecture are hardly similar to television, radio, computer games or other media with which modern students are surrounded (Sarason, 1983). Though we live in an age where any number of distant events can be conveyed to us almost instantly through diverse media, educators still frequently regard students as empty vessels into which doses of knowledge can enter mainly via rote forms of teaching and learning (Jackson, 1986). Numerous standardized tests are given to provide "objective measures" to teachers and administrators which indicate that these doses have, in fact, been dispensed and stored. This testing continues even though the benefit of such compact, numerical feedback upon students' thinking and problem-solving skills is uncertain, at best (Burgess and Adams, 1985; Gardner, 1991).

If we think of students as empty vessels (or, as we often do in the United States, as "products") it becomes more defensible to maintain a traditional, assembly-line or uniform approach. In schools that use a uniform approach, each child is taught the same thing, in the same way, at the same time, and evaluated with the same bulldozer methods (Gardner, 1987, 1991). The early grades tend to centre on the rote learning of reading, writing and arithmetic, and the drilling of these skills on prescribed problems. Collaboration between students is rare, and hands-on activities are infrequent. There may be opportunities for young children to work in the arts, but these diminish as the student advances (Gardner, 1980; Gulbenkian Foundation, 1982). It is even possible in the early years of schooling for a student to get by on linguistic memory alone. Later, as a child develops, some degree of logical-mathematical intelligence will be demanded. Opportunities to engage other forms of thinking are limited.

Traditional schooling usually yields more uniform results, although it also tends to muffle curiosity and breed lack of interest, both in students who are not particularly gifted in linguistic and logical-mathematical intelligences, and among students who have high abilities in these standard school intelligences (Jackson, 1968). Moreover, traditional schooling diminishes the possibility that students will be able to apply to new problems and settings what they learn at school. Transfer, which is always difficult to effect, requires multiple and varied exposure to problems (Perkins and Salomon, 1987). The back-to-basics movement, which the United States has experienced in the last six years, with its increased emphasis on memorization of facts (National Commission on Excellence, 1983; Hirsch, 1987; Ravitch, 1983) reflects a return to uniform schooling. While potentially useful for notions of national solidarity, this effort largely ignores these long-term effects on learning in exchange for modes and—perhaps spurious—gains on standardized, largely short-answer tests (Cannell, 1987).

In schools that follow a more progressive philosophy, efforts are made to provide a context for learning. Rather than making wide use of short-answer formats and drills, students often work over a period of time on problems that intrigue them. They may pursue these inquiries both on their own and with other students. And, like our three critical thinkers, they can determine the tactics by which to answer their inquiries as well as present their results in a variety of ways (Yeomans, 1981). In progressive schools, there are more opportunities to work in the arts and to use the forms of intelligence we associate with them. There are also more apprentice-like encounters with adults who can model some degree of expertise in a range of skills and disciplines.

Some people may find it unreasonable or unrealistic to expect young children to engage in pint-size versions of what Tuchman, Bakker and Stravinsky have done. Yet, in many pre-schools and "open" classrooms one encounters ample evidence that even young children are very good at carrying out modest projects (Fraiberg, 1987; Paley, 1986; Malkus, Feldman and Gardner, 1988). Issues of school organization tend to obscure the reality that there is absolutely no need for children first to fill up on rote lessons and only later be allowed more running room.

In fact, the allocation of running room has advantages for the development of critical thinking. Because progressive schools give students more extensive and varied exposure to the problems, because they afford opportunities to see how experts solve problems, and because they allow problems to be tackled by a range of intelligences, students are more likely to transfer knowledge and skills from one project to the next (Perkins and Salomon, 1987). In reasonably well-run progressive schools (as opposed to those with unbridled *laissez-faire* tendencies), student outcomes may be much more variable than they are in traditionally oriented schools. Yet, there is a far greater likelihood that students will be imaginative, exercise initiative, and have acquired a desire for lifelong learning (Aiken, 1942).

While neither traditional nor progressive education is found in its pure form, as is no doubt evident by now, we favour the latter orientation, at least in United States education (Gardner, 1987, 1989a). In other societies, which may be guided by long-standing values that are shared by a homogeneous population, traditional schooling may be both appropriate and fruitful. However, in the United States as well as many Western European countries, there is a highly heterogeneous population with diverse sets of values, modes of interaction, and attitudes towards education (Gulbenkian Foundation, 1982; Hargreaves, 1982; Lightfoot, 1978; Ogbu, 1978). We cannot successfully expect that all students will want to, or be able to, master the same material, in the same way and at the same rate. Further, in societies undergoing rapid technological changes, we believe that progressive approaches afford the best means of sustaining educational interest and flexibility. This preference therefore is consonant with societal events and imperatives, as well as with what we have ascertained from research on intelligence and individual development.

Curriculum and Assessment for a Range of Critical Thinking

In keeping with our work in developmental and cognitive psychology, our research unit, Harvard Project Zero, has begun to devise curriculum and assessment techniques that are "intelligence fair" and which make use of richer, more real-life contexts. In standard intelligence testing, a student may be confronted by a relative stranger who poses questions that are at some remove from what the student ordinarily thinks about. Though such tests may detect certain aspects of logical-mathematical and linguistic intelligence, they have little to say about thinking skills in other areas. Another flaw of standardized tests is their lack of "ecological validity" (Gardner, 1991; Ramos-Ford and Gardner, 1990). They do not reveal a person's cognitive style: the degree of persistence, playfulness or boredom which he or she may bring to different problems (Baron, 1987; Sternberg, 1984). Nor do they give insights into how people handle problems with which they have some familiarity and interest, features that enabled Tuchman, Bakker and Stravinsky to accomplish their work.

The problems posed by standardized testing led researchers at Project Zero to develop more ecologically valid assessments at the pre-school, middle school and high school levels. At the pre-school level, Project Zero researchers, in collaboration with David Feldman of Tufts University, are engaged in Project Spectrum. Project Spectrum has devised attractive classroom materials and activities which have become regular features at a university-based pre-school. These materials enable young children to develop their various intelligences, while teachers (and researchers) can uncover, in a non-intrusive way, the range of strengths, interests and working styles that individual children employ (Malkus, Feldman and Gardner, 1988; Ramos-Ford, Feldman and Gardner, 1988; Wexler–Sherman, Gardner and Feldman, 1988).

One example of Spectrum's assessment-cum-curriculum materials is the dinosaur game. This game uses two dice: one indicates the direction a small dinosaur can travel along the back of a large dinosaur; the other indicates the number of spaces the little dinosaur can move. While the game helps children to learn number concepts in a congenial setting, it also allows the teacher to gauge the child's comprehension and development. In addition, one can elicit information on a wide range of skills, from the child's capacity to interact with other individuals, to the facility with which he or she shakes the dice and moves the "pieces".

The Project Spectrum classroom materials have helped to demonstrate that there are great early variations in thinking skills. As early as age three or four, children are strong in some intelligences and not in others. Rather than using this information to rank children, Project Spectrum's staff provides parents with a report describing each individual's relative strengths and weaknesses. The report also suggests activities which can be undertaken in the home, school or community that may be helpful and interesting to a particular student (Gardner, 1991; Ramos-Ford and Gardner, 1989).

At the middle school and high school levels, researchers from Project Zero are working with teachers in the Pittsburgh Public Schools, and the Educational Testing Service on Arts PROPEL. PROPEL is a combined curriculum-and-assessment method that encourages production, perception and reflection in the areas of music, visual arts and imaginative writing. PROPEL's primary vehicles are student portfolios and domain projects: rich activities within each of these three disciplines (Gardner, 1989b; Harvard Project Zero, 1988).

An example of a domain project in the area of imaginative writing is dialogue writing. For this project, teachers might encourage students to work in pairs to create a dialogue. This first draft would be revised several times: after students reflect on their work, perform it for their peers, submit it to their teacher for comments, or hear other dramatic works. These various activities help the students to perceive other ways to construct their dialogue. Each of these revised constructions, the comments they received, as well as student reflections on what sparked their re-writing, are kept in a student's portfolio.

Portfolios (which might more accurately be termed "process folios") are repositories of a student's drafts, notebooks, teachers' comments, and other documents pertinent to his or her development in one or more art form or discipline. Portfolios help students keep track of their progress and development, and provide them with food for further reflection. Because they are not just limited to graded final projects, but rather record a process (including initial plans and critiques, revisions, collections of related materials), they also provide teachers with a richer means to assess a student's progress (Brown, 1987; Zessoules, Wolf and Gardner, 1988). We are not alone in this belief. Recently, the use of portfolios has been widely adopted within the British educational system (Kirkman, 1988; Medway and Yeomans, 1988). We also find it encouraging that several states are now considering portfolio methods (Rothman, 1988).

A more recent effort to develop critical thinking skills, undertaken in collaboration with Yale University researchers, is called Practical Intelligence for Schools (PIFS). PIFS attempts to use subject-matter content as a springboard for acquiring learning skills. It does not establish a new curriculum. Instead, PIFS tries to infuse thinking skills into curricula that are already in place. It does so by encouraging sixth graders (and especially those "at risk" for difficulties in school) to reflect on and monitor their own thinking skills while working on a specific subject. Thereby, it seeks to build a bridge between decontextualized general skills—such as taking notes, using references and writing reports—and the demands and requirements of specific subject matter.

As one example, students are often confronted with an assignment or problem for which they must use resources. While one can offer some generic advice about resources, our approach is to help students learn to distinguish between the kinds of resources which could be useful in solving a mathematics problem (e.g. experience of problems already solved) and those resources relevant to the preparation of a term paper (e.g. help from knowledgeable individuals). By the same token, exercises on how to choose a topic, or how to revise a first draft, are crafted with respect to the contexts of specific school disciplines.

Knowing how to define problems or topics, using resources to solve them, and revising one's work, are characteristic of many human endeavours and are essential to critical thinking as exemplified by Tuchman, Bakker and Stravinsky. Within their own discipline, each recognized when they had "a spectacular subject", one which intrigued and compelled them. Each knew the range of appropriate resources: from battlefields to fossil beds to folk song collections available hundreds of miles away. Finally, Tuchman, Bakker and Stravinsky did not rest with their "first drafts". Tuchman not only constructed a chronology, but selected details, interpreted them and shaped them into narratives. Bakker did not stop when he formulated his hypothesis about warm-blooded dinosaurs. Using this theory and his knowledge of dinosaur and bird anatomy, he generated a hypothesis about dinosaur evolution. Stravinsky's revisions spanned a decade of work until, at last, he found a unique, new sonority which suited the portrayal of a traditional ritual.

We believe that curriculum and assessment methods like Arts PROPEL and Project Spectrum build on important insights about how competent human beings ordinarily learn. They also are more representative of the ways people usually demonstrate mastery of a discipline or craft. While the PIFS project is still in its early phase, we maintain that fostering a mindful approach to problems in various disciplines is akin to methods of "real-world" thinkers. We hope it will expand the problem-solving repertoire typically employed by students and that it will effect a more flexible use of knowledge and skills.

Conclusion

We have argued for the recognition of different forms of intelligence, each with its own representative forms of thinking. Each of these varieties of intelligence has its own developmental path which leads to quite separate forms of adult competence. We noted that it is rare for any form of thinking to operate in isolation. Given this, and the heterogeneous and rapidly changing societies of Western Europe and the United States, it is especially appropriate for schools and teachers to recognize and educate the full range of human intelligences.

As our discussion of Project Spectrum, Arts PROPEL, and PIFS illustrates, we also believe that thinking and learning, as well as assessment, operate best in meaningful contexts. Such contexts allow the learner to shape questions and to devise means of solving them. They encourage the development and deployment of a wider array of human intelligences, both separately and in consort with one another. In addition, such contexts more closely resemble those afforded nearly all young learners until the relatively recent advent of mass education. They are also more similar to the environments in which our three critical thinkers carried out their work.

We cannot expect that an emphasis on the array of human competences and their deployment in richer contexts will result in vast increases in the number of gifted historians, scientists, composers or other disciplinary experts. At a more modest level, our approach should convey to a greater number of students what it takes to become a competent adult practitioner, and enhance their appreciation of some of the achievements of which human beings can be most proud. We believe that such an emphasis is more responsive to human diversity; that it will allow more students to engage their unique strengths; that they will thereby feel more proficient and possibly more prone to engage in co-operative activities with other competent individuals; and that by employing their strengths and skills in appropriate arenas, they will be better equipped to deal with events that none of us can yet envisage.

References

Adams, E. (1986). "The outcomes of education," in Burgess (1986a).

Aiken, W. (1942). *The Story of the Eight-Year Study*. Harper and Brothers, New York.

Bakker, R. (1986). *The Dinosaur Heresies*. Kensington, New York.

Bakker, R. and Galton, P. (1974). "Dinosaur monophyly and a new class of vertebrates", *Nature*, **248**(5444), pp. 168–171.

Baron, J. (1987). "A hypothesis about the training of intelligence", in Perkins, Lochhead and Bishop (1987).

Binet, A. and Simon, T. (1905). "Méthodes nouvelles pour le diagnostic du niveau intellectuel des anormaux", *L'année psychologique*, **11**, pp. 245–236.

Brown, N. (1987). "Pivotal pieces", *Portfolio*, **1**(2), pp. 9–13.

Burgess, T. (ed.) (1986a). *Education for Capability*. NFER-Nelson, Windsor, Berkshire.

Burgess, T. (1986b). "New ways to learn", in Burgess (1986a).

Cannell, J. (1987). *Nationally Normed Elementary Achievement Testing in America's Public Schools: How All Fifty States are Above the National Average*. Friends for Education, Daniels, WV.

Craft, R. and Harkins, W. (1972). "Stravinsky's *Svadebka* (*Les Noces*)", *New York Review of Books*, **19**(10), pp. 23–31.

Damon, W. (1989). *Child Development Today and Tomorrow*. Jossey Bass, San Francisco.

Feldman, D. (1980). *Beyond Universals in Cognitive Development*. Ablex, New York.

Feldman, D. (1986). *Nature's Gambit*. Basic Books, New York.

Fraiberg, S. (1987). *Selected Writings of Selma Fraiberg*. Ohio State University, Columbus, OH.

Gardner, H. (1980). *Artful Scribbles: The Significance of Children's Drawings*. Basic Books, New York.

Gardner, H. (1983). *Frames of Mind: The Theory of Multiple Intelligences*. Basic Books, New York.

Gardner, H. (1987). "An individual centered curriculum", in *The Schools We've Got, the Schools We Need*. Council of Chief State School Officers and the American Association of Colleges of Teacher Education, Washington DC.

Gardner, H. (1991). "The school of the future", in Brockman J. (ed.), *Ways of Knowing Reality Club*, Vol 3, 199–217.

Gardner, H. (1991). "Assessment in context: The alternative to standardized testing", in Gifford B. and O'Connor, M. C. *Future assessments, changing visions of aptitude, achievement, and instruction*, Kluwer, Boston MA.

Gardner, H. (1989a). *To Open Minds: Chinese Clues to the Dilemma of American Education*. Basic Books, New York.

Gardner, H. (1989b). "Zero-based arts education", *Studies in Art Education*, **30**(2), pp. 71–83.

Gardner, H. (1990). "The difficulties of school: Probable causes, possible cures", *Daedalus*, **119**(2), 85–113.

Gardner, H. and Wolf, D. P. (1983). "Waves and streams of symbolization", in Rogers, D. R. and Sloboda, J. A. (eds.), *The Acquisition of Symbolic Skills*. Plenum Press, London.

Gould, S.J. (1981). *The Mismeasure of Man*. Norton, New York.

Guilford, J. P. (1967). *The Nature of Human Intelligence*. McGraw Hill, New York.

Gulbenkian Foundation (1982). *The Arts in Schools: Principles, Practice and Provision*. Calouste Gulbenkian Foundation, London.

Hargreaves, D. H. (1982). *The Challenge of the Comprehensive School; Culture, Curriculum and Community*. Routledge & Kegan Paul, London.

Harvard Project Zero (1988). *Portfolio*, **1**(3).

Hirsch, E. D. (1987). *Cultural Literacy*. Houghton Mifflin, Boston.

Jackson, P. (1968). *Life in Classrooms*. Holt, Rinehart and Winston, New York.

Jackson, P. (1986). *The Practice of Teaching*. Teachers College Press, New York.

John–Steiner, V. (1985). *Notebooks of the Mind: Explorations of thinking*. University of New Mexico Press, Albuquerque, NM.

Kirkman, S. (1988). "A liberating influence", *Times Educational Supplement*, 4th March 1988, 3740, p. 24.

Lightfoot, S.L. (1978). *World's Apart: Relationships between families and Schools*. Basic Books, New York.

Lowenfeld, V. and Brittain, W.L. (1982). *Creative and Mental Growth*. Macmillan, New York.

Lowry, K., Wolf, C. and Gardner, H. (1988). *Arts Education in China: A Cross-cultural Perspective*. Technical report. Harvard Project Zero, Cambridge, MA.

Malkus, U., Feldman, D.H. and Gardner, H. (1988). "Dimensions of mind in early childhood", in Pelligrini, A. D. (ed.), *The Psychological Bases of Early Education*. Wiley, Chichester, UK.

Medway, P. and Yeomans, D. (1988). *Technology Projects in the Fifth Year*. Technology and Vocational Educational Initiative, University of Leeds.

Messenger, J. H. (1958). "Reflections on esthetic talent", *Basic College Quarterly*, **4**, pp. 20–24.

National Commission on Excellence in Education (1983). *A Nation at Risk: The Imperative for Educational Reform: A Report to the Nation and the Secretary of Education, United States Department of Education*. The Commission on Excellence in Education, Washington DC.

Ogbu, J. (1978). *Minority Education and Caste: The American System in Cross-cultural Perspective*. Academic Press, New York.

Olson, L. (1988). "In Pittsburgh: New approaches to testing tract arts 'footprints'", *Education Week*, **8**(11), pp. 1, 22–23.

Paley, V. (1986). *Mollie is Three: Growing up in school*. University of Chicago Press, Chicago.

Perkins, D. N., Lochhead, J. and Bishop, J. (eds.) (1987). *Thinking: The Second International Conference*. Erlbaum, Hillsdale, NJ.

Perkins, D. N. and Salomon, G. (1988). "Teaching for Transfer", *Educational Leadership*, 41, (September).

Perkins, D. N. and Simmons, R. (in press). "Patterns of misunderstanding: An integrative model of misconceptions in science, math and programming", *Review of Educational Research*.

Piaget, J. (1965). *The Child's Conception of Number*. W. W. Norton, New York.

Piaget, J. and Inhelder, B. (1969). *The Psychology of the Child*. Basic Books, New York.

Polanyi, M. (1958). *Personal Knowledge: Towards a Post-critical Philosophy*. University of Chicago Press, Chicago.

Ramos-Ford, V., Feldman. D. H. and Gardner, H. (1988). "A new look at intelligence through Project Spectrum", *New Horizons for Learning (On the beam)*, **8**(3), pp. 6–7, 15.

Ramos-Ford, V. and Gardner, H. (1990). "Giftedness from a multple intelligences perspective", in Colangelo N. and Davis G. (eds.), *The Handbook of Gifted Education*, Allyn and Bacon, Boston, MA.

Ravitch, D. (1983). *The Troubled Crusade: American Education*, 1945–1980. Basic Books, New York.

Rothman, R. (1988). "Vermont plans to pioneer with 'work portfolios' ", *Education Week*, **8**(8), pp. 1, 11.

Russell, Bernard (1917/1963). *Mysticism and Logic and Other Essays*. George Allen and Unwin, London.

Sarason, S. (1983). *Schooling in America: Scapegoat and Salvation*. Free Press, New York.

Spearman, C. (1923). *The Nature of "Intelligence" and the Principles of Cognition*. Macmillan, London.

Sternberg, R. J. (1984). "Testing intelligence without IQ tests", *Phi Delta Kappa*, **65**(10), pp. 694–698.

Sternberg, R. J. (1988). *The Triarchic Mind*. Viking, NY.

Stravinsky, I. and Craft, R. (1962). *Expositions and Developments*. Faber and Faber, London.

Terman, L. (1916). *The Measurement of Intelligence: An Explanation of and a Complete Guide for the Use of the Stanford Revision and Extension of the Binet-Simon Intelligence Scale*. Houghton Mifflin, Boston.

Terman, L. (1923). *Intelligence Tests and School Reorganization*. World Book Company, Yonkers-on-Hudson, New York.

Thurstone, L. (1935). *The Vectors of Mind*. University of Chicago Press, Chicago.

Thurstone, L. (1938). *Primary Mental Abilities*. University of Chicago Press, Chicago.

Tuchman, B. (1981). *Practising History*. Ballantine Books, New York.

Walters, J. and Gardner, H. (1985). "The development and education of intelligences", in Link F. (ed.), *Essays on the Intellect*. Curriculum Development Associates, Washington DC.

Wexler–Sherman, C., Gardner, H. and Feldman, D. (1988). "A pluralistic view of early assessment: The Project Spectrum approach", *Theory into Practice*, **27**(1), pp. 77–83.

Woolf, V. (1929). *A Room of One's Own*. Harcourt Brace Jovanovich, New York and London.

Yeomans, E. (1981). *A Teacher's Odyssey*. Windflower Press, Cambridge, MA.

Zessoules, R., Wolf, D. P. and Gardner, H. (1988). "A better balance: Arts Propel as an alternative to discipline-based arts education", in Burton, J., Lederman, A. and London P. (eds.), *Beyond DBAE: The Case for Multiple Visions of Art Education*. University Council on Art Education, Cambridge MA.

Commentary
by François Bresson

Centre d'étude des processus cognitifs et du langage,
Ecole des Hautes études en sciences sociales,
Paris, France

Both in his paper and in his book, Frames of Mind (*1983*), *Professor Howard Gardner insists on the plurality of intelligence. He bases his argument on the diversity of forms of intellectual creation and activity, for which he proposes seven categories: linguistic, logical-mathematical, musical, spatial, bodily kinesthetic, interpersonal and intrapersonal.*

One has to agree with the assertion that there are a number of intellectual capacities. This variety in forms of intellectual activity stems from abilities which correspond to differences between the various processes of dealing with information. Examples such as Barbara Tuchman, Robert Bakker or Igor Stravinsky illustrate this theory. They present these different intelligences as both specific and critical. Many other cases of writers, musicians or scientists could be added to these examples. They have all produced, each in their own specialized field, original works of value which reveal their abilities, knowledge and critical capacities.

The success of these various forms of intelligence has always been recognized and appreciated, even if the school curriculum has not always attached the same importance to different cognitive capacities. These distinguished people have proved capable of producing what they wanted to create, and schools are neither for nor against such achievements. These creative minds have made as much use of the knowledge they were given, as that which they found out for themselves.

One also has to agree with the conclusion that schools need to broaden their curriculum and offer pupils the possibility of expressing their interest in various types of knowledge and in all their critical abilities. Nevertheless, schools are not expected to cater for the development of the exceptionally talented.

My aim here is rather to suggest ways in which the greatest number of people will be able to express their various abilities, people who would otherwise remain less productive or might fail. Gardner's conclusions, however, give rise to two questions:

> (*i*) *What is the relationship between specific types of intelligence and the general curriculum?*
> (*ii*) *What is the relationship between knowledge and the procedures of intellectual activity?*

Relationship Between Specific Intelligence and the General Curriculum

The different types of intelligence which Gardner talks about appear to be governed by specific processes. Cognitive psychology, and in particular neuropsychology, have shown quite clearly that lesion of some cortical areas disturbs or prevents certain sorts of comprehension or intellectual activity. However, these are necessary but not sufficient conditions for these particular intelligences to develop. This does not mean that these processes govern only the intellectual activities that we have observed, nor that this intelligence does not bring into play other systems of comprehension or action.

The different kinds of knowledge and the different forms of intellectual acitivities (such as mathematical, musical or linguistic ones) do not result from unitary operations. Depending on the methods or the kinds of action—sometimes even on circumstances—similar results can be obtained by different people in various activities. In their reasoning, mathematicians such as Gauss and physicists such as Maxwell have stressed the role of imagined figural models, in contrast to algebraic analytical reasoning. Fermat used classes of figural numbers in his theorem on whole numbers (Bresson, 1987).

It is now known that what the neuropsychologists call "acalculies" (the inability to carry out basic arithmetic) is not the result of the same processes depending on whether there are lesions in the right or left hemisphere (Bresson, de Schumen and Tzortzis, 1972). We also know that although we speak of language as if it were a single entity, in reality it is not. It comes from a complex system in which speech, reading and forms of writing must be considered as the sum of many modular activities (Petersen et al., 1988), as is illustrated by neuropsychological observations on dyslexia, dysphasia and the various forms of aphasia.

Intellectual activities do not involve a single kind of intelligence; rather, they bring into play a number of processes which exist, as far as we know, in all normal people, but the way they function varies according to the type of comprehension or result that each of us can aim for and achieve. Some processes play an essential role in the functioning of certain intellectual categories. Their organization appears to be a combination of modular systems and the interactions which exist between them. Preferential development of one of these ways of thinking in a particular person does not mean that the rest of the thinking process will not continue with other or even all possible functions. Thus, in a child, walking, language, spatial organization and the perception of shapes can be seen to develop simultaneously. This does not rule out different strategies in the exercise of these functions, so that one child may be able to speak earlier or later than another.

Different kinds of intelligence can therefore co-exist. The capacity of knowing how to succeed in some intellectual activities does not mean that we cannot perform as well in others. Dominique Ingres (1780–1867) is famous not only because he was a great artist but also because he was a very talented violinist. Philidor (1726–1795), the composer of operas, was also one of the most famous chess players. Exceptional capacities probably depend on a number of cognitive factors, both affective and social, which determine a hierarchy of links between the cognitive capacities, all universal, of these different forms of intelligence.

Does critical thought and reasoning develop as a general function common to all specific intelligence, or is there a function for each intellecual form? Whilst it is impossible to give a precise answer, one can say that these ways of thinking develop only in situations where specific cognitive capacities can function. Cognitive, affective and social factors make this development possible, and transfer to other intellectual capacities depends on analogous possibilities to exercise them in other situations.

In the present social and economic climate, particularly in high-tech societies, it is essential to acquire many types of knowledge and to develop a high level of efficiency in a range of activities. Several factors must therefore be taken into account: first, one must establish a pattern of the various capacities and preferences which correspond to the different kinds of intelligence, and then another of the various social demands.

There is no reason why these two patterns should be compatible. The problem is simple at primary school level. It remains so at secondary school level for those whose particular intellectual development corresponds with prevailing curriculum demands. For those whose intellectual development is highly specific, however, this relationship may not exist, resulting in underachievement.

What is the Relationship Between Knowledge and the Procedures of Intellectual Activity?

The three examples given by Gardner reveal as much a command of specific knowledge, in their particular intelligence, as a capacity for critical thinking. One can say that these two forms of competence correspond respectively to knowledge and metaknowledge. Here, teaching encounters the same difficulties, at different levels, for each of Gardner's seven categories of intelligence.

The various disciplines are taught as conceptual knowledge, along with the rules which make it possible to link the concepts and to make the application procedures quite clear. The pedagogic techinques depend on the nature of the communication between the person with the knowledge and those who must acquire it. The essential part of this communication is based, as always—whatever the discipline—on language, whether written or spoken, even if it only accompanies or illustrates examples of actions.

There are thus two difficulties in teaching both knowledge and metaknowledge:

(i) How does one move from this knowledge to practical knowledge?

(ii) How does one move from communicated knowledge to critical thinking?

Transition from declarative to procedural knowledge

Verbal communication in pedagogy is what the computer scientists call "declarative". It allows conscious knowledge to be acquired. But procedural knowledge—know-how, the process that underlies practical actions and their application—is largely implicit and unconscious.

Learning to talk and read is a good example of this. Children acquire their mother tongue spontaneously, without having to be taught. As early as the last quarter of their first year, children start to produce the phonemes of their language and to progress, as in the adult, from the acoustic recognition of consonantal sounds to the auditory recognition of these individual syllabic consonants (Werker and Tees, 1984; Werker and Lalonde, 1988; Best, McRoberts and Sithol 1988). The procedural knowledge of phonetic, intonational, syntactic and semantic rules which produce comprehensible speech remains implicit, even in adults.

However, learning to read alphabetical writing gives rise to different problems, whether for children or adults. The recognition of phones is never spontaneous: we have to tell children how to recognize phones by analysing syllables. The process of learning to read is declarative and this knowledge remains explicit. Dyslexics can have serious difficulties in this regard, and it is not sufficient to be able to speak in order to read (Bertelson, 1986; Morais et al., 1986).

There is not always a direct transition from the declarative to the procedural or the other way round. We may be able to repeat something that we have learned but be incapable of applying this knowledge. This is what has been demonstrated in cognitive psychology, in experiments where problems are set and the subjects are then asked to describe the rules used to obtain the solution, or vice versa. It was realized that there could be no connection between knowing how to proceed carefully and making mistakes in verbal answers to the same question. The more data there are, the more complex becomes the problem of dealing with implicit procedures, and the less capable we are of describing correctly the rules that we should follow (Broadbent, Fitzgerald and Broadbent, 1986; Hayes and Broadbent, 1988).

This explains why we cannot always teach the necessary rules for approaching a problem. It is quite clearly the case with language. To know how to speak and write texts, how to recognize whether or not a phrase is correct, does not mean that we can formulate the synactic, semantic or stylistic rules which we have followed. Knowledge of a language is not made up of a series of algorithms that we have to learn in order to speak or write.

Even though mathematics appears to be a field organized with great precision— knowledge that can be communicated explicitly—there is also a large amount of procedural knowledge where the rules cannot be taught. This is the case, for example, with the acquisition of the knowledge necessary for transforming the algebraic expressions which must be found in order to solve a problem.

Even in straightforward situations, the transition from declarative conceptual knowledge to practice does not result from a formulation that can be put into words and communicated. There are no directly teachable algorithms. Even when the aim of a task can be clearly conveyed, the procedures have to be understood before it can be achieved. One can only present similar examples, suggest exercises which increase in difficulty, and give rules for checking, so that the implicit procedure will be spontaneously discovered.

Procedural knowledge is easier to acquire if one can sort out not only the effects but also the actions which lead to them. There is then a difference between the kinesthetic or musical form of intelligence and linguistic or logical-mathematical understanding. The results we want to achieve by physical means can be governed both by internal and external information and by visual or auditory means, during the process itself as well as in the outcome. Seeing or hearing what others are doing, or what we ourselves are doing, judging effects while they are being produced, is not equally feasible, however, in all the different areas of intelligence.

Transition from Communicated Knowledge to Critical Thinking

The various kinds of intelligence or critical thinking are not only possibilities for directly applying what is known already but they include the capacity to compare different kinds of knowledge, to combine them and draw conclusions, to develop analogies from them, and to invent.

Critical thinking constitutes procedural knowledge and remains implicit: only its effects, its explicit and conscious results—not the process involved—are judged. Mathematical discoveries are a good example: many mathematicians have written about the role of intuition and about a moment of surprise following their own discoveries (Poincaré, 1907; Hadamard, 1945). There is thus no form of direct learning which can develop critical intelligence. One can only try to induce the spontaneous acquisition of these ways of thinking.

One tactic, emphasized by Gardner, is to discover which kinds of intelligence are, for each student, the most highly developed, and which ones best motivate. Another tactic is to increase the opportunities for exercising this procedural knowledge. These strategies augment those which were mentioned in connection with the direct application of knowledge.

Experience tells us that there are conditions which relate to a specific field of knowledge and others which enable generalizations covering several fields. The teacher can explain, for example, a fairly large number of possible relations between conceptual categories, and lead the student to find others spontaneously. This transformation of representations is a way of helping meta-knowledge to develop.

But this critical thinking, this metaknowledge is not directly transferable, even if identical processes can be applied in several different intellectual fields. A critical intellectual activity in one category is not isolated but interacts with its context. It implies a procedure linked to results of processes arising from a system of relationships peculiar to that field.

There is no need whatsoever for general transfers, even if the processes are identical. Expertise in one field can coincide with partial or even total incapacity in another. Even if all normal individuals start with the same capacities in the various intelligences, this does not mean that their development will be similar.

It is, however, possible to encourage operation systems to function in parallel and thus enable critical thinking to be exercised in several fields, whether it be checking, reasoning, analysis, synthesis or analogy. Such transfers between specific kinds of intelligence can also take place when relationships established between various fields can be analysed. This is what is known as "an abstraction system", where a new kind of knowledge is brought into being. Examples of such knowledge are becoming quite common, particularly with the development of artificial intelligence.

Conclusion

The different kinds of specific intelligence can be studied from two viewpoints:

> *(i) By looking at the processes necessary for specific cognitive activities: nevertheless these processes and their interactions depend on modules and on their interactions that are in all likelihood universal.*
>
> *(ii) By examining the process in experts in a particular field, whose recognized talents develop only when a range of cognitive, motivational and social factors come together. These specific kinds of intelligence do not rule out the possibility that they might develop simultaneously in the same individual.*

Educational curricula must take into account the different characteristics of individuals, as well as the practical necessity of providing a broad training. One of the enduring difficulties is the implicit nature of procedural learning.

References

Bertelson, P. (1986). "The onset of literacy: Liminal remarks," *Cognition*, **24**, pp. 1–30.

Best, C. T., McRoberts, G. W. and Sithol, N. M. (1988). "Examination of perceptual reorganization for non-native speech contrasts: Zulu click discrimination by English-speaking adults and infants," *Journals of Experimental Psychology: Human Perception and Performance*, **14**, pp. 345–360.

Bresson, F. (1987). "Les fonctions de représentation et de communication," in Piaget, J., Mounoud, P. and Bronckart, J.-P. (eds.), *Psychologie* (Encyclopédie de la Pléiade), Paris, Gallimard, pp. 933–982.

Bresson, F., de Schonen, S. and Tzortzis, C. (1972). "Etudes des perturbations dans des perfomances logico-arithmétiques chez des sujets atteints de diverses lésions céré-brales," *Langages*, **25**, pp. 108–122.

Broadbent, D. E., FitzGerald, P. and Broadbent, M. H. P. (1986). "Implicit and explicit knowledge in the control of complex systems," *British Journal of Psychology*, **77**, pp. 33–50.

Gardner, H. (1983). *Frames of Mind: The Theory of Multiple Intelligences*. Basic Books, New York.

Hadamard, J. (1945). *The Psychology of Invention in the Mathematical Field*. Princeton University Press, Princeton.

Hayes, N. A. and Broadbent, D. E. (1988). "Two modes of learning for interactive tasks," *Cognition*, **28**, pp. 249–276.

Morais, J., Bertelson, P., Cary, L. and Alegria, J. (1986). "Literacy training and speech segmentation," *Cognition*, **24**, pp. 45–64.

Petersen, S. E., Fox, P. T., Posner, M. I., Mintun, M. and Raichle, M. E. (1988). "Positron emission tomographic studies of the cortical anatomy of single-word processing," *Nature*, **331**, pp. 585–589.

Poincaré, H. (1907). *Science et Méthode*. Ernest Flammarion, Paris.

Werker, J. F. and Lalonde, C. E. (1988). "Cross-language speech perception: Initial capabilities and developmental change," *Developmental Psychology*, **24**, pp. 1–12.

Werker, J. F. and Tees, R. C. (1984). "Cross-language speech perception: Evidence for perceptual re-organization during the first year of life," *Infant Behavior and Development*, **7**, pp. 49–63.

13

Methods and Approaches

JOHN NISBET

Honorary Senior Research Fellow and formerly Professor of Education,
University of Aberdeen, Scotland,
United Kingdom

Introduction

To claim that we can teach thinking is perhaps pretentious, and many who work in the field of education are sceptical of such claims. It may be more acceptable to express the aim as "accelerating cognitive development", but it is still an ambitious and unproven claim. On the assumption that the idea is at least worth considering seriously, the question then arises: which of the various ways of teaching thinking offers the best promise of success? The purpose of this paper is to review a range of approaches and methods which have been adopted over the past 20 years, when there has been a flood of interest in the idea worldwide. (I shall use *methods* in a specific way, to describe techniques and procedures which have been commonly used in teaching thinking. I use *approaches* as a more general term, to express different theoretical standpoints, though in fact my classification is based largely on the medium or subject-matter content through which thinking is taught.) I see this as an initial step towards building a conceptual framework for the teaching of thinking, within which we may analyse the various approaches and methods, and examine the psychological or pedagogical theories on which they are based. There is no ideal framework: different writers use different frameworks for different purposes. I shall follow the classification adopted for the review of research in the Background Report which distinguishes between the "skills" and the "infusion" approach, and proceeds to suggest subdivisions within these two broad categories.

No Simple Answer

Suppose that a teacher (or an educational administrator) comes to us and says: "I am interested in this idea. I believe we should try to teach thinking. How should I proceed? What methods or approaches do you recommend?" This is a question which Sternberg says he is often asked (Baron and Sternberg, 1987). His answer is:

> There is no one programme that is best for everybody or every place ... One must learn about the principles of thinking and the programmes available ... and then make a carefully thought out decision as to what will work best in a given setting.

I think we would all agree, but I hope that we may be able to set out the options within a conceptual framework that will help our practitioner to make appropriate choices and decisions. I suggest that we keep our practitioner in mind during our discussions, in the hope that we can give comprehensive information and practical guidance. In this chapter I shall try to answer the teacher's questions: "How can we teach thinking? What methods or approaches do you advise?"

I wish to say at the start that my experience is mainly of programmes and publications in the English-speaking area, especially in the United States. There is a different tradition in educational thinking in many European countries, a tradition more closely linked to psychological and philosophical theories of cognitive development, especially Piagetian and neo-Piagetian theories. Piagetian theory identifies stages in cognitive development, and one influential group of researchers interpret teaching thinking as assisting, or accelerating, the progress from one state to another. The American approaches tend to be more pragmatic, weaker in their theoretical base; but they are developed from practical trials in schools and colleges with methods which they claim to be effective (though often on limited evidence). I think that the broad two-fold classification still applies, in that cognitive acceleration may be attempted through specific training, but it is more commonly introduced as a component in the teaching of conventional subjects, especially science. There is also a European network of educational and cognitive psychologists, EARLI (European Association for Research on Learning and Instruction). Their work is published mainly in psychological journals and has made a significant contribution to research on learning. This includes learning to learn, metacognition and problem solving.

Skills or Infusion?

The first decision which the teacher has to make is whether to adopt a separate course or package of materials on thinking, or to adopt the method of infusing thinking into all his or her regular teaching. The decision to adopt materials specifically designed for teaching thinking is often criticized as implying that thinking is an "add-on" element, something to be learned in the way one learns to read, to write and to count. This is an unfair criticism: those who have developed separate courses or materials for teaching thinking do not necessarily make this assumption. Their courses and materials are designed to focus attention on the processes of thinking, to rescue thinking from the neglect it suffers in much of our educational practice, and thus to empower learners in the wider application of thinking skills to other aspects of learning and to the world outside the classroom.

But there are two assumptions implicit in this approach which require closer scrutiny (and I shall return to those later). One assumption is that there are identifiable thinking skills which can be abstracted from their contexts. The other assumption which it is easy to fall into is that this transfer of thinking skills from specific exercises to other fields will occur spontaneously. Consequently, teachers who choose to adopt the separate-course approach must pay particular attention to the question of transfer.

The other alternative, teaching thinking through "infusion", is more likely to be immediately acceptable to most teachers. Indeed, our imaginary teacher who asks for advice is likely to respond to the idea of infusion by saying that she or he is doing this already. The notion of problem solving as a technique for involving learners in the active application of knowledge and skills in specific domains of the curriculum—and thereby ensuring a clearer understanding and firmer grasp of that knowledge—is widely accepted in educational practice today. Teachers often adopt a problem-solving approach, however, because they see this as a more effective way of teaching their specialist subject, not as a means to teach thinking. The distinctive contribution of the "teaching thinking movement" is its focus on a whole range of thinking across the curriculum: not just problem solving but also defining problems, decision making, guarding against premature judgement, looking for contrary evidence, creative thinking, the use (and dangers) of analogies, metacognitive monitoring and so on. This brings in the issue of transfer again: if the teacher's choice is to work through infusion within a specific domain of the curriculum, particular attention must be paid to ensuring that there is transfer beyond that domain, for transfer does not occur automatically.

The distinction between teaching thinking as a separate course and teaching thinking by infusion throughout the curriculum is the main division in the conceptual framework of approaches and methods. We can extend this classification into subdivisions, though it becomes increasingly difficult to fit individual schemes into precise categories, as many writers advocate a mixture of approaches.

The Skills Approach: Subdivisions

If the teacher decides to introduce a separate course of thinking, he or she must make a choice between those which are "content free" and those which teach procedures for dealing with practical problems. For example, the materials in Feuerstein's Instrumental Enrichment (Feuerstein *et al.*, 1980) have abstract headings—patterns, comparisons, orientation, analytic perception—derived from a psychological theory. Edward de Bono's CoRT material (1973, 1976) seems to me an example of the other category, recommending a range of procedures (Plus/ Minus/Interest, Consider All Factors, First Important Priorities, Other Points of View, etc.) as practical strategies for tackling problems as they arise. Other examples in this second category are Bransford's IDEAL algorithm (Bransford and Stein 1984): Identify the problems, Define, Explore, Act and Look at effects; and the formidable list in the recent book by Marzano *et al.*, *Dimensions of Thinking* (1988), which identifies eight "thinking processes" (e.g. concept formation, principle formation, comprehending, etc.) and 21 "core thinking skills" (focusing skills, information-gathering skills, remembering skills, etc.). Marzano's list has been criticized on the grounds that these are not "dimensions" but are more appropriately described as practically derived procedures. Courses which are more firmly based on an explicit psychological theory derive strength from that theory, but also suffer the weakness that they have a less obvious appeal unless one fully understands and accepts the underlying psychological theory. The other type, which recommends "self-evident" procedures, has an immediate face validity but suffers the weakness that they are derived from psychological theories which are implicit and therefore questionable.

Sternberg's *Intelligence Applied* (1986) seems to bridge the gap, being derived from his triarchic theory of intelligence and proceeding to work out practical implications for learning. Thus, he distinguishes three components of intelligence: the metacomponents (executive processes for managing and monitoring thinking), the performance components (for implementing strategies) and the knowledge acquisition components (for learning). The programme includes training in "coping with novelty" (an aspect of transfer) and in "automizing information processing".

The assumption common to all these courses is that there are identifiable thinking skills or procedures which can be abstracted from the context in which we normally learn them, which can be taught separately, and which can then be applied generally. This assumption is challenged by some of those who argue for teaching thinking by infusion throughout the curriculum.

Infusion: Subdivisions

Under the heading "infusion approach", the Background Paper adopts a subdivision into three approaches: problem-based teaching and learning, study of the humanities, and information technology and computers.

The first of these, a problem-based approach to the teaching of the conventional subjects and disciplines of the curriculum, is the field in which there is the greatest volume of published work (cf. Appendix. pp. 211–212). Those who advocate this approach may be classified into three groups:

(i) those who see this as the most effective way of teaching these subjects;

(ii) those who aim to teach thinking, and see this as a feasible and sensible way of introducing thinking into the curriculum without radical change; and

(iii) those who are sceptical of efforts to teach "disembodied" thinking skills on the grounds that reasoning abilities are closely tied up with the particular knowledge domains in whose context they were acquired.

For the first two groups, transfer is again a crucial issue. Their standpoint raises the issue of the aims of education. Is the aim to produce knowledgeable practitioners or rational thinkers? Is the first of these a precondition of the second? The third group raises deeper issues on the nature of knowledge and thinking. They argue that each domain of knowledge has its own distinctive styles of thinking: therefore, training in thinking should be "domain specific", and transfer across domains is likely to be limited to a few very general and broadly applicable strategies. We shall return to this issue later.

The claim that thinking can be taught through the humanities is more limited, but it too has a respectable tradition which can be traced back to the study of rhetoric and logic in classical and medieval times. There may be a lesson here for those who favour this approach, for rhetoric and logic (and grammar too) became formal exercises divorced from everyday life, and their potential as an introduction to thinking was lost in the minutiae of scholarly complexities. This approach to the teaching of thinking attempts to recover that potential. Courses in "informal logic" and "critical thinking" (Paul, 1984, 1985) and "philosophy for children" (Lipman, Sharp and Oscanyan 1980) make this their explicit aim (cf. Appendix pp. 212–213). Although these can also be classified as separate courses, they are more appropriately seen as an aspect of the infusion approach, since they introduce thinking through the medium of an established discipline. The full potential of language as a means to teaching thinking seems to me to remain unexplored in the English-speaking world, but perhaps this is an aspect in which we have much to learn from other cultures.

The growth of information technology and the use of computers have opened up a new approach to teaching thinking. Two aspects can be distinguished: training in programming as an analytic exercise in thinking, and the use of computer programs (often in the form of games) which stimulate thinking. Papert's LOGO (1980) is a computer language designed for easy programming: its author's aim is "to contribute to mental processes not only instrumentally but in more essential, conceptual ways" (p. 4). Evaluation studies, however, indicate that training in computer programming does not enhance cognitive skills more generally, perhaps because those who teach it are not concerned with teaching for transfer, or because the learners are too preoccupied with the complexities to look beyond the specific skill. In contrast, computer games seem able to tap an under-used source of energy in some learners, and publishers' catalogues of computer programs are full of claims for educational benefits, not only for more effective teaching and learning within a subject domain but also more generally as a stimulus to thinking. These claims depend on the extent of transfer. With computer games as in other learning situations, transfer is more likely to occur if it is planned and deliberate before, during and after the activity, through discussion of strategies, metacognitive monitoring of processes and retrospective analysis of outcomes. Transfer is thus a key factor in all the approaches which we have reviewed.

Transfer

Thus, the teacher who asks for advice on the teaching of thinking has a wide range of choice of approach. The main choice is between what we have called "skills" and "infusion". In the preceding paragraphs, both of these options have been expressed in terms of skills to be taught and learned: either general thinking skills to be taught through separate courses, or "domain specific" skills taught within specified domains of knowledge. Irving Sigel (1984) challenges the concept of thinking skills: "The skills approach disengages thinking from its subject matter" (p. 11).

In this approach, skills are abstracted from their knowledge base, and taught and practised as "content-free" procedures. The transfer problem is then their application in context: the danger is that the skills remain inert ideas, abstractions which we cannot apply. However, the infusion approach, insofar as it uses the concept of "skills", also requires an abstraction of thinking from its subject matter, but this comes after the learning and practising of skills in context. Transfer in this case involves a decontextualization by the learner after mastery of the skill; in the course approach, decontextualization is done by the course designer, and the learner's task is to find the appropriate context. This line of argument suggest a link with the analysis of transfer by Perkins and Salomon (1988) which is referred to in the Introduction (p. xxviii) and to which more comprehensive reference is made in the Appendix (p. 220).

Skills and Strategies

If we are to build a sound conceptual structure of this field of teaching thinking, we shall have to define precisely the way in which we are using terms like *skills* and *strategies*. In particular, the use of the word *skill* carries with it a number of implications which require examination. In *Learning Strategies* (Nisbet and Shucksmith, 1986), the process of learning is analysed in terms of three "levels": skill, strategy and style. The term *skills* is used specifically for procedures often closely tied to the subjects of the curriculum. Strategies are generalizable combinations of skills or procedures. Style is much more general, an approach or attitude or disposition to learning. If strategies are practised sufficiently until they become routinized, then they become superordinate skills which in turn can be organized into superordinate strategies, thus moving towards a general disposition to learning being built up in this way. I make no special claim for this interpretation but quote it only as an example of the kind of conceptual structure which is needed.

It also fits in with what might be described as a consensus view on the approaches to teaching thinking, as expressed in the Background Report: "Any effort to teach thinking is unlikely to be as effective as it could be unless it combines these two approaches to some degree" (Nickerson, 1988, pp. 33–34).

Are there distinctive modes of thinking within specific domains of knowledge, or are there general rules which apply across domains? The answer is yes to both questions. Number (or quantitative reasoning) is one example of a procedure or skill which, though transferable, is clearly domain specific: but there are also broadly applicable strategies (or "mental habits", as one psychologist called them in a personal communication) which cut across domains: the de Bono procedures mentioned earlier, for example.

Methods and the Teacher's Role

An alternative way to answer the teacher's question is to describe methods—specific techniques as distinct from the general approaches—which are commonly used in teaching thinking. In addition to direct instruction, four methods are referred to in the Background Report: modelling, co-operative learning, metacognition and questioning. All these methods have been applied across a range of approaches. Methods are complementary to approaches: it is necessary to make a choice of methods as well as a choice of approach. Feuerstein in particular sees training in method as an essential element in Instrumental Enrichment. All the methods listed require sophisticated skills and a change of role for the teacher.

Metacognition may be seen as a common element in these methods: heightening awareness of the processes of thinking, externalizing these processes (by the teacher modelling, by peers' comments, by the teacher's questioning), opening up possibilities of more effective self-management of thinking. Metacognition is open to the objection that thinking about thinking is a disruptive process because of excess cognitive load. But there are techniques for reducing overload which can become automated with practice (see Perkins, 1989), such as alternating attention and interrupting the task to review process or, more simply, to "stop and think". Our conceptual framework should provide an analysis of method as well as of approach.

The word *mediation* is a useful concept in understanding the change in the teacher's role. Teaching thinking seems to require a mediator to bring the process out into the open and give learners access to their own thinking. Socrates used the metaphor of the midwife to describe his role as a mediator; but that metaphor has the defect of implying that the ideas are already there and that the mediator's role is to help them to emerge. There is more to it than this: the mediator has to provide a stimulus to thinking, and appropriate materials or exercise for practice, but he or she also requires a framework within which to work and a clear understanding of that framework. The conclusion that all approaches have a contribution to offer is unsatisfactory in one respect, in that we need to establish principles by which appropriate choices can be made. We cannot expect to teach thinking if the teachers themselves are not thinking. The FACE programme in Finland (see Voutilainen's paper in this volume) takes up this point. It is tempting to suggest that it is the teachers who should study the programmes on thinking skills so that they can then apply the principles through infusion into curriculum generally. But that is only part of what is required. Schon's book, *The Reflective Practitioner* (1983), analyses "how professionals think in action": "[They] often reveal a capacity for reflection on their intuitive knowing in the midst of action and sometimes use this capacity to cope with the unique, uncertain and conflicted situations of practice."

The reflective practitioner requires a sound basis of knowledge and experience, and also a framework of understanding as a guide to "reflection-in-action". Schon's hope is "to make what some of us do on rare occasions into a dominant pattern of practice". Development on these lines must accompany the constant evaluation and refinement of materials, methods and approaches in the teaching of thinking.

References

Baron, J. B. and Sternberg, R. J. (1987). *Teaching Thinking Skills: Theory and Practice.* Freeman, New York.

Bransford, J. D. and Stein, B. S. (1984). *The IDEAL Problem-Solver).* Freeman, New York.

Bono, E. de (1973). *CoRT I: Teachers' Handbook.* Pergamon, Oxford.

Bono, E. de (1976). *Teaching Thinking.* Temple Smith, London.

Feuerstein, R., Rand, Y., Hoffman, M. B. and Miller, R. (1980). *Instrumental Enrichment: An Intervention for Cognitive Modifiability.* University Park Press, Baltimore, MD.

Lipman, M., Sharp, A. M. and Oscanyan, F. S. (1980). *Philosophy in the Classroom.* Temple University Press, Philadelphia, PA.

Marzano, R. J., Brandt, R. S., Hughes, C. S., Jones, B. F., Presseisen, B. Z., Rankin, S. C. and Suhor, C. (1988). *Dimensions of Thinking: A Framework for Curriculum and Instruction.* Association for Supervision and Curriculum Development, Alexandria, VA.

Nickerson, R. S. (1988). "On improving thinking through instruction", *Review of Research in Education,* 15, pp. 3–57.

Nisbet, J. and Shucksmith, J. (1986). *Learning Strategies.* Routledge & Kegan Paul, London.

Papert, S. (1980). *Mind-Storms: Children, Computers and Powerful Ideas.* Harvester, Brighton, UK.

Paul, R. W. (1984). "Critical thinking: Fundamental to education for a free society". *Educational Leadership,* September, pp. 4–14.

Paul, R. W. (1985). "The critical thinking movement: A historical perspective." National Forum, *Phi Kappa Phi,* 65, pp. 2–3.

Perkins, D. N. (1989). "Teaching cognitive and metacognitive strategies". Oral presentation, American Educational Research Association Conference, San Fransisco, May, 1989.

Perkins, D. N. and Salomon, G. (1988). "Teaching for Transfer", *Educational Leadership,* 41, pp. 22–32.

Schon, D. A. (1983). *The Reflective Practitioner: How Professionals Think in Action.* Temple Smith, London.

Sigel, I. (1984). Quoted in Benderson, A. *Focus 15: Critical Thinking.* Educational Testing Service, Princeton, NJ, p. 11.

Sternberg, R. J. (1986). *Intelligence Applied.* Harcourt Brace Jovanovich, San Diego, CA. Also in Baron and Sternberg, *op. cit.,* Chapter 10.

Commentary by Christiane Gilliéron

University of Geneva,
Switzerland

Professor Nisbet quotes Sternberg's answer to the question of how to teach thinking:

> There is no one programme that is best for everybody or every place . . .
> One must learn about principles of thinking and the programmes
> available . . . and then make a carefully thought out decision as to what
> will work best in a given setting.

He adds: "I think we would all agree . . ."

In these lines, the term thinking *or* thought *occurs three times. In one case it concerns the student: it is after all the student that matters when one wants to inquire into the principle of thinking. In another it is the teacher who has to make a carefully thought-out decision. And finally it is us, or the programme designer. Are all of these the same kind of thinking?*

It is because we are convinced that we think that we set out to make students resemble us as much as possible. Schools do not claim to create geniuses, but rather endeavour to provide conditions in which a majority of children will be able to achieve something that we believe we know and possess. We think, and so what must we do for children to do the same?

Now, if we present the problem in this form, it seems to me that we are superficially confusing two separate ways of thinking. The thought processes we want to develop in a child can be taught, whereas ours must be worked out for ourselves (carefully thought-out decisions). Students' thought processes can be programmed: they need to be given good techniques, good habits. But for me, things are quite different: it is not some external method that enables me to develop this line of argument.

This difference in levels brings to mind the difference between a problem in the context of problem solving, and a problem in the context of somebody who says: I have a serious problem. In the first case someone is setting a problem for someone else: the teacher for the student; the psychologist for the subject, whether it be an animal or a human being. In the second case, it is the person who sets himself or herself the problem (since what he or she sees as problematic does not present itself as a problem, but rather as an obstacle). There is a crucial difference between the two: in the first case, everyone knows that there is a solution: if not, A would not have presented the problem to B. In other words: A is placed ahead of B, who is aware of this and has corresponding expectations. It is an exercise, a test, in which B is measured in relation to A. This is not what

187

happens in "real" thinking, and we should remember this when problem solving is proposed as an infusion method.

Such a gap is fundamental both on the practical level in education and on the theoretical level in genetic psychology. In both cases, the starting point depends on what one knows already. Psychologists reconstruct the stages of a development from what they know of the final phase. Teachers lead students towards something which they know or think they know. This brings me to an essential point (of Nisbet's final section on Methods and the Teacher's Role*), which is the teacher's attitude to the "method" or the teaching programme, the attitude of a teacher who asks the specialist(s) questions. In actual fact, teachers look to other disciplines: psychology, cognitive science, computers, neuropsychology, and so on. As a result, they have to act as if knowledge in these fields was definitive, to act as if we knew what thinking was, as if there was one accepted theory of intelligence (in the same way as we talk about the theory of evolution). And it is not only practitioners who ask questions, but also programme designers, decision makers, employers. It will take years for the knowledge provided by disciplines outside pedagogy actually to materialize, be expressed and integrated in an educational programme. Should the programme be modified at the same pace as progress in fundamental research? This dependence leads to a double problem: for the teacher and for the planner.*

The difficulty for teachers is that this may encourage in them an attitude which is contrary to all they ought to be fostering in the students: being teacher-centred and dogmatic. This attitude is an occupational disease among teachers, although of course not all are affected. But by claiming to distribute packages to produce the "perfect little thinker" in schools, one is merely reinforcing this tendency, when in fact it is the opposite of what personal experience teaches us when we are really thinking. Adaptive and creative thinking is humble, full of questions. A teacher whose training includes the constant exercise of child centring, of questioning things, will be in a far better position to understand the students' difficulties (and to be able to help them) than the teacher who has ready-made answers. This approach, however, is not spontaneous but rather the result of both reflection and interaction with others, and it is this particular kind of training which should be encouraged above all (see Duckworth, 1986, for a specific illustration).

At the policy level, the inherent danger is that such a procedure makes the programme dependent on fashions, of which the metacognitive is a good example.

The first "meta" discipline was metaphysics. By analogy, the term metalanguage *was coined to designate the language required to discuss the symbolism (itself a kind of language) that a formal system constitutes. The notions of object language and metalanguage only make sense in this context. For shorthand purposes, logicians then spoke of metatheories or metamathematics. But if these distinctions are clear when one sets up a formal system, they have nothing to do with psychological levels. On the contrary, a psychologist will doubt that the mind or thinking will proceed in different ways when one demonstrates a theorem as against a metatheorem.*

In reality, the prefix "meta" is used to designate that which relates to the "introspective" and the "theoretical", when it is the innocent student who is in question. Metalinguistics is spontaneous grammar; the metacognitive is psychology, which relates to knowledge. The first question concerns the status of this "cognition" that is said to be "meta". Is knowledge "metaperception"? And, in advocating "sustained metacognition" what does one intend to encourage in the students? Either one hopes that students will benefit from recognizing and identifying certain processes (behaviour, attitudes, states of mind) which the psychologist has already identified, categorized and labelled. Or, one hopes that they *will gain access to the way* they *function through introspection. Most probably Professor Nisbet is referring to the first meaning, but it presupposes a preliminary framework that can be used for interpretation; this framework must also be universal* (quid *of the age or the "cognitive styles"?* quid *of the idiosyncrasies?*); *and there must be the possibility of immediate diagnosis and also self-diagnosis.*

It is not therefore the disruptive effect of distancing oneself or the need for greater attentiveness which constitutes the main problem of "sustained metacognition", but rather its efficiency.

One can see that this meaning is not really substantially different from the second one, since it presupposes that self-observation leads to self-understanding. In other words, the corrections or the expected progress depend on accurate measurement of mental activity, which is in addition directly accessible by the person concerned.

This postulate seems to me wrong. There is no reason to believe in the accuracy of the image which people *construct of* themselves, *but considerable grounds for believing quite the opposite. This is not to say that what* people *are* aware of *in* themselves *has a negligible influence on* their *mental activity. On the contrary, it is quite easy to imagine thematization playing an essential role in cognitive progress. But it is necessary to distinguish between what is "useful" and what is "truthful".*

Here is a sensorimotor example: the art of juggling. Someone who is juggling with three balls will tell you that in order to succeed you must throw the second ball when the first ball has reached its highest point; similarly, the third ball leaves the hand once the second is suspended, immobile, neither rising nor falling. Objectively, this description is false, as video recordings in fact show. But as far as jugglers are concerned, this description makes sense: they *think* they are *succeeding because* they are *doing it in that way. If* they *do not "do"* (in their *head, not in reality) what* they *think* they are *doing,* they *will fumble. This is thus the best way of teaching timing.*

Where the content of a problem is more abstract, the same things can happen. Certain "tricks" may then be useful, but only an empirical test can show it. (In fact, an introspective account could just as well have a blocking effect.) It is also important to note that sometimes awareness comes spontaneously and stems from the repeated use of one particular mechanism, whether it be mental or symbolic (Gilliéron, 1988). Activity and practice lead to reflective knowledge, but the awareness that comes with this knowledge is focused on the matter in view. Such realizations, just like any biological phenomena, undoubtedly have a specific adaptive role to play; however, they should not be confused with an objective description such as a psychologist would make. To use a well-known example, children *who reason operatively are* not *conscious of* their *thought processes. However,* they are *not conscious of the same things as a younger child. They bring to bear some obvious facts on* their *thought processes. They project what* they *know from experience onto what* they are *thinking about. They expect a ball of clay to stay the same, whereas in fact this necessity comes not from reality, but from the composition of the mental transformations which* they *have mastered.*

Enough said about metacognition. The last point which I will deal with is the approach "inspired by Piaget". Professor Nisbet suggests that teaching thinking can make it possible to progress from one stage to another. To this, I would say that it is necessary to distinguish between stages (with a small "s") and Stages (with a capital "s"), of which there are three. At the Sensorimotor Stage, action and calculation are possible with respect to what is real. At the Concrete Stage, calculation is possible on representations. At the Formal Stage, calculation is possible on the representation of thought processes. Two years, ten years, fifteen years: is it possible, through ad hoc teaching, to make a child pass from one Stage to another? If one has enough faith to say yes, then one will have to solve all kinds of problems first, such as: should one deal with a five-year-old child in the same way as an eight-year-old? Should one be careful about using certain material before the child is ready for it? Thus, many fundamental problems are raised by the "application" of Piaget to schools (cf. Vinh Bang, 1971; Duckworth, 1987).

As far as the stages (with a small "s" are concerned, these are steps that have been identified from the procedures used in different tasks. There are as many hierarchies as there are different tasks. The transition from one behaviour to another can be explained by giving it a structure which is the consequence of a construction process; but the mismatches show that each part must be (re)constructed. In other words, the levels of each procedure have nothing general about them and it is metaphorical to talk of a "transfer". The structuring process, which explains progress in any field, is dependent upon all the recognized development "factors", above all the person's mental activity. Like adults, children are *shaped by the way they* shape themselves.

In conclusion, I must stress three points:

> (*i*) *resources, which are always limited, mean that choices have to be made; it seems to me important for investment to be made in teacher training. Teachers play a crucial role as observers* and *clinicians, and it is they who can show* students *how they function* and *act as someone to emulate, provided* they have *the necessary training.*
>
> (*ii*) *A recurrent problem when a new curriculum is introduced is also linked to the "teacher" factor. During the development phase, the results are promising. But once it is widely used, the curriculum is disappointing. This short-lived success can usually be put down to the selection of teachers to take part in experiments, which is never random.*
>
> (*iii*) *If reflective knowledge helps* individuals *make progress and allow effective control over action, decisions and judgements, that is because the* individuals themselves *do the organizing. When a decision is taken by a group of people, who is the main organizer? How can one give this group a way to get to know itself better so that it can learn and progress? One would also like to be able to answer this question when making fundamental decisions relating to education.*

References

Duckworth, E. (1986). *Inventing Density*, North Dakota Study Group on Evaluation, Grand Forks, ND.

Duckworth, E. (1987). *The Having of Wonderful Ideas and Other Essays on Teaching and Learning*, Teachers College Press, New York.

Gilliéron, C. (1988). Logique, épistémologie génétique, et développement de la réflexivité chez l'enfant. Presentation at the XII Incontro di logica matematica, Istituto Matematico Guido Castelnuovo, Università La Sapienza, Rome, 6th–9th April.

Vinh Bang (1971). "La psychologie de J. Piaget et ses applications pédagogiques", in Rusk, B. (ed.). *Alternatives in Education*, General Publishing Company, Toronto, pp. 29–41.

14

Issues Related to the Whole Child: Implications for Curriculum Development

HIROSHI AZUMA

Professor Emeritus of Education
Tokyo University,
Japan

Why Make Them Think?

I started my career as a teacher of a slow learners class, and once gave to a 14-year-old boy a maths problem involving two one-digit numbers with carry-over. He thought for a moment and produced a number of answers, but all were off target. I asked what he was thinking. He answered: "I have been wondering which number you will call right."

I knew I had failed in making the boy think as I had wanted him to. But why did I want him to think in a particular way? What did I expect the boy to gain by thinking in the way I wanted? The goal was definitely not to make him capable of producing the correct answer to that particular problem. If that had been the case, the strategy which the boy employed was not a bad one. Perhaps I wanted him to acquire the skill which would transfer the need for carrying over to other problems. In that case, it would have been better to have had him memorize an algorithm. More probably, I was operating under the belief that there is something called general thinking ability and that that ability can be fostered by thinking reflectively and analytically.

Today, I still believe that reflective thinking will greatly help us cope with the problems in this highly industrialized society and that children should therefore be guided to think reflectively when confronted with any significant problem. I do not believe, however, that merely presenting a problem and telling children to think will lead to a readiness to think reflectively.

Pragmatics of Thinking

Now, what is a significant problem? No single problem is categorically significant. For every problem there is some context that makes the given state of affairs problematic. The content domain is only one ingredient of the context. But, abiding by my theme—issues related to the whole child—I will talk primarily about personal contexts.

Historically, the limited methodology of orthodox psychological studies has tended to express contextual factors in error terms. Recently, however, the idea that contexts are integral parts of thinking and intelligence has become a widely acknowledged fact. Other contributors to this volume— Dr Edward de Bono, who has pointed out the relevance of feeling and ego development to thinking (de Bono, 1978), and Dr Howard Gardner, who has persuasively discussed "personal intelligence" (Gardner, 1983)—are among those who have led the trend to give due consideration to contexts and personal backgrounds of thinking. However, in charting the development of the field of cognitive psychology, Gardner noted that: "provisionally, most cognitive scientists attempt to so define and investigate problems that an adequate account can be given without resorting to these murky concepts (like effect, context, culture and history)" (1985).

Only four years after the publication of Gardner's book, the scene has already changed. The progress of cognitive science, and especially the rapid expansion of its applied fields, is forcing cognitivists to grapple with these "murky" concepts. Those working with machine translation must try to cope with the contextual nature of human discourse, and those working with artificial intelligence are struggling to simulate effect (e.g. Toda, 1987). The system would not be practical otherwise.

If we want our students to learn to think, we should look not only into the process of thinking but also at the context where thinking takes place. It is analogous to pragmatics as a linguistic concept.

People think in order to gain control over a frustrating situation. The solution is a state of regained control. The solution we usually ask for in classrooms represents a form of control over some aspect of the external world. Students think in order to find a way through the barrier that thwarts them from reaching their goal. But a cross-cultural study by Weisz, Rothman and Blackburn (1984) postulated the need for another kind of thinking effort directed at internal control. The effort of thinking may lead to a changed perception of a frustrating situation where the problem may not be solved in the external sense but suddenly seems so trivial that the frustration effectively dissipates.

So far, the studies of thinking have almost solely dealt with solution-directed efforts, but mental efforts leading to an altered perspective on a situation may equally well be an important form of thinking. Whether thinking will lead to a solution or to a change of perception will depend on various conditions, among which personal and sociocultural contexts play the leading role.

In this context it seems appropriate to refer to a couple of cross-national studies I have conducted. The purpose is not to show how Japan and the United States, for example, differ. A national culture is a surrogate concept. Every country has a wide variety of subcultures, down to a microculture consisting of each individual person. The power of a nation or a larger ethnological unit to create uniformity highlights the prevalent subculture alone, overshadowing other cultural alternatives to the extent that people are not aware that they exist. Cross-national differences show that there should be a significant distribution of intranational subcultures encompassed in the prevalent culture. This is particularly important in view of the fact that modern schooling methods and curricula have developed into the Euro-American mainstream culture and are not necessarily representative of a number of ethnic subgroups.

When and Where to Think

As part of a cross-cultural study on the influence of maternal teaching styles on a child's cognitive development which I directed jointly with Robert D. Hess of Stanford University (Hess et al., 1986), children at the age of five took tests which supposedly measured their reflectivity. Later, when the children were aged 11 to 12, the scores were correlated with their mathematics and reading achievement scores. A puzzling incongruity was found between Japanese and American results. In Japan, the score of a modified version of the Matching Families Figures (MFF) test at age five correlated substantially with later school achievement. In the United States, the corresponding correlation was insignificant. Conversely, the score of the Tactual and Visual Matching (TVM) correlated highly with later school achievement in the United States, but the corresponding correlation was barely significant in Japan.

Such differences were puzzling because we assumed that both of the tests measured the same trait of reflectivity. But a closer look revealed the obvious difference between the two tests. Most children were excited by TVM. Some of them even insisted on continuing when the test was over. Such excitement was not found with MFF. Malone (1981) has experimentally shown that the components of intrinsic motivation are challenge, fantasy and curiosity. TVM appeals to all three of these elements. Groping for a hidden figure is naturally curiosity-arousing. The subject must imagine how it looks in order to match it with one of the figures presented visually. The figures are different enough for the success to be self-evident when attained.

The MFF test lacks all three components. The correct answer is reached by the method of elimination rather than by direct identification, and therefore that feeling of "this is it" seldom accompanies the experience of applying MFF. Simple pictures of familiar objects are not curiosity-arousing, and differences amongst alternative figures are relatively meaningless in the life of the child. The subject has to stick to the given details, and fantasy becomes an interference.

Going back to our results, self-control in the sense of suppressing impulsive reaction was required for children in both countries in order for them to be successful at school. But the depth of the required control was different: in Japan, motivation itself needed to be subjected to internal control. Behaviour was directed by the will to live up to the passive sociocultural expectation of diligence rather than by intrinsic motivation. The hidden curricula of when and where to stop and think, or the pragmatics of reflectivity, were different.

Even the explicit curricula and teaching methods of the two cultures defined "when and where to think" differently. In the 1970s in schools in the San Francisco Bay area, the influence of the open education and individualized curriculum movement was more or less prevalent. Children were encouraged to follow through self-chosen tasks. In Japan, classes closely followed the textbooks, which in turn conformed with the government-edited course of study. Children had much less freedom to take initiatives in deciding what to do and what to learn during a given class-hour in Japan. Such differences in learning environments would have required different mental sets regarding when and where to think.

Watch people play chess. They all think. But good players know when and where to think. This knowledge of when and where to think is just as important in learning school subjects, solving scientific problems, and coping with matters of everyday life. In school learning, which involves social interaction with the teacher and fellow learners, the when and where to think depends very much on the cultural context.

What to Think

Suppose two people tackle the same problem independently. Of course, they will both engage in thinking. But although the problem is identical, the questions they will ask themselves may be quite different. Here again, culture exerts considerable influence upon what comes into the scope of a person's thinking. One of the studies I have recently conducted compared American (Ann Arbor) and Japanese (Tokyo) students' choice of information needed to judge the moral acceptability of the actions of a fictitious person. A scenario was outlined in very rough form. For example: "Person A has been caught cheating in a maths final". The subject had to choose additional information which he or she required in order to clarify the situation and to make a better judgement. American students tended to ask for factual information, such as the number of times the person in question had committed a similar offence in the past. The Japanese asked more often for feeling-oriented information, such as how the person felt at the time of the action or how he or she felt about the action subsequently. The domain of facts they required in order to make better judgements differed between the two groups. A similar Japan–United States comparison with high school students corroborated this finding.

The difference discussed above reflects the difference in materials used for constructing thinking. The thinking of a typical Japanese may differ from the thinking of a typical American with respect of the fundamental level at which basic perceptual cues are picked up. Moreover, I would not be surprised if the Japanese strategy worked better in the Japanese context, and the American approach gave a solution more acceptable in the American context.

Another continuing study of mine—looking into what type of person is perceived as being intelligent—will provide an indirect reinforcement of this point. It is a follow-up to my previous study (Azuma and Kashiwagi, 1987), which compared American and Japanese students regarding the functional concept of intelligence. They were asked to identify, from among people they knew personally, one highly intelligent male, one highly intelligent female and a person of mediocre or lower intelligence of the same sex as themselves. Each one of the three "targets" was then rated on scales of 32 personal characteristics, for example "listens well to what people say".

The results show which characteristics are effective in separating people perceived to be intelligent from those who are perceived to be unintelligent. While a number of characteristics were related to verbal intelligence and the speed of judgement, which were amongst effective items in both cultures, there were some items that were effective in one culture but not in another. "Insight into others' feelings" contributed significantly in Japan to judging a person intelligent, but not in the United States. "Originality of thought and opinions" was important in the United States but not in Japan. If the Japanese had developed their definition of thinking without any knowledge of Western philosophy and psychology, interpersonal feeling would have been a more integrated part of the concept.

I do not quote these studies in order to stress cultural differences. An empirical rule of thumb of mine is that a truth in one culture has at least some generalizability to other cultures. Explicit beliefs may be radically different but are actually more accurately perceived as being part of a continuum. Our knowledge of thinking has progressed, like other sciences, under the Euro-American cultural tradition. The ability to think is conceptualized as something residing in the mind of each individual. But evidence suggests that the Japanese view of thinking as a social and interpersonal phenomenon may also be important. Fujinaga has conducted a 10-year follow-up of two children who, at ages five and seven, were found in isolated confinement in which they had been put by their insane father (Fujinaga *et al.*, 1989). At the time they were found, they were so severely retarded because of their long social deprivation that they were not capable of verbal communication, and their intelligence test scores were extremely low. Their "spurt" in intellectual development closely followed their establishing attachment to their care-givers.

The Right to be Unintelligent

A colleague of mine, having learned about the famous slogan of Dr Machado of Venezuela to the effect that all people should have the right to be intelligent, once muttered: "Well, it is a great idea. In our so-called developed countries, however, isn't it equally important to protect the right to be unintelligent?"

It is an unwelcome but undeniable fact that that in our society, schools are functioning as agents of social selection. If as a result of school pressures on children, thinking comes to mean nothing more than the need to think alone, and if this ability for isolated thinking becomes one more hurdle in the rat race for academic and social promotion, then the right to remain a poor thinker needs to be protected. When we think together, a person who can ask a naive and honest question is just as important as a person who can provide a sophisticated answer or a creative proposal.

Of course, thinking is important in our civilization. Our school curricula should encourage thinking and foster the ability and readiness to think. However, it should be kept in mind that although thinking ability which is content and culture free does exist, it will not alone account for a major portion of variance in the actual attainment of the goal of thinking. Motivation, the organization of workmates, and the Aptitude Treatment Interaction (ATI) in a broad sense will perhaps carry greater weight as long as we are dealing with the normal range of general intellectual ability. A successful programme for encouraging thinking must include plans for embedding the problem in a meaningful context, motivating children and organizing a peer culture which will encourage thinking. Speaking intuitively, I think the success of the de Bono method owes more to the fact that it systematically removes the learned helplessness related to the problem-solving domain, revitalizes the student's constructive motivation, and helps to improve relationships among peers, than to the actual materials used in the method.

Many of the instructional programmes claiming to promote thinking that I have seen in my own country have ended up either as an élitist selection programme to weed out less efficient thinkers, or as a drill in sequential reasoning in which the particular developer believed, or even as an exercise for training children to read the mind of the teacher. Common to most of these programmes were the poor self-confidence, poor group organization, and lack of warmth they engendered among the students in the class. This result was further exacerbated by the academic pressure for short-range excellence, that is, success in the entrance examination (Kashiwagi, 1984).

If I were to advise Japanese curriculum developers how to make their products more thinking-oriented, I would suggest they retain the current subjects as far as content is concerned. Children are in school only for a limited time. How to allocate this limited time to various activities is the greatest practical concern of those who write courses of study for actual use. If new content claims an added portion of this time, unnecessary friction is caused. I would, however, ask them to be especially creative in designing activities both for teachers and students:

(i) The teacher should see each child as an integral part of the context in which learning takes place. The teacher should know not only all the children's learning readiness and intelligence, but also their pride, their aspirations, and the meaning they attribute to themselves.

(ii) An honest, supportive and co-operative classroom culture should be fostered. The way the teacher relates to the children will have a significant influence upon this classroom culture.

(iii) The teacher him or herself must be a thinker who is open to asking and to being asked questions.

(iv) The learning tasks should be so designed that problems arise in a context which is meaningful in some way.

(v) Interpersonal interaction and co-operation should be encouraged in tackling problems. Good classes are usually moderately noisy.

(vi) Incentive systems should be designed so that the attainment of self-control in the form of patience and co-operation is encouraged, as well as the attainment of an effective solution.

What I have written is particularly relevant to Japanese schooling today. I hope the issues I have raised and the points I have discussed are, nevertheless, generalizable to education systems in other cultures.

References

Azuma, H. and Kashiwagi, K. (1987). "Descriptors for an intelligent person," *Japanese Psychological Research*, **29**, pp. 17–26.

Bono, E. de (1978). *Teaching Thinking*, Penguin Books, Harmondsworth.

Fujinaga, T. *et al.* (1989). *Shoki-kankyo to Chiteki Hattatsu (Early Environment and Cognitive Development)*, Tokyo:

Gardner, H. (1985). *The Mind's New Science*, Basic Books, New York.

Gardner, H. (1983). *Frames of Mind: The Theory of Multiple Intelligences*. Basic Books, New York.

Hess, R. D. *et al.* (1986). "Family influences on school readiness and achievement in Japan and the

United States: An overview of a longitudinal study," in Stevenson, H.; Azuma, H.; and Hakuta, K. (eds.), *Child Development and Education in Japan*, Freeman, New York, Chapter 11.

Kashiwagi, K. (1984). *Ninchimen oyobi joimen ni okeru jukenatsuryoku no eikyou ni kansuru shinrigaku-teki kenkyuu* (*A Psychological Study of the Cognitive and Affective Influences of the Pressure of Entrance Examination*), A report on 1983 Ministry of Education Science Research Grant, Tokyo.

Toda, M. (1987). *Kokoro wo motta Kikai* (*A Machine with its Mind*), Diamond-sha, Tokyo.

Weisz, J. R., Rothman, F. M. and Blackburn, T. C. (1984). "The psychology of control in America and Japan." *American Psychologist*, pp. 970–971.

IV

Appendix

15

Background Report:
The Key Issues and Literature
Reviewed

BY THE SECRETARIAT

Centre for Educational Research and Innovation,
OECD, Paris

Introduction

Can thinking be taught? Many are sceptical about the idea, in some cases because they regard thinking as an activity which comes naturally, like walking or talking. Others reject the idea because they see thinking as dependent on intelligence; and believing this to be an innate quality, they doubt if teaching can have any lasting effect on it. This view of intelligence is increasingly challenged, and even those who hold the view may accept that, with appropriate training and experience, potential can be realized more fully.

> We think without being taught to do so . . . It does not follow from the fact that we think spontaneously that we think as effectively as we might . . . the challenge is not so much to teach thinking as to teach good thinking. (Nickerson, 1988, p. 3)

The issue proves to be more complex than the simple question, "Can thinking be taught?" Following the procedures of those who aim to teach problem solving, we need to examine our definitions and to formulate our questions more precisely. Developing capable learners has long been accepted as a prime aim of education. Does this involve more than the acquisition of knowledge, and if so, what more? Thinking involves the appropriate use of knowledge, and we should not assume that this competence will develop spontaneously. Thinking is an imprecise term which includes problem solving, decision making, critical thinking, logical reasoning and creative thinking (Nickerson, 1988, p. 9, lists 12 references which give numerous definitions of thinking). These are activities which go beyond knowledge acquisition, and there is reason to believe that current educational practice has not given adequate attention to these aspects of thinking.

The conclusion of many working in this field is that some of these aspects of thinking can be developed or strengthened by appropriate teaching (for example, Nickerson, 1988, p. 3–9; Marzano *et al.*, 1988, pp. 1–3; Presseisen, 1987, pp. 1–10; Resnick, 1987, pp. 46–47; Baron and Sternberg, 1987, pp. 182–217; Glaser, 1984, pp. 102–103). Even if this claim is considered as still unproven, the aim is so important that it is reasonable at least to try to achieve it.

The crucial question which runs through the whole argument is this: what is "appropriate teaching"? Should we be concerned with teaching "thinking skills" in specially designed programmes, or can it best be done by changing the style of teaching the established disciplines?

There are over 100 programmes on the market which claim to improve thinking skills. But other researchers equally vehemently argue for an infusion of thinking through the traditional subjects of the curriculum, using a problem approach to alert students to, and train them in, the thinking skills and strategies at the heart of these subjects.

The concept of transfer is crucial, whatever the method: the criterion of effective teaching of thinking is whether specific learning can be transferred to new and unfamiliar situations. This issue is discussed in the final section.

The section on "Methods and Approaches" reviews the issue of "separate skills courses versus infusion" more fully, subdividing the "infusion" approach to cover: (i) the problem-based teaching of subjects such as science and mathematics; (ii) the humanities, including language and literature, writing and philosophy; (iii) computers and information technology.

Which of these is likely to be the most effective? The answer depends partly on how we define thinking. We must distinguish between those who aim to teach thinking explicitly and those who advocate the use of "discovery methods" and "active learning" as the best way of teaching a particular subject. The second group is not teaching thinking unless one believes that there are different forms of thinking—mathematical thinking, scientific thinking, legal thinking, historical thinking and so on—and there are no common elements among these which can be applied more generally. It is not enough to teach the separate forms and hope that students will make the necessary generalization and application spontaneously (Perkins and Salomon, 1988, call this the "Bopeep Theory": "Leave them alone and they'll come home . . ."). Transfer is again the key issue here. This aspect, referred to in the literature as the "local knowledge" issue, is discussed further at the end of this paper.

In the long term, the question, "Can thinking be taught?" will be answered by evaluation studies. Relatively few programmes have been evaluated systematically and critically: Nickerson (1988, p. 43) warns of "unsubstantiated claims . . . one–sided assessments . . . (and) excessive promotionalism". (Evaluation is discussed more fully below.)

Historical Background

Influences which have shaped developing theories on the nature of reasoning and the teaching of thinking are reviewed here under four broad headings: *developments in psychology*; in philosophy and logic (*philosophical approaches*); in computer science, information processing and artificial intelligence (*information technology*); and in pedagogical theories and educational reform generally (*curriculum innovation*). These influences overlap and interact.

The idea, of course, is not new. Improvement of the intellect has long been one of the aims of formal education, from Plato through the centuries. Montaigne recognized that "mieux vaut une tête bien faite qu'une tête bien pleine", whilst Goethe noted that "every new object, well contemplated, opens up a new organ within us". In the nineteenth century, the study of languages (especially Latin with its systematic grammatical structure) and mathematics was seen as "mental discipline" for exercising the "faculty" of reason.

Developments in Psychology

The faculty psychology on which nineteenth-century educational theory was based was discredited by Thorndike and others (Thorndike, 1906; Thorndike and Woodworth, 1901), who showed that transfer of training from "mental discipline" was very limited. In its place, a theory of innate general intelligence dominated much of the educational practice of the first half of the twentieth century. Ability to reason was seen as a quality of the mind which was largely inborn and relatively unchanging. This view is still widely held in popular thinking.

Developments in cognitive psychology since 1950, however, have led to a rather different interpretation of intelligence (Bruner, Goodnow and Austin, 1956; Brunner, 1960), linking reasoning to the structuring of experience, the development of schemata and the formation of concepts. Intelligence has also been closely linked to language acquisition (Chomsky, 1972; Vygotsky, 1961). Studies of the relationship between language and learning achievement (Bernstein, 1961) have important implications for schooling.

While Vygotsky and Bruner argue that it is by acquiring the means to communicate that cognitive and linguistic processes develop, Piaget's theory of intelligence is more closely linked to neurophysiological development. Put simply, the theory (Piaget and Inhelder, 1964) sees the functioning of intelligence as linked to progressive stages of neural development in which cognitive structures form and reform. Progress is stimulated by the continuing engagement with environmental factors such as social interaction and communication. For a number of years, Piaget's theories dominated teacher education and played an important part in helping teachers to understand the child's capacity for learning and its natural limitations.

Cognitive psychology has developed these ideas extensively in recent years. New theories of intelligence have emerged, such as Gardner's "multiple intelligence" (1983) and Sternberg's "triarchic intelligence" (1985), while Flavell's "metacognition" (1976) is one of several new approaches to how thinking can be learned. In the analysis of reasoning, Sternberg (1983) distinguished between "executive" and "non-executive" processes, the executive processes being those which manage the operation of the others, a terminology derived from information processing. The fields of artificial intelligence and information science generally (see below) have provided a stimulus to these developments and helped to establish a theoretical basis for the current phase of programmes in thinking and problem solving.

Philosophical approaches

In the medieval university curriculum, the study of logic was seen as a training in rational thinking. The concepts of formal logic have had a profound influence on our understanding of thinking and the analysis of argument; but the skills taught in the traditional logic course are not readily transferable to thinking about practical problems which are ill defined, unstructured and "fuzzy". In the twentieth century, in the field of educational philosophy, Dewey's writings made an early and significant contribution to the analysis of thinking and implications for teaching it. Several of the ideas mentioned in the previous paragraphs were foreshadowed by Dewey. In *How We Think* (1910) he stated that, "The intellectual side of education consists in the formation of wide-awake, careful, thorough habits of thinking" (pp. 28); and "There is no single and uniform power of thought, but a multitude of different ways" (p. 45).

Dewey's analysis of reflective thinking (summarized by Cuban, 1984, p. 664), comprising five steps (identify the problem, define the problem, generate hypotheses, refine a hypothesis, test the hypothesis) was the first of many attempts to analyse the reasoning process into a sequence of steps. Kilpatrick, the founder of the Project Method, wrote in the 1920s that "American education discovered the problem approach as a teaching device" from Dewey's analysis of reflective thought (quoted in Dykhuisen,

1973, p. 140). The project method and the problem approach, however, were seen at the time as ways of improving the teaching of knowledge and subject-related skills, rather than as a means to teach thinking and general reasoning.

Philosophical interest in thinking as an educational objective was stimulated by a seminal paper by Ennis in 1962 on the concept of critical thinking. Ennis defines critical thinking as "reasonable reflective thinking that is focused on deciding what to believe or do" (see Baron and Sternberg, 1987, p. 10).

A further stimulus to philosophical interest has come from the writings of Lipman (Lipman, Sharp and Oscamyan 1980) and Paul (1984). Lipman's "Philosophy for Children" programme uses a technique of story-telling to highlight philosophical issues in everyday life, and these issues are discussed by the characters in his books (see Lipman, in this volume; Baron and Sternberg, 1987, pp. 151–167). Paul's approach stresses "dialogical thinking"—seeing problems and their solutions from different points of view—as a basis for teaching critical thinking (see Baron and Sternberg, 1987, pp. 125–148). He distinguishes between the "weak" and "strong" meanings of critical thinking: the "weak" sense merely takes account of other viewpoints to protect one's own beliefs, while the "strong" sense of the term implies a fair-minded capacity to understand counter-arguments (Paul, 1984).

Information technology

A third category of influences which have shaped ideas about thinking is associated with computers, programming, information processing and artificial intelligence. The task of designing programmes and procedures for information processing and retrieval has necessarily drawn upon our knowledge of human mental processes for doing these things; and though there are (probably) basic differences, the rapid growth of sophistication of computers has resulted in a stimulus to the study of similarities between human thinking and machine "thinking" or artificial intelligence.

A second strand within this category is the writing of computer programs explicitly to make students think or to train them in thinking by giving them guided practice. Claims of this kind are made for the computer language LOGO (cf. p. 182). Programming obliges one to analyse processes and thus to think about how the mind works. Some educational computer programs aim to teach mental strategies by exercising them in games which hold the learners' interest. However, Perkins and Salomon (1988), quoting reviews by Clements (1985), Dalbey and Linn (1985), and Salomon and Perkins (1987), conclude that "The track record of efforts to enhance cognitive skills via programming is discouraging. Most findings have been negative" (p. 24).

Curriculum innovation

The fourth category of influence, that of educational reform and curriculum development generally, is difficult to summarize because of its overlap with the other three; but it represents an important underlying factor in creating a climate which is receptive to the idea of teaching thinking. Reference has already been made to studies of language acquisition and their impact on teacher education and classroom practice. Curriculum reform in the 1960s introduced a range of new programmes which emphasized a problem approach to promote the active involvement of learners. In the United States, projects in the sciences especially, and others such as Bruner's "Man a Course of Study" (MACOS); and the Nuffield and Schools Council programmes in the United Kingdom all adopted this approach. In various subjects (again, especially science and mathematics), analyses of concepts—and of misconceptions (Novak, 1987; Novak *et al.*, 1989) which act as a barrier to learning—have switched attention to the process of learning instead of only the knowledge content. In the teaching of mathematics, Polya's (1957), analysis of problem solving, outlining recommended heuristic procedures, has influenced a generation of authors of books on this subject. The process of writing and the thinking which accompanies it have been analysed to provide guides on how it may best be taught (Scardamalia and Bereiter, 1981; Scardamalia, Bereiter and Steinbach, 1984; Applebee, 1984).

These developments. however, have aimed essentially at devising more effective means of teaching subjects and their related skills, rather than at teaching thinking. Work in the area of "special needs", with children of below-average attainment, has focused more precisely on processes of thinking, learning and memory (Presseisen, 1988). For the rest, the major question is, once again, whether educational methods which stress discovery, active learning and problem solving within subject disciplines, transfer their effects to other spheres; and this question is discussed further below.

Current Interest

The principal concern amongst OECD member countries is to achieve higher quality education to meet changing and more complex social and economic demands. Whilst the minimal requirements of schooling are often described in this respect as mastery of "the basics" (mathematics, science, reading and writing), it is becoming increasingly clear that broader competencies are required by all school leavers to meet the needs of the labour market and democratic citizenship (OECD, 1987).

A number of significant trends have been identified, such as:

(i) the increasing need for a flexible work-force capable of being retrained, perhaps repeatedly;

(ii) production tasks which increasingly require the application of intelligent judgement to technological tasks and systems rather than dexterity in manual skills;

(iii) the need for workers to comprehend, interpret and communicate, not between discrete processes but as participants within, often intricate, human and machine systems;

(iv) the emergence of enterprise skills in societies where possibilities seem limitless, but in which increasingly the prevailing culture seldom provides clear references for good practice; linked to this are

(v) the increasingly complex demands of good citizenship, where intersubjective truth becomes less easy to identify.

A new range of cognitive skills is called for to meet the demands of this changing context. Whilst memorizing, translating and calculating are still important capacities, the need is widely recognized for "the basics" to be redefined in terms of higher-order thinking skills, and the influences mentioned above (developments in psychology, philosophical approaches, information technology and curriculum innovation) have opened up possibilities of meeting that need.

At a deeper level of analysis, interest in the topic can be interpreted as "a democratization of thinking", extending what was formerly an objective for education only of the élite to a new interpretation of "literacy" in mass education: "It is a new challenge to develop educational programmes that assume that all individuals, not just an élite, can become competent thinkers" (Resnick, 1987, p. 7).

The concern with effective education for thinking and reasoning has been raised by a number of OECD member countries in the recent survey of trends in curriculum development (OECD, 1990). In Canada, for instance, the curriculum is currently under review in several provinces. There is a redefinition of basic skills taking place which goes beyond the "three R's". In Saskatchewan, in particular, "essential learnings have been identified, which include learning to think". It is significant that at a recent conference on the curriculum ("Curriculum at the Centre", Montreal, May 1989), two sessions were devoted to the topic, whilst no session directly addressed the subject matter more traditionally associated with basic skills.

Finland has made a strong investment in the FACE programme (Formal Aims of Cognitive Education; see Voutilainen in this volume), which aims to help teachers understand the nature of cognition, and review their own teaching method. There is a recognition that it is more important to increase the ability to think rather than teach factual information; skills of analysis and the ability to use information technology appropriately are being stressed.

In France, teaching in the Lycée has been traditionally founded on the importance of the process of reasoning and abstraction and the development of students' independence in the organization of their work. There is a new commitment at ministerial level to the aim of effective thinking as an important outcome of education. *Initiative et Formation*, a training agency sponsored by the Ministry, monitors the implementation of the ideas of de la Garanderie on attention, reflection, memorization and imagination (see, for example, de la Garanderie and Caltar, 1988).

In Italy a reappraisal of the curriculum is taking place following the Fassino Report (1982). The new curriculum is to be based on the notion of the child as a cognitively active individual. There is a major reform of primary education under way, and fundamental skills are being redefined, such as the acquisition of language and a basic mastery of the conceptual areas, skills and research procedures which are necessary for understanding.

In Japan the fundamental role of the school is stated as being to develop abilities to think, judge and express oneself. The Report of The National Council on Educational Reform (1986) argues for emphasis on logical thinking, imagination and inspiration. "Problem study" is proposed as a new "subject", and an important objective of education is to achieve "affluent humanity" by means of appropriate social and moral education; the aim is to create a society where personal and social values underpin material success.

In curriculum guidelines issued in Norway in 1987, problem solving is an important aspect of study in several curricula. Reports from other countries also mention this concern. In the United Kingdom, for example, the new syllabuses for GCSE (the national examination at 16), emphasize a problem-solving approach in many areas (Association of Teachers of Mathematics, 1984), as do the new Standard Grade syllabuses for SCE, the equivalent examination in Scotland. An influential report on the teaching of mathematics (*Mathematics Counts*, The Cockcroft Report, 1982) states: "The ability to solve problems is at the heart of mathematics". Local initiatives in England include the Somerset Thinking Skills Course (Blagg, Ballinger and Gardner, 1988), the Oxfordshire Skills programme and the Hertfordshire Achievement Project.

It is especially in North America that the idea of teaching thinking has been taken up most energetically. There, the explosion of interest in teaching thinking was sparked by concern over educational standards. Following the introduction of "minimum competency testing" in many states in the 1970s, there is now concern that the test programmes are testing the wrong things, and that it is possible to get through 12 years of schooling without ever having to think at all. Various national commissions in the United States have stressed the importance of critical thinking, especially in our rapidly changing post-industrial society (see Ennis in Baron and Sternberg, 1987, p. 9). California, Connecticut, Michigan and Pennsylvania are among the states which have introduced mandatory testing of critical thinking; and California's state universities specify the study of critical thinking as a requirement for graduation. Courses in thinking skills (usually within subject disciplines) have been offered in some universities for more than 10 years. In Canada, to take only one example, York District of Ontario appointed a thinking skills consultant to their advisory staff some four years ago. In response to this pressure, there has been a flood of programmes and books: Paul (1989, in interview) estimated the number of programmes currently on the market at over one hundred.

To illustrate the extent and range of publication, an Annex lists a selection of reviews, books and programmes on the topic. These lists are incomplete, especially in respect of programmes and materials for schools: to cover these adequately would require a listing of virtually all the publishers' catalogues of school texts. There are also many computer programs designed to develop reasoning, none of which has been included in these lists.

It is difficult to avoid overweighting the North American work in this review because so much has been published. Parallel developments in other countries have not been reported so extensively, possibly because many of the initiatives are still at a relatively early stage, or because they use different conceptual structures, thus limiting international exchange of ideas. In the United States, there are several networks of agencies involved in this area of development: for example, the Association for Supervision and Curriculum Development (ASCD) Collaborative on Teaching Thinking; a committee of the nine regional laboratories producing annotated bibliographies (Boswell and Coan, 1989, Kanach, 1989); a network centred on Montclair State University; and various other centres. The organizations of conferences on thinking provides a less formal but more extensive network of contacts for those working in this field. Presseisen (1986a) lists 29 conferences held on this theme within a span of 28 months. An International Conference on Critical Thinking is held annually at Sonoma in California; and there has been a series of international psychological conferences, each of which has resulted in a major publication (e.g. Tuma and Reif, 1980; Segal, Chipman and Glaser, 1985; Perkins, Lochhead and Bishop, 1987).

Finally, research on the psychological, philosophical and pedagogical aspects of teaching thinking is being undertaken at many universities, colleges and research centres throughout North America. Possibly the largest research programmes are at the University of Pittsburgh and Harvard University in the United States and at the Ontario Institute for

Studies in Education in Canada; but significant work is being done by researchers in at least 30 other centres in North America, as well as in Australia and several European countries.

Methods and Approaches

The extensive range of development described in the last section has produced a wide variety of methods in, and approaches to, the teaching of thinking. At first sight there seem to be almost as many different lists of thinking skills, processes, procedures and strategies as there are writers, and as many different methods recommended. The aim of this section is to categorize the different methods and approaches, distinguishing a "skills" approach and three variants of the "infusion" approach. Those who adopt a "skills" approach identify component skills in thinking, and practise these skills through exercises which are usually "content-free" or not closely linked with any one subject discipline. A contrasting view is held by those who argue for "infusion", embedding the teaching of thinking within the traditional curricula, on the grounds that the process of thinking is inseparable from the content. The skills approach has the advantage of focusing attention on the process of thinking: this, together with an understanding of metacognition (Flavell, 1976) or "executive processes" (Sternberg, 1983), makes possible a more efficient "management" of one's thinking. Those who reject this argue that much (perhaps even all) of the thinking we do is "domain specific" (such as the manipulation of number in basic mathematical thinking according to procedures which have to be learnt).

Skills approach

If there are skills involved in thinking, independent of specific content, then the idea of training people in these skills is at least worth considering. Examples of such generalizable skills might include: looking for evidence, using analogies, quantifying as percentages for comparisons of unequals, stopping to think, seeking counter-arguments, being suspicious of evidence which confirms your strongly held prejudices, and so on. If good advice like this can carry over into action (how do we ensure that?), it seems sound sense to teach it. But are these really "skills"? Many authors have produced lists of what they variously call skills or strategies or processes or procedures or heuristics. Some are in plain terms: Bransford and Stein (1984) offer IDEAL: Identification of problems, Definition, Exploration of strategies, Acting on ideas, Looking for effects. Feuerstein et al (1980) use materials described as "content-free", in the form of "instruments", for example, organization of dots, orientation in space, comparisons, numerical progressions, and so on, each designed to foster particular mental skills with a teacher's guide covering objectives, methods and suggestions for lessons. Others are more detailed: Marzano *et al.* (1988) offer 21 core thinking skills, two concerned with focusing, two with information gathering, two with remembering, four with organizing, four with analysing, three with generating, two with integrating and two with evaluating. Arter and Salomon (1988) have produced a matrix of no fewer than 53 thinking skills, distilled from a range of publications.

This skills approach is criticized by Sternberg (in Baron and Sternberg, 1987. p. 253) under a heading "Is having the right thought processes tantamount to being a good thinker?". To this question he asserts that the answer is "a resounding no". Also required (as many of those he criticizes would agree) are: knowing how to combine skills into workable strategies for solving problems; effective mental representations, to be able to see both sides of a case; a knowledge base, since thinking must be performed in the context of knowledge; and motivation to use the skills learnt. Glaser (1984, p. 99) attributes the popularity of this "skills" approach to the influence of information-processing theories. While recognizing a limited utility in teaching general processes, he argues that higher-order thinking is best learned through the study of "knowledge-rich" domains of subjects in the traditional curriculum of education.

Infusion approach 1: Problem-based teaching and learning

Teaching thinking through a problem-based approach within the conventional curriculum subjects is usually associated with mathematics and science. Mathematicians, for example, for many years have used the teaching method of setting problems for students to solve. Since the ability to solve mathematical problems is a relevant area of competence in the subject, practice in problem solving is an acceptable activity. But students benefit from guidance in how to go about finding solutions (e.g. Polya, 1957; Schoenfeld, 1985), rather than leaving them to sink or swim. It is certainly not sufficient merely to tell them the solution: they have to apply the recommended procedures to other new examples. If new examples are closely similar to the context in which a procedure has been learned, there is relatively little transfer; but in the study of mathematics one hopes for larger leaps and broader generalizations. Can such thinking become generalizable beyond the bounds of mathematics? How might the teaching of mathematics encourage more extensive transfer, so that we are teaching thinking rather than mathematical thinking?

Scientific thinking has similarly been the subject of intensive inquiry in many countries. In the United Kingdom, for example, the science education journals carry a running debate on the topic (Hodson, 1985; Driver and Oldham, 1986; Millar and Driver, 1987). Earlier work had proceeded on the lines of identifying scientific skills to be taught (like observing, hypothesizing and inferring), leading to a "process approach" to science teaching which some rejected indignantly as "content-free science". The argument is relevant to the teaching of thinking (as distinct from the teaching of science) if the purpose of teaching science is to prepare people to cope with everyday problems, rather than to produce scientists. Clearly the knowledge component is essential, but the application of scientific knowledge and skills must extend beyond the traditional limits of discipline.

History and social studies, and professional training programmes in engineering, medicine and law, are other examples of areas in which the problem approach has been adopted with the aim of developing thinking within a context of specialized knowledge. The rationale underlying the techniques involved has been outlined by Swartz (see Baron and Sternberg, 1987, pp. 106–126) who describes in detail how infusion can be done in a variety of subject-matter areas in a way that reinforces thinking skills.

While this style of approach commands wide support among educational writers, the crucial question is how to ensure that specific skills and strategies are applied more generally. This would seem to require some coherent policy of "thinking across the curriculum" if the approach is not to be merely a more efficient means of teaching subjects. This assertion is based on the belief that the aim of education is not just to produce good lawyers or scientists or historians, but to produce good thinkers.

Infusion approach 2: Study of the humanities

The study of literature has traditionally been seen as an essential component in general education, since literature extends our experience vicariously, alerts us to moral issues and opens up new insights. The study of philosophy similarly can extend our understanding of the nature of knowledge and experience. These aims, however, will be attained only if they are clearly accepted as objectives by those who teach. Traditional philosophy has not been notably successful in achieving transfer of training to practical issues. The analysis of terms like "premise", "inference" and "assumption" can provide insights into logical thinking (Paul, 1984); and courses in "informal logic" come closer to the handling of practical problems than the inflexible structures of formal logic. If we interpret "thinking" as including judgements based on values—surely we must, since thinking is not just an intellectual puzzle-solving activity—then the fields of moral education and ethics are brought in. In the moral dimension of teaching thinking, is the aim to teach insight or virtue (or is the first necessary for the second)?

Methods of teaching thinking through philosophy are reviewed in the publications, mentioned previously, by Lipman (Philosophy for Children) and Paul (Dialogical Thinking and Socratic Questioning). For example,

Lipman's first novel, *Harry Stottlemeier's Discovery*, introduces Aristotle's class logic, transitivity and symmetry, and propositional logic, in the context of a children's story. Paul (1989) extends his methods of teaching critical thinking into other fields such as social studies by "critical-thinking writing-prompts" which focus attention on issues and judgements.

The strength of the approach through the humanities is that it recognizes the importance of uniquely human capacities such as motivation and emotion. In arguing for the place of the arts in the curriculum, Greene (1989) reminds us that cognitive development is the product of an intersubjectively lived world, a world of ambiguous meaning in which the young learner progresses by intuition and imagination as well as analysis. To those who hold this view, the skills model is an insult to the human mind, a mechanical assembly-line interpretation of education.

Infusion approach 3: Information technology and computers

This "mechanical" criticism readily springs to mind when we turn to the contribution of information technology and computers. But the introduction of computers across the curriculum, if done self-consciously with the aim of developing thinking, can promote the same "infusion" as the other approaches in our classification. It may even do it more effectively, because computers allow individual working, active involvement and instant feedback, and they do this in a way which clearly holds the interest of many young learners. Whatever evaluation studies may say about LOGO, for example, there is no doubt that its use generates interest and insight into the processes of problem solving (Papert, 1980). The evidence (Perkins and Salomon, 1988, p. 24) that training in programming does not seem to transfer may be explained in terms of the difficulty which students experience with it, and the failure of those who teach it to extract transferable principles in their concern to teach limited techniques. It may also be argued that evaluation in this developing field is premature: few people would have believed in the potential of air travel on the evidence available in, say, 1905.

One particularly promising line of development, not necessarily linked with computers, is the devising of "thinking games" for children (and for adults too). Computer games already have a large and growing market, but there are similar games which require no mechanical apparatus. Torbert (1980), for example, describes a large range of games designed to exploit the contribution which play can make to mental development. The chapter headings in her book include: attention span and concentration, listening skills, self-control, and development of thinking processes. Here again, transfer is crucial. The crossword puzzle may enlarge our vocabulary, or it may be only an artificial diversion with its own highly specific, non-transferable, "useless" skills.

At a more specific level, when we turn to examine methods which various writers recommend for the teaching of thinking, we find that these cut across the categories outlined earlier: "The effectiveness of strategy training appears to depend not only on what strategies are taught, but how they are taught" (Nickerson, 1988, p. 18).

Most writers suggest using a range of methods, of which the following is only a selected list:

> (i) *direct instruction* in the component skills of thinking, with exercises and guided practice;
>
> (ii) *modelling*, the teacher or parent providing a demonstration of procedure for the learner to follow, sometimes talking through one's thought processes in order to externalize them for the learner; Collins, Seely-Brown and Newman (1989) use the term *cognitive apprenticeship* for the way experts apply modelling, with the ancillary stages of "scaffolding" and "fading";
>
> (iii) *co-operative learning*, in small group discussion or working in pairs (Whimbey and Lochhead, 1984); Palincsar and Brown's (1984) "reciprocal teaching" combines this with modelling, in that the teacher models initially and then the learner takes over; de Bono (1973) also uses co-operative learning;
>
> (iv) *metacognition*, used to raise awareness of mental process and to provide leverage for regulating one's thinking (Flavell, 1976; Haller, Child and Walberg, 1988); cognitive maps (Novak and Gowin, 1984) similarly help to externalize mental processes;
>
> (v) *questioning*, using a Socratic or "dialogical" method (Paul, 1984).

These and other methods may be used to promote thinking, whether one adopts a "separate skills" approach or when problem-based instruction is infused throughout the curriculum (or within the context of a single field of study). One feature which they have in common is that they imply a change in classroom climate. Presseisen (1986b) writes: "Creating a climate that will support critical-mindedness and thoughtful reflection is a primary step. Opening teachers' minds to new ideas that may be found in this research literature can be the initial act of this process" (p. 26).

Glaser (1984), reviewing a range of methods within specialized subjects, concludes:

> The pedagogical implication that follows from this is that an effective strategy for instruction involves a kind of interrogation and confrontation. Expert teachers do this effectively, employing case method approaches, discovery methods and various forms of Socratic inquiry dialogue ... Such interactive inquiry methods are powerful tools for teaching thinking in the context of subject matter. (p. 101)

Evaluation

There has been relatively little evaluation of programmes designed to teach thinking. The evaluations which have been reported tend to be small-scale, involving disappointingly small numbers or using only a limited measure of effectiveness. Inevitably, evaluations are short-term, since there is insufficient time to follow up any group for long-term effects. It is also difficult to decide what should be taken as firm evidence of success, or to distinguish between the merits of the materials and the methods adopted in using them, or to take account of the quality of teaching.

Baron and Sternberg (1987, pp. 221–247) devote a full chapter to evaluation in their review of the field, but mostly on what should be done rather on what has been done. They recommend using a variety of styles of evaluation for different purposes. Their list of 10 "concerns" for summative evaluation is fairly demanding and probably has not been fully satisfied by any of the studies reported. They recognize the value of less rigorous procedures for formative evaluation as a guide to further development.

Resnick (1987) notes that "the most common evaluation is mastery performance—that is, performance in exercises similar to those included in the programme itself". This is a necessary part of the task, but not sufficient in itself, since it neglects the important question of transfer: "Useful evaluations of higher order skill training programmes require that the educational outcomes of interest be directly assessed" (pp. 32–34). She argues against relying on evidence from test scores because of the risk of coaching, which "can have the effect of suppressing efforts to expand higher order skill teaching". Her summary of evaluation studies (p. 47) reports findings of some improvement in reading comprehension and grade averages, and improved problem solving in mathematics and science, but "not demonstrating (and not necessarily seeking) transfer to other disciplines or to practical life".

Evaluation studies of Feuerstein's Instrumental Enrichment ("one of the best documented programmes", according to Nickerson, 1988. p. 41) have been summarized by Savell, Twohig and Rachford (1986). These generally show beneficial effects, though some of the measures used are scores in tests which resemble the training material. The original report by Feuerstein *et al.* (1980) includes evaluative data. An extensive evaluation in the United Kingdom by the Schools Council (Weller and Craft, 1983), covering five English local education authorities, was unfortunately cut short by the closure of the Council. "The evidence was mixed but largely positive", they report (p. 83). Perhaps more usefully, the study helps to identify "the possibilities and problems associated with the introduction of Instrumental Enrichment" (*ibid.*), the enthusiasm engendered in teachers and pupils, and difficulties in sustaining motivation and in classroom organization.

Edward de Bono reports evaluation data of the CoRT Programme in *Teaching Thinking* (1976) and *CoRT: Teachers' Handbook* (1973):

> Some of the larger, more global objectives of the thinking programmes indicate positive changes in the general nature of many students regarding intelligent behaviour ... the confidence of those who have had training in thinking, the focus of their thinking, their structured approach and breadth of consideration. Teachers often sum up these factors as "maturity" in commenting about these children who come to their classrooms after some training in thinking (de Bono, quoted in Presseisen, 1988).

An independent evaluation by the United Kingdom Schools Council (Hunter-Grundin, 1985) covered the final year classes in 10 primary schools. Feedback from the children was "generally favourable", and the report showed that those who had taken CoRT Thinking Lessons had significantly fewer irrelevant points and ideas. Evidence of improved quality of thinking, however, was not statistically significant: de Bono (private communication, cf. also pp. 12–13) attributes this to the inadequacy of the criterion measures. An Australian evaluation (Edwards, 1988) shows significant gains from the CoRT-1 Programme on a number of measures, including IQ and a Thinking Approaches questionnaire.

Reports on several other projects and programmes have been published, but often with insufficient detail for the reader to judge their adequacy. Evaluations of three general programmes and four subject-based courses reviewed in Nickerson *et al.* (1985) show positive effects of training, as did a detailed evaluation of Project Intelligence (Herrnstein *et al.*, 1986) covering 400 seventh graders in Venezuela, together with a control group (using mental tests as a criterion measure).

The psychological literature also includes studies which, while not evaluating programmes, report experimental tests of the effectiveness of different methods (see Nickerson, 1988, pp. 18–19, for example).

Clearly, we need more and better evaluation if teaching thinking is to avoid the kind of backlash criticisms which have been levelled against the progressive education movement. Indeed, progressive education may provide a relevant warning of the danger of a "bandwagon" enthusiasm for an idea which neglects the hard task of evaluation. Nickerson (1988) comments:

> The field also needs more self-criticism. It is a bit paradoxical that some developers of programmes to teach critical thinking have had less than severely critical attitudes toward their own work. This is unfortunate. Unsubstantiated claims ... one-sided assessments ... excessive promotionalism ... are serious threats to an extremely important area of research and educational endeavour. They invite the kind of destructive criticism that can undermine the whole field,

when what is needed is the kind of sympathetic but uncompromising criticism that can help progress without an excessive amount of wasted effort. (p. 43)

Emerging Trends

Which are the promising lines in current research and writing on teaching thinking? Can we identify emerging trends which may help to indicate priorities and predict development? Three areas of current interest are suggested in this section.

There is a tendency to see the teaching of thinking in a wider context, challenging and changing existing pedagogical styles, and to see this as possibly in the long term a more important influence for education than novel materials or methods. To introduce the teaching of thinking into the curriculum involves more than the addition of a course on reasoning skills. Resnick (1987, p. 49) refers to reasoning as "a new enabling discipline in the school curriculum"; but this is not meant to suggest that it is another "subject" to be taught. Indeed, if students are required to attend a class in thinking, teachers of established subjects may be less inclined to give proper attention to thinking in their own teaching. Resnick (*ibid.*) argues that the movement implies "reorienting instruction". White (in Novak *et al.*, 1989) describes the objective as not the acquisition of knowledge about thinking but a restructuring of knowledge itself. In an interview with Brandt, the editor of *Educational Leadership*, Resnick outlines the implications (Brandt, 1989). Current testing and teaching are often based on a perception of knowledge as a collection of bits of information: the educated person is thus seen as one who knows the answers to questions. In contrast, teaching thinking is based on a perception of knowledge as organized systems of thought, with appropriate strategies for finding answers to questions.

This approach implies radical change in objectives and method. Cuban (1984) writes of changing the old "architecture of schooling", "a jumble of old blueprints for the efficient mass production of schooling", which in the past obstructed attempts to introduce the teaching of reasoning as advocated by Dewey, Kilpatrick and the New Education Movement.

These deeper implications may be a reason for possible hostility to the idea. Certainly, knowledge is an integral element of thinking—one cannot think without thinking about something—and detailed knowledge is a characteristic of expert thinking. But a change of emphasis from content to process, from knowledge acquisition to modes of learning, may be seen as challenging traditional conceptions in education and society (Scriven, 1985, p. 11). Goldman (quoted in Baron and Sternberg, 1987, p. 35) reminds us of Socrates' experience of the danger of cultivating the spirit of inquiry in the young.

There is an implicit change in the role of the teacher (Marzano *et al.*, 1988, p. 134) as a mediator of experience. Paul's "dialogical thinking" is an example of a method very different from traditional didactic modes. In her presidential address at a recent American Educational Research Association Conference in San Francisco, Cole (1989) said: "The 'active learner' is incompatible with 'teacher as teller' and 'learner as accumulator' ". Consequently, if the teaching of thinking is to be implemented effectively, we need a radical change in the professional training of teachers (Lipman, Paul and others in Benderson, 1984 pp. 16–17). This topic is reviewed in detail by Nickerson (1988, pp. 37–39).

One interesting idea is that it is the teachers, not the students, who can benefit most from courses in thinking skills, for a better understanding of how to organize their teaching and the students' learning (see, for instance, the Finnish Project FACE).

Glaser's summary (1984) brings the various points together:

> The cognitive skills developed by people in a society are profoundly influenced by the ways knowledge and literacy are taught and used ... The task is to produce a changed environment for learning—an environment in which there is a new relationship between students and their subject matter, in which knowledge and skill become objects of interrogation, inquiry and extrapolation. As individuals acquire knowledge, they should also be empowered to think and reason (pp. 102–103).

A second trend in current research is the assessment of critical thinking, the search for ways of testing reasoning rather than facts and memory. In many countries, and especially in secondary and tertiary education, the examination system is a major determinant of what is taught, how it is taught and how students set about their learning. Existing systems of competency testing and formal examinations are an obstacle to change (Glaser, in Wagner *et al.*, 1989); but new methods of assessment, if they can be developed, would act as a powerful level to influence content, method and aims in the curriculum.

Development of new styles of testing is already a priority for the Educational Testing Service in the United States, which has organized conferences on the topic. The College Entrance Examination board Task Force on "Learning Strategies and Thinking" (Nickerson *et al.*, 1985) recommended the development of tests "to assess the extent to which a student has acquired effective learning and thinking strategies". In California's school test programme, by 1985 one third of all the test items had been designed to test critical thinking skills (Paul, 1985). A symposium at the American Educational Research Association Conference (Glaser, in Wagner *et al.*, 1989) discussed examples of approaches to testing which might measure (and thus encourage the teaching of) reasoning. Existing measures of critical thinking are summarized by Presseisen (1986b, pp. 25–26), but these are mostly psychological tests, unrelated to curriculum or instruction. Ennis has developed an essay-type test which measures "cogency of analysis" of an argument (Benderson, 1984, p. 17). In the United Kingdom, the new syllabuses for GCSE in England and SCE Standard Grade in Scotland include provision for new forms of assessment, such as "investigations" (small projects undertaken by students) which cumulatively build a portfolio of work for subjective assessment. New styles of criterion-related assessment are being considered in many countries. The Records of Achievement Schemes of the Curriculum Development Council in Australia, for example, are a major force for change in school-based assessment. They involve students in goal setting, establishing criteria for success, and self-evaluation; the higher-order thinking skills of formulation, analysis and reflection are actively exercised (Mortimore, Keene, Nuttall *et al.* in Broadfoot, 1986).

Reference has already been made to the study of students' misconceptions, where over-simple or erroneous concepts and knowledge structures are a barrier to learning and understanding (Novak, 1987; Novak *et al.*, 1989). Work on diagnostic assessment and error analysis may thus also contribute to research on thinking.

The third trend is the recognition that attitudes and motivation play an important part in thinking. Resnick (1987) refers to this as:

> the *disposition* to higher order thinking. The term disposition should not be taken to imply a biological or inherited trait. As used here, it is more akin to a *habit* of thought, one that can be learned, and, therefore taught. Engaging in higher order thinking with others seems likely to teach students that they have the ability, the permission, and even the obligation to engage in a kind of critical analysis that does not always accept problem formulations as presented or that may challenge an accepted position. We have good reason to believe that shaping this disposition to critical thought is central to developing higher order cognitive abilities in students. (p. 41)

Thus, effective thinking requires not only knowledge about thinking but also the capacity and will to use that knowledge, "not just to teach children new processes but to get them to use these processes widely and frequently" (*ibid.*, p. 42). This aspect is stressed also by others who review the field (Nickerson, 1988, pp. 25–27; Paul in Baron and Sternberg, 1987, pp. 141–142; also Lipman, *ibid.*, p. 160; Sternberg, *ibid.*, pp. 212–213 and 254). How can such attitudes be shaped or encouraged? McGuinness (1988, p. 10) sees Feuerstein's concept of mediation as "central to the role which social interaction plays in cognitive change". The extensive use of "co-operative learning" (Whimbey and Lochhead, 1984 and 1986; and others) is another indication of the importance of social factors. Resnick (1987, pp. 40–41) outlines various ways in which "thinking aloud" in a social setting can improve thinking, allowing others to critique and shape one's performance, providing "scaffolding" through group support, providing occasions for modelling, and through motivation. Garner (1989) suggests that high self-esteem and an internal locus of control are needed, and White (in Novak *et al.*, 1989) notes the need for confidence in developing one's own construction of knowledge in the face of the authority inherent in schooling.

The interdependence of these various factors, cognitive, pedagogical, dispositional, epistemological, is stressed by Nickerson (1988):

> One implication of the interrelatedness of the many aspects of thinking is the need to be aware that the fact that a programme focuses on one aspect does not mean that it will have no effects on others ... Numerous writers ... have cautioned against unbalanced approaches that focus on a single critical component without acknowledging the importance of the others. (pp. 27–29)

Issues

Two major issues deserve special attention: the question of transfer; and the controversy over whether the teaching of thinking is best done by separate courses on general aspects of thinking or by teaching "domain-specific" thinking, the characteristic modes of thinking of the traditional subjects of the curriculum.

Transfer

A critical test of the approach adopted in teaching thinking is whether the competence acquired from instruction can be applied in a context different from that in which it was learned. At the start of the century, Thorndike's analyses (1906) had suggested that transfer depended on identical elements in the material learned and the situation to which it was applied; and he recommended that we should teach for transfer by emphasizing the commonality of elements in situations and the potential applications of knowledge.

The recent work of Perkins and Salomon (summarized in Baron and Sternberg, 1987. p. 51; Perkins and Salomon, 1988) explores the process in clearer detail. They identify "two distinct mechanisms for transfer": high-road and low-road transfer. Low-road transfer occurs as an "automatic triggering of well-rehearsed schemata", as when the ability to drive a car is applied to driving a pick-up truck. High-road transfer is more a conscious choice of action: it involves "active decontextualization and restructuring ... the deliberate mindful abstraction of a principle and its application to a different context" (Perkins, 1989). Low-road transfer depends on perceptual similarities—whether we see two situations as "near" or "distant" is partly a matter of perception—and it could be described as "backward reaching" (finding related experience from the past). High-road transfer involves abstract thinking and metacognitive management of one's thinking: it is "forward reaching" in aiming to predict or anticipate.

This analysis of transfer has implications for teaching. If we wish to improve the likelihood of transfer, we should be clear about which processes we are aiming to encourage. Perkins (Baron and Sternberg, 1987, p. 51) criticizes instructional programmes on thinking skills for failing to establish the necessary conditions for transfer. Both forms of transfer are needed, and one needs to know when each is appropriate. Much of the learning in the early stages of education (reading and number, for example) is applied in low-road transfer, while at advanced stages of education the "domain-specific" knowledge and skills can only be transferred by high-road processes.

Sternberg (Baron and Sternberg, p. 258), who describes transfer as "the fundamental question in the teaching of thinking", lists six ways of maximizing the probability of transfer in a thinking skills programme. The first two in his list are the teaching of "executive skills" (or metacognitive monitoring), and presenting principles and rules of thinking in the context of a variety of academic disciplines. A comprehensive review of the issue in popular language is to be found in a recent article in *Educational Leadership* by Perkins and Salomon (1988). For maximizing transfer, they recommend "hugging" and "bridging". "Hugging" is teaching so as to facilitate low-road transfer: this is done by demonstrating linkages, applications and examples wherever possible. In "bridging", the teacher "mediates the needed processes of abstraction and connection making" (pp. 28–29) to help high-road transfer, pointing out principles and encouraging students to make generalizations.

Separate courses or infusion throughout the curriculum?

Can thinking be taught in the form of general skills which operate across a range of knowledge, or only as "domain-specific", in that each field of knowledge has its own distinctive style of knowledge? Resnick (in Brandt 1989, p. 15) describes this as "probably the single most important theoretical issue in the field of learning research". Most programmes and books designed to teach thinking are based on the assumption that there are general aspects of thinking which can be taught separately and be applied through transfer to specific situations. Marzano *et al.* (1988) was quoted above as an example in which eight "thinking processes" and 21 "core thinking skills" (such as defining problems, observing, comparing, classifying, inferring, restructuring, verifying) are identified. This "general skills approach" adopts a curriculum based on a synthesis of activities common across various forms of critical thinking. In contrast, the "domain-specific approach" (Polya, 1957, in mathematics;

Rubenstein, 1975, in engineering; Schoenfeld, 1985, in mathematics; and so on) is based on the assumption that the forms of thinking involved in different domains have relatively little in common and are best taught by an infusion of thinking (questioning, discussion, problem solving, etc.) in the teaching of each of the school subjects.

McPeck (1981) represents the extreme position that all thinking is "domain-specific". He was the originator of the saying: "Thinking is always thinking about something". But as Siegel (1988, pp. 18–23) points out in his review of this issue, while we can recognize that "assumptions" made in a mathematical argument are different from "assumptions" made in a political debate, there is still a common element in knowing what an assumption is and understanding the tentative thinking which necessarily follows from assumptions. There are particular styles of thinking in law, history, accountancy, physics, medicine, business and so on (see Becher, 1981). The study of a discipline gives the student a particular mode of approach to problems, and the accompanying skills and techniques associated with that discipline. Thus, thinking in specific ways can be taught: is such learning generalizable? If "appropriateness" or "selection of appropriate strategies", is one of the skills of thinking, the answer would appear to be yes.

Perkins and Salomon (1988) describe this controversy as the problem of "local knowledge" (p. 24): whether skills and knowledge tend to be "local"—more specialized, more specific to their context—rather than "general and crosscutting". The issue is highlighted dramatically in a recent article by Perkins and Salomon (1989) which asks whether a world chess-master should be put in command of a country's armies. Their conclusion, however, is that local knowledge and general transferable knowledge "are not rivals: rather they are members of the same team that play in different positions" (1988, p. 31).

The curriculum implications of this controversy are reflected in the policies of providing separate courses in thinking skills and of aiming to develop thinking within the teaching of the conventional subjects. The arguments for and against these policies are summarized by Sternberg (Baron and Sternberg, 1987, pp. 254–255). Separate courses focus attention on skills, but the application of these skills is not guaranteed if they are taught out of context. Teaching thinking in context may be effective within that context, but transfer to other applications may be limited.

Writers from the field of cognitive psychology tend to be critical of the skills approach: "Thinking is not a collection of skills", says Resnick (Brandt, 1989, p. 14). The College Entrance Examination Board Task Force (Nickerson et al., 1985) recommended "that the teaching of thinking and learning strategies be closely coupled with the teaching of conventional content material". Glaser (1984, p. 96) argues that much of the evidence favouring the notion of general skills comes from experiments of puzzles and material with a "lean" knowledge base, not applicable to thinking in domains with a rich knowledge base. Puzzle solving may be done by following heuristic procedures; but in science, mathematics, history or business, one cannot think effectively except on the basis of comprehensive knowledge and experience of the field. On the other hand, de Bono (1976) argues that there is a catalogue of easily learned skills which can quickly transform the learner's capacity to think.

The conclusion of most writers is that the dichotomy is false:

> For the most part, the various approaches are compatible and deal with different aspects and methods of teaching thinking skills. Ultimately, the most profitable program of instruction will probably be one that combines the best elements of the various approaches. (Baron and Sternberg, 1987, p. 5)

A similar conclusion is reached by Glaser (1984, p. 102). Ennis (1985) also argues strongly for a middle stance in this controversy: "A thorough knowledge of the subject about which one is thinking is essential for critical thinking ... [But] there are general principles that bridge subjects, that have application to many subjects" (p. 29).

There is a place for teaching general thinking skills and heuristic procedures, but such teaching leads to inert knowledge if it is not set in a context to which it can be applied. Resnick (1987) also sees value in both approaches: "Good thinking depends on specific knowledge, but many aspects of powerful thinking are shared across disciplines and situations" (p. 45).

Nickerson (1988) provides a balanced summary: "Any effort to teach thinking is unlikely to be as effective as it could be unless it combines these two approaches to some degree" (pp. 33–34).

Annex

I. Recently Published Reviews

Comprehensive reviews of research on the teaching of thinking have been published recently by Nickerson (1988), Marzano et al (1988), Resnick (1987), Baron and Sternberg (1987), Presseisen (1986a, 1987) and Nickerson, Perkins and Smith (1985). Collections of papers from conferences on thinking include Gilhooly et al. (1989), Perkins, Lochhead and Bishop (1987) and Segal, Chipman and Glaser (1985). The annual programmes of the Conference on Critical Thinking (Paul, 1981 on) and the journal, *Educational Leadership* (Association for Supervision and Curriculum Development, 1988), are also rich sources of relevant material.

II. Selected Examples of Publications Incorporating Programmes on Thinking or Outlining an Underlying Rationale

The entries in this list are arranged in chronological order of latest publication:

Swartz, R. J. and Perkins, D. N. (1989). *Teaching Thinking: Issues and approaches*, Midwest Publications, Pacific Grove, CA.

Beyer, B. K. (1988). *Developing a Thinking Skills Program*, Allyn and Bacon, Boston, MA.

Seigel, H. (1988). *Educating Reason: Rationality, Critical Thinking and Education*. Routledge & Kegan Paul, London.

Fisher, R. (1987). *Problem Solving in Primary Schools*, Blackwell, Oxford.

Bono, E. de (1986). *Six Thinking Hats*, Pelican Books, London; Little, Brown, New York.

Perkins, D. N. (1986). *Knowledge as Design*, Erlbaum, Hillsdale, NJ.

Whimbey, A. and Lochhead, J. (1986). *Problem Solving and Comprehension*, Erlbaum, Hillsdale, NJ.

Costa, A. (1985). *Developing Minds: A Resource Book for Teaching Thinking*, Association for Supervision and Curriculum Development, Alexandra, VA.

Bransford, J. D. and Stein, B. S. (1984). *The IDEAL Problem Solver*, Freeman, New York.

Halpern, D. F. (1984). *Thought and Knowledge: An Introduction to Critical Thinking*, Erlbaum, Hillsdale, NJ.

Novak, J. D. and Gowin, D. B. (1984). *Learning How to Learn*, Cambridge University Press, Cambridge.

Anderson, J. (1983). *The Architecture of Cognition*, Harvard University Press, Cambridge, MA.

Whimbey, A. (1983). *Analytical Reading and Reasoning*, Innovative Sciences, Stamford, CT.

Hayes, J. R. (1981). *The Complete Problem Solver*, Franklin Institute, Philadelphia, PA.

McPeck, J. E. (1981). *Critical Thinking and Education*, Robertson, Oxford.

Lochhead, J. and Clement, J. (1979). *Cognitive Process Instruction: Research on Teaching Thinking*, Erlbaum, Hillsdale, NJ.

Bono, E. de (1978). *Teaching Thinking*, Pelican Books, London. (Also Temple-Smith, London, 1975).

Rubenstein, M. F. (1975). *Patterns of Problem Solving*, Prentice-Hall, Englewood Cliffs, NJ.

Jackson, K. (1975). *The Art of Solving Problems*, Bulmershe College, Reading, UK.

Covington, M. V., Crutchfield, R. S., Davies, L. and Olton, R. M. (1974). *The Productive Thinking Programme: A Course in Learning to Think*, Merrill, Columbus, OH.

Wickelgrin, W. (1974). *How to Solve Problems: Elements of a Theory of Problems and Problem-Solving*, Freeman, San Francisco, CA.

Newell, A. and Simon, H. A. (1972). *Human Problem Solving*, Prentice-Hall, Englewood Cliffs, NJ.

III. Selected Examples of Programmes on Thinking　'

This list is not comprehensive and often refers to local programmes where further documentation is not always easily available. The order is alphabetical, by author:

Adams, M. and others. *Odyssey* (derived from Project Intelligence, Harvard and Venezuela), Harvard, Cambridge, MA.

Blagg, N. *Somerset Thinking Skills*, Somerset, UK.

Bono, E. de *The CoRT Thinking Program*, SRA/Pergamon, Chicago, IL.

Draze, D. *OPTIONS: A guide for creative decision making*, California.

Feuerstein, R. *Instrumental Enrichment*, Israel and the United States.

Lipman, M. *Philosophy for Children*, Montclair, NJ.

Marzano, R. and Arredondo, D. *Tactics for Thinking*, Association for Supervision and Curriculum Development.

McCarthy, B. *4MAT*, Minnesota.

McTighe, J. *Thinking Improvement Program*, Maryland.

Mirman, J. and Perkins, D. N. *NE/IS Reg Lab and Connections*. Harvard, Cambridge, MA.

Pogrow, S. *Higher Order Thinking Skills (HOTS)*, Tucson, AZ.

Schlichter, C. L. *Talents Unlimited*, Alabama, GA.

Schoenfeld, A. *Heuristic Instruction*.

Seagull, B. and Erdos, G. *Problem Solving for Adult Students*, Rutgers, NJ.

Sternberg, R. J. *Intelligence Applied*, Yale, CT.

Swartz, R. *Critical and Creative Thinking Programme*, Boston, MA.

Wales, C. E. and Stager, R. A. *Guided Design*, Morgantown, VA.

Warsham, A. and Stockton, A. *Inclusion Process*, Maryland.

Wincour, L. *Project Impact*, Maryland.

ADAPT (Accent on Development of Abstract Processess of Thought), Nebraska.

BASICS, Florida.

Cognitive Studies Project, New York.

COMPAS (Consortium for Operating and Managing Programs for the Advancement of Skills), Louisiana.

DOORS (Development of Operational Reasoning Skills), Illinois.

DORIS (Development of Reasoning in Science), California.

McRAT (Multicultural Reading and Thinking), Arkansas.

Practicuum of Thinking, Cincinnati.

Science – A process approach, American Association for the Advancement of Science.

Structure of Intellect.

Think About (Skills Essential to Learning Project).

See also a list of 22 references in Presseisen (1986b), p. 32; and 49 references in Presseisen (1987), pp. 63–71.

Computer programs designed to develop reasoning are not included in this list.

Note

This paper was prepared with the assistance of Dr John Nisbet, Honorary Senior Research Fellow and formerly Professor of Education, University of Aberdeen, Scotland. It has since been published in *Research Papers in Education*, 5 (1) as "The Curriculum Redefined: Learning to think— thinking to learn" (John Nisbet and Peter Davies, 1990).

References

Applebee, A. N. (1984). "Writing and reasoning", *Review of Educational Research*, **54,** pp. 577–596.

Arter, J. N. and Salmon, J. R. (1988). *Assessing Higher Order Thinking Skills: A Consumer's Guide*, Educational Regional Laboratory, Portland, OR.

Association for Supervision and Curriculum Development (ASCD). (1988). "Teaching thinking", *Educational Leadership*.

Association of Teachers of Mathematics (1984). *Working Investigationally: Ideas for investigational approaches to standard topics, a resource for GCSE*, ATM, London.

Baron, J. B. and Sternberg, R. J. (1987). *Teaching Thinking Skills: Theory and Practice*, Freeman, New York.

Becher, T. (1981). "Towards a definition of disciplinary cultures", *Studies in Higher Education*, **6,** pp. 109–122.

Benderson, A. (1984). *Focus 15: Critical Thinking*, Educational Testing Service, Princeton, NJ.

Bernstein, B. (1961). "Social class and linguistic development: A theory of social learning", in Halsey, A. H.; Floud, J.; and Anderson, C. A., *Education, Economy and Society*, Free Press of Glencoe, New York, pp. 288–314.

Blagg, N., Ballinger, M. and Gardner, R. (1988). *Somerset Thinking Skills Course: Handbook*, Blackwell, Oxford.

Bono, E. de (1973). *CoRT-1: Teachers' Handbook*, Pergamon, Oxford.

Bono, E. de (1976). *Teaching Thinking*, Temple-Smith, London.

Boswell, A. & Coan, B. (1989). *On Thinking Skills in Mathematics*, SE Regional Laboratory, Research for Better Schools, Washington DC.

Brandt, R. (1989). "On learning research: A conversation with Lauren Resnick", *Educational Leadership*, **46,** pp. 12–16.

Bransford, J. D. and Stein, B. S. (1984). *The IDEAL Problem-Solver*, Freeman, New York.

Broadfoot, P. (ed.) (1986). *Profiles and Records of Achievement: A Review of Issues and Practice*, Holt, Rinehart and Winston, London.

Bruner, J. S. (1960). *The Process of Education*, Harvard University Press, Cambridge, MA.

Bruner, J. S. , Goodnow, J. J. and Austin, G. A. (1956). *A Study of Thinking*, Wiley, New York.

Chipman, S. F., Segal, J. W. and Glaser, R. (1985). *Thinking and Learning Skills*, Vol. 1, Erlbaum, Hillsdale, NJ.

Chomsky, N. (1972). *Language and Mind*, Harcourt Brace Jovanovich, New York.

Clements, D. H. (1985). "Research on LOGO in education: Is the turtle slow but steady, or not even in the race?" *Computers in the Schools*, **2**, pp. 55–71.

Cockcroft Report. (1982). *Mathematics Counts*, HMSO, London.

Cole, N. (1989). *Conceptions of Educational Achievement*, Presidential Address, American Educational Research Association Conference, San Francisco.

Collins, A., Seely-Brown, J. and Newman, S. E. (1989). "Cognitive apprenticeship: teaching the craft of reading, writing and mathematics", in Resnick, L. B., *Cognitive Instruction: Issues and Agendas*, Erlbaum, Hillsdale, NJ.

Covington, M. V., Crutchfield, R. S., Davies, L. and Olton, R. M. (1974). *The Productive Thinking Program: A Course in Learning to Think*, Merrill, Columbus, OH.

Cuban, L. (1984). "Policy and research dilemmas in the teaching of reasoning: Unplanned designs", *Review of Educational Research*, **54**, pp. 655–681.

Dalbey, J. and Linn, M. C. (1985). "The demands and requirements of computer programming: A literature review". *Journal of Educational Computing Research*, **1**, pp. 253–274.

Dewey, J. (1910). *How We Think*, Heath, Boston, MA.

Driver, R. and Oldham, V. (1986). "A constructivist approach to curriculum development in science". *Studies in Science Education*, **13**, pp. 105–122.

Dykhuisen, G. (1973). *The Life and Mind of John Dewey*, S. Illinois University Press, Carbondale, IL.

Edwards, J. (1988). The Direct Teaching of Thinking Skills: CoRT-1, An Evaluative Case Study. Ph.D. thesis, James Cook University of North Queensland, Australia.

Ennis, R. H. (1962). "A concept of critical thinking", *Harvard Educational Review*, **32**, pp. 81–111.

Ennis, R. H. (1985). "Critical thinking and the curriculum. National Forum", *Phi Kappa Phi*, **65**, pp. 28–31.

Fassino, G. (1982). *Relazione all'On, le Ministro della Pubblica Istruzione sui Lavori della Commissione incaricata della elaborazione preliminare delle Linee generali dei nuovi programmi della scuola elementare* (Ministerial Report), Rome.

Feuerstein, R., Rand, Y., Hoffman, M. B. and Miller, R. (1980). *Instrumental Enrichment: An Intervention for Cognitive Modifiability*, University Park Press, Baltimore, MD.

Fisher, R. (1987). *Problem Solving in Primary Schools*, Blackwell, Oxford.

Flavell, J. H. (1976). "Metacognitive aspects of problem solving", in Resnick, L. B., *The Nature of Intelligence*, Erlbaum, Hillsdale, NJ.

Garanderie, A. de la and Caltar, G. (1988). *Tous les enfants peuvent réussir*, Centurion, Paris.

Gardner, H. (1983). *Frames of Mind: The Theory of Multiple Intelligences*, Basic Books, New York.

Garner, R. (1989). When Children Do Not Use Metacognitive Strategies. Oral presentation, American Educational Research Association Conference, San Francisco.

Gilhooly, K. J., Keane, M. T., Logie, R. H. and Erdos, G. (1989). *Lines of Thinking*, Wiley, New York and Chichester.

Glaser, R. (1984). "Education and thinking: The role of knowledge", *American Psychologist*, **39**, pp. 93–104.

Greene, M. (1989). "Educate the fortunate fifth to care," in *Summary Report, Curriculum at the Centre Conference on Curriculum, Instruction and Leadership, Montreal, Quebec, 19th May, 1989*, Infolink Consultants, Inc, Ottawa, Ontario.

Haller, E. P., Child, D. A. and Walberg, H. J. (1988). "Can comprehension be taught? A quantitative synthesis of metacognitive studies", *Educational Researcher*, **17**(9), pp. 5–16.

Hayes, J. R. (1981). *The Complete Problem Solver*, Franklin Insitute Press, Philadelphia, PA.

Herrnstein, R. J., Nickerson, R. S., de Sanchez, M. and Swets, J. A. (1986). "Teaching thinking skills", *American Psychologist*, **41**, pp. 1279–1289.

Hodson, D. (1985). "Philosophy of science, science and science education", *Studies in Science Education*, **12**, pp. 25–57.

Hunter-Grundin, E. (1985). *Teaching Thinking*, SCDC, Schools Council, London.

Jackson, K. (1983). *The Art of Solving Problems*, Bulmershe College, Reading, UK.

Kanach, A. (1989). *On Thinking Skills in the Language Arts*, NE/IS Regional Laboratory, Research for Better Schools, Washington DC.

Lipman, M., Sharp, A. M. and Oscanyan, F. S. (1980). *Philosophy in the Classroom*, Temple University Press, Philadelphia, PA.

Lochhead, J. and Clement. J. (1979). *Cognitive Process Instruction: Research on Teaching Thinking Skills.* Erlbaum, Hillsdale, NJ.

McGuinness, C. (1988). Talking about Thinking. Paper read to the International Conference on Thinking, Aberdeen.

McPeck, J. (1981). *Critical Thinking and Education,* Robinson, Oxford.

Marzano, R. J., Brandt, R. S., Hughes, C. S., Jones, B. F., Presseisen, B. Z., Rankin, S. C. and Suhor, C. (1988). *Dimensions of Thinking: A Framework for Curriculum and Instruction,* Association for Supervision and Curriculum Development, Alexandria, VA.

Millar, R. and Driver, R. (1987). "Beyond processes", *Studies in Science Education,* **15,** pp. 3–57.

Newell, A. and Simon, H. A. (1972). *Human Problem Solving,* Prentice-Hall, Englewood Cliffs, NJ.

Nickerson, R. S. (1988). "On improving thinking through instruction", *Review of Research in Education,* **15,** pp. 3–57.

Nickerson, R. S., Perkins, D. N. and Smith, E. E. (1985). *The Teaching of Thinking,* Erlbaum, Hillsdale, NJ.

Nickerson, R. S. *et al.* (1985). "Curriculum reform and instructional strategies related to learning strategies and thinking: Task force report 2", in *Excellence in Our Schools: Making it Happen.* College Entrance Examination Board, New York.

Novak, J. D. (1987). *Human Constructivism: Toward a Unity of Psychological and Epistemological Meaning Making, Proceedings of the 2nd International Seminar, Misconceptions and Educational Strategies in Science and Mathematics,* Vol. 1. Cornell University, Ithaca, NY.

Novak, J. D. and Gowin, D. B. (1984). *Learning How to Learn,* Cambridge University Press, Cambridge.

Novak, J. D., Resnick, L. B., West, L. H. T. and White, R. T. (1989). *A Conversation about Trends in Research on Misconceptions and Conceptual Change and its Potential vs. Actual Contribution to Education.* Symposium, American Educational Association Conference, San Francisco.

OECD (1987). *Information Technologies and Basic Learning. Reading, Writing, Science and Mathematics.* OECD, Paris.

OECD (1990). *Curriculum Reform—An Overview of Trends.* OECD, Paris.

Palincsar, A. S. and Brown, A. L. (1984). "Reciprocal teaching of comprehension—Fostering and metacognitive strategies", *Cognition and Instruction,* **1,** pp. 117–175.

Papert, S. (1980). *Mind-Storms: Children, Computers, and Powerful Ideas,* Harvester, Brighton.

Paul, R. W. (1981 on). *Annual Programme of the Conference on Critical Thinking,* Sonoma State University, Sonoma, CA.

Paul, R. W. (1984). " Critical thinking: Fundamental to education for a free society", *Educational Leadership,* **41,** pp. 4–14.

Paul, R. W. (1985). "The critical thinking movement: A historical perspective. National Forum", *Phi Kappa Phi,* **65,** pp. 2–3.

Paul, R. W. (1989). Personal communication in interview.

Paul, R. W., Binker, A. J. A., Martin, D., Vetrano, C. and Kreklau, H. (1987). *Critical Thinking Handbook: 6th–9th Grades.* Sonoma State University, Sonoma, CA.

Perkins, D. N. (1989). Teaching Cognitive and Metacognitive Strategies. Oral presentation, American Educational Research Association Conference, San Francisco.

Perkins, D. N., Lochhead, J. and Bishop, J. (1987). *Thinking: The Second International Conference.* Erlbaum, Hillsdale, NJ.

Perkins, D. N. and Salomon, G. (1988). "Teaching for transfer", *Educational Leadership,* **41,** pp. 22–32.

Perkins, D. N. and Salomon, G. (1989). "Are cognitive skills context-bound?" *Educational Researcher,* **18**(1), pp. 16–25.

Piaget, J. and Inhelder, B. (1964). *The Early Growth of Logic in the Child,* Routledge & Kegan Paul, London.

Polya, G. (1957). *How to Solve it: A New Aspect of Mathematical Method,* Princeton University Press, Princeton, NJ.

Presseisen, B. Z. (1986a). Critical Thinking and Thinking Skills: State of the Art Definitions and Practice in Public Schools. Oral presentation, American Educational Research Association Conference, San Francisco.

Presseisen, B. Z. (1986b). *Thinking Skills: Research and practice,* National Education Association, Washington, D.C.

Presseisen, B. Z. (1987). *Thinking Skills Throughout the Curriculum*: A Conceptual Design, Phi Lambda Theta, Bloomington, ID.

Presseisen, B. Z. (1988). *At-Risk Students and Thinking*: Perspectives from Research, National Education Association and Philadelphia: Research for Better Schools, Washington, D.C.

Resnick, L. B. (1987). *Education and Learning to Think*, National Academy Press, Washington, D.C.

Rubenstein, M. F. (1975). *Patterns of Problem Solving*, Prentice-Hall, Englewood Cliffs, NJ.

Salomon, G. and Perkins, D. N. (1987). "Transfer of cognitive skills from programming: When and how?", *Journal of Educational Computing Research*, **3**, pp. 149–169.

Savell, J. M., Twohig, P. T. and Rachford, D. L. (1986). "Empirical status of Feuerstein's Instrumental Enrichment (IE) technique as a method of teaching thinking skills", *Review of Educational Research*, **56**, pp. 381–409.

Scardamalia, M. and Bereiter, C. (1981). *Writing for Results*, Curriculum series, **44**, OISE, Toronto.

Scardamalia, M., Bereiter, C. and Steinbach, R. (1984). "Teachability of reflective processes in written composition", *Coginitive Science*, **8**, pp. 173–190.

Schlichter, C. L. (1986). "Talents unlimited: An inservice education model for teaching thinking skills", *Gifted Child Quarterly* **30**, pp. 119–123.

Schoenfeld, A. (1985). *Mathematical Problem Solving*, Academic Press, New York.

Scriven, M. (1985). "Critical for survival. National Forum", *Phi Kappa Phi*, **65**, pp. 9–12.

Segal, J. W., Chipman, S. and Glaser, R. (1985). *Thinking and Learning Skills*, Vol. 2, Erlbaum, Hillsdale, NJ.

Siegel, H. (1988). *Educating Reason: Rationality, Critical Thinking and Education*. Routledge & Kegan Paul, London.

Sternberg, R. J. (1983). "Criteria for intellectual skills training", *Educational Researcher*, **12**(2), pp. 6–26.

Sternberg, R. J. (1985). *Beyond IQ: A Triarchic Theory of Human Intelligence*, Cambridge University Press, New York.

Sternberg, R. J. (1986). *Intelligence Applied*, Harcourt Brace Jovanovich, San Diego, CA.

Thorndike, E. L. (1906). *Principles of Teaching*, Seiler, New York.

Thorndike, E. L. and Woodworth, R. S. (1901). "The influence of improvement in one mental function upon the efficiency of other functions", *Psychological Review*, **8**, pp. 247–261, 384–395, 553–564.

Torbet, M. (1980). *Follow Me: A Handbook of Movement Activities for Children*. Prentice-Hall, Englewood Cliffs, NJ.

Tuma, D. T. and Reif, F. (1980). *Problem Solving and Education: Issues in Teaching and Research*. Erlbaum, Hillsdale, NJ.

Vygotsky, L. S. (1961). *Thought and Language*. Edited and translated by Haufmann, E. and Vakar, G., MIT Press and Wiley, New York and London.

Wagner, R., Gardner, H., Snow, R. and Glaser, R. (1989). *Assessment Models Focussed on New Conceptions of Achievement and Reasoning*, Symposium, American Educational Research Association Conference, San Francisco.

Wales, C. E. and Stager, R. A. (1977). *Guided Design*, West Virginia University Center for Guided Design, Morgantown, VA.

Weller, K. and Craft, A. (1983). *Making Up Our Minds: An Exploratory Study of Intellectual Enrichment*. Schools Council (now SCDC Publications), London.

Whimbey, A. and Lochhead, J. (1984). *Beyond Problem Solving and Comprehension: An Exploration of Quantitative Reasoning*, Erlbaum, Hillsdale, NJ.

Whimbey, A. and Lochhead, J. (1986). *Problem Solving and Comprehension* (4th edn), Erlbaum, Hillsdale, NJ.

White, R. T. (1988). *Learning Science*. Blackwell, Oxford.

Wickelgrin, W. (1974). *How to Solve Problems: Elements of a Theory of Problems and Problem Solving*, Freeman, San Francisco.

Name Index

Adams, E. 162, 163
Adey, Philip xxi
Adey, P. S. and Shayer, M. 89, 90
Adey, P. S., Shayer, M. and Yates, C. 80
Aiken, W. 164
Anderson, J. R., Boyle, C. F., Corbett, A. and Lewis, M. 98
Ansermet, Ernest 150
Applebee, A. N. 206
Arendt, Hannah 65, 76
Arter, J. N. and Salomon, J. R. 211
Atwood, Margaret 74
Azuma, Hiroshi xxiii–xxiv
Azuma, H. and Kashiwagi, K. 195

Bacher, F. 53
Bakhtin, M. 71
Bakker, Robert 148–9, 150, 151, 157, 161, 167, 171
Baldauf, R. B. Jr, Edwards J. and Matthews, B. 22
Baron, J. 165
Baron, J. B. and Sternberg, R. J. 178, 202, 205, 209, 211, 212, 215, 217, 219. 220, 221, 222
Baulac, Y. 98
Becher, T. 222
Bell, Richard 68–9
Benderson, A. 218, 219
Bernstein, B. 203
Bertelson, P. 174
Best, C. T., McRoberts, G. W. and Sithol, N. M. 173
Binet, Alfred 127, 153, 154
Binet, A. and Simon, T. 50
Biran, Maine de 127
Bishop, Elizabeth 76
Blagg, N., Ballinger, M. and Gardner, R. 208
Bono, Edward de see de Bono
Boswell, A. and Coan, B. 209
Brandt, R. 217, 221, 222
Bransford, J. D. and Stein, B. S. 180, 210
Bresson, François xviii–xix, 172
Bresson, F., de Schonen, S. and Tzortzis, C. 172

Briggs, K. C. and Briggs Myers, I. 23
Briggs Myers, I. 23
Broadbent, D. E., Fitzgerald, P. and Broadbent, M. H. P. 174
Broadfoot, P. 219
Brown, J. S., Collins, A. and Duguid, P. 96
Brown, N. 166
Bruner, Jerome S. 69, 116, 206
Bruner, J. S., Goodnow, J. J. and Austin, G. A. 116, 203
Burgess, T. 162, 163
Burloud, Albert 127

Caillot, Michel xx, xxvii
Cannell, J. 164
Cassierer, Ernst 152
Chomsky, N. 203
Clements, D. H. 205
Cohen, R. 90
Cole, N. 218
Collins, A., Seely-Brown, J. and Newman, S. E. 214
Conrad, Joseph 73
Costa, A. 25
Craft, A. and Weller, K. 45
Craft, Robert 150
Craft, R. and Harkins, W. 149
Cuban, L. 204, 217
Cunningham, Merce 157

Dalbey, J. and Linn, M. C. 205
Damon, W. 159
de Bono, Edward xi–xiii, xv, xvi, 15–17, 19, 22, 26, 180, 183, 192, 196, 214, 216, 223
Debray, Rosine xiv–xv, 49, 50, 59
Descartes, René 151, 152
Dewey, John 66, 69–70, 204, 217
Dilthey, Wilhelm 152
diSessa, A. A. 100
Dostoevsky, Fyodor 74
Driver, R. and Oldham, V. 211
Duckworth, E. 188, 190

Subject Index